*Judicial Politics in the
D.C. Circuit Court*

# Judicial Politics in the D.C. Circuit Court

CHRISTOPHER P. BANKS

THE JOHNS HOPKINS UNIVERSITY PRESS
*Baltimore and London*

© 1999 The Johns Hopkins University Press
All rights reserved. Published 1999
Printed in the United States of America on acid-free paper
9 8 7 6 5 4 3 2 1

The Johns Hopkins University Press
2715 North Charles Street
Baltimore, Maryland 21218-4363
www.press.jhu.edu

Library of Congress Cataloging-in-Publication Data will be found
at the end of this book.
A catalog record for this book is available from the British Library.

ISBN 0-8018-6184-5

*For Diane*

# Contents

# Figures and Tables

## FIGURES

# TABLES

# Preface

In his influential *Courts of Appeals in the Federal Judicial System* (1981), J. Woodford Howard, Jr., suggested that little was really known about the enormous judicial role that federal courts in the middle tier play in the American political system.[1] As one legal writer put it in 1983, circuit courts "remain courts of relative invisibility."[2] Regrettably, not that much has changed in increasing the awareness about the intermediate tier of courts, because public law scholars still tend to concentrate on understanding the judicial behavior of the Supreme Court of the United States to the exclusion, it seems, of virtually all else. This book was written, in part, to change that emphasis and perhaps the related perception that circuit courts are relatively insignificant actors in the judicial process. In particular, it describes the importance of the political transformation of the U.S. Court of Appeals for the District of Columbia Circuit, or, as it is commonly known, "the D.C. Circuit," after 1960.

Curiously, with few exceptions very little has been written about the D.C. Circuit even though it occupies a central place in the federal court system.[3] Situated in the nation's capital and once seen as an anomalous federal circuit court that had the unusual duty of taking care of federal law and superintending certain local matters arising from the District of Columbia, it emerged as a "dominant judicial force" in the modern era for some of the reasons explained in this book.[4] Perhaps the most telling one, though, is the fact that it is a political institution, a circumstance that goes against the popular myth that courts, especially influential ones, are apolitical. As the following pages suggest, perceiving the legal and political significance of the circuit court in Washington, D.C., begins from the premise that much of what defines today's court, and most likely what it will be tomorrow, is a function of a special brand of D.C. Circuit judicial politics.

Since 1960 the D.C. Circuit has enjoyed two distinct reputations in the legal community. Both have had an impact on the political scope of the court's work and its judicial role in the American legal system. Once primarily known as a progressive court that expanded the rights of criminal defendants in the district in the 1960s, it evolved into a different judicial forum in the 1970s and thereafter because of several changes in the external political environment which ultimately affected the court's docket, membership, and jurisprudence. The political transformation, in essence, altered the court's function and serves as the focus for acknowledging the court's present operation as a quasi-specialized, de facto court of administrative law.

After presenting a brief historical summary of the court's genesis, the first chapter explores the reasons why in the 1960s the D.C. Circuit established its reputation for being a progressive, if not activist, court that allegedly coddled criminals with its liberal tendency to expand the constitutional rights of the accused. Judicial workload statistics demonstrate that the court's decision-making influenced its ability to set its agenda and act as a court of last resort in making criminal law policy that irked conservatives in Congress and the presidency. The purported judicial activism of the circuit prompted a conservative response as well, allowing Congress to enact legislation that increased the power of the police to fight street crime and, in the end, curb the liberal bench that was in place when David Bazelon was its chief judge.

Chapter 2 thus undertakes to explain why conservatives in Congress opted to enact court reform at a time when a return to law and order became the preferred policy position of presidential hopefuls like Richard M. Nixon. Liberal courts, including the mollycoddling judges of the D.C. Circuit, were increasingly being seen as more of the problem rather than the solution in combating violent street crime in the 1960s. As a result, the executive and the legislative branches combined forces to produce the District of Columbia Court Reform and Criminal Procedure Act of 1970 (D.C. Circuit Crime bill), an innovative piece of legislation that in part tried to remove much of the circuit court's capacity to act as an anomalous, *liberal* court of great authority in criminal law.

Even with its power to act as a local state supreme court in the district over criminal appeals essentially curtailed by partisan politics, the D.C. Circuit ironically forged a new reputation during a time of burgeoning regulation in the 1970s and its aftermath. Since the composition of the bench remained intact throughout most of the new decade, judicial reform only succeeded in redirecting the court's focus toward controlling the legal and policy initiatives of administrative agencies, which now enjoyed broad delegated power to act legislatively in matters of social regulation. With the excision of many local criminal appeals but with plenty of administrative law cases on its docket to choose from, the D.C. Circuit bench developed the hard-look doctrine as the substantive and procedural means to curb agency policy-making. As a self-anointed judicial guardian of the public interest, the court's decision-making impelled the High Court to respond politically in an effort to modify the lower court's activism. In the end, therefore, the politics of D.C. Circuit court reform had the unintended consequence of not only exposing the ideological differences between the U.S. Supreme Court and the circuit court, but also initiating the process of transforming the D.C. Circuit into a de facto, quasi-specialized administrative law court of last resort.

Chapter 3 describes how the judicial politics of the D.C. Circuit was a key aspect of the court's regulatory decision-making in the 1980s. Quite clearly, internal *and* external political forces shaped the nature and scope of the court's administrative law jurisprudence at a time when almost half of the court's docket consisted of agency appeals. An important political event—the election of Ronald Reagan to the presidency in 1980—provided the impetus for transforming the court's membership as President Reagan seized several opportunities to make the D.C. Circuit more conservative through the judicial selection process. The rapid turnover in judicial personnel had profound ideological implications as the court's liberal majority—which in some ways was still very committed to maintaining the substantive goals of the earlier, pro-regulatory decade—began to dissipate in a time of increasing deregulation and political conservatism. As the chapter reveals, judicial politics affected legal decisions concerning litigant access to the court and whether agencies, rather than the court, had the constitutional authority to make regulatory policy decisions in the first place. This latter question, in particular, not only brings into sharp relief how opposing ideologies on the bench competed for judicial supremacy, it also demonstrates that modern administrative law jurisprudence is essentially framed by a very old political debate concerning the legitimacy of the New Deal and the underlying concern of whether courts should play an active role in controlling regulation. Chapter 3, however, does not conclude that political ideology completely drives policy decision-making in the circuit. Indeed, it suggests that political *and* nonideological variables affected the court's work and conjoined to produce case outcomes that are meaningful in the modern administrative state.

Chapter 4 examines the critical issue of whether the D.C. Circuit is a court of last resort for most federal litigants who bring agency appeals to the circuit court in Washington, D.C. It approaches the subject from two vantage points. First, it investigates, in some detail, the history of en banc review, at first generally, and then specifically, in the D.C. Circuit. The discussion highlights the subtle point that internal, collective review of panel judgments has a key impact on whether circuit courts are agents of final social and legal change. In observing that en banc review was originally perceived as an efficient method of deciding cases of exceptional importance, the argument nonetheless reiterates the oft-repeated criticism that the procedure is fraught with a variety of weaknesses, including the possibility that it can be politically abused by result-oriented judges. Since President Reagan had the chance to fill the D.C. Circuit bench with several judicial appointments, the chapter looks at the court's new membership and if it was prone to making en banc review political when the liberal majority on the court was losing influence. Through a brief description of cases and judicial workload statistics, the discussion suggests that this form of internal judicial review is susceptible to political manipulation; and, more importantly, that decisions produced from en banc courts are likely to be ratified by the U.S. Supreme Court upon further appeal.

This latter point raises, therefore, the second issue addressed in the chapter: whether the nation's highest court uses its discretion to condone or reject D.C. Circuit decision-making. A detailed inspection of the grant and denial rates of certiorari petitions emanating from all circuit courts and the D.C. Circuit illustrates that the lower court in Washington, D.C., has considerable clout in shaping legal policy. As a result, the politics of en banc review, when combined with the political reality that the U.S. Supreme Court does not supervise the circuit courts that closely, indicates that the D.C. Circuit is, in fact, a court of last resort for most federal litigants in administrative law, its dominant area of jurisprudence.

Although it is a unique policy-maker in regulation, the D.C. Circuit must still confront many of the basic issues that command attention as the federal judiciary enters the new millennium. Chapter 5 thus describes the contemporary function of the D.C. Circuit as a de facto administrative law court in light of the so-called caseload crisis and the possibility of enacting subject matter reform. For most public law scholars, the fact that the courts of appeals are in the midst of a burgeoning caseload is probably unremarkable, as is the reluctance of Congress to help ameliorate it by adding more judges or enacting legislation that would alter the organization of the federal court system. Indeed, as this book and the recent work of the Commission on Structural Alternatives for the Federal Courts of Appeals (which explored whether the Ninth Circuit and the rest of the courts of appeals should be reconstituted) attests, the issue of judicial reform is often a function of partisan politics. Apart from political considerations, though, the concluding chapter suggests that Congress or the Judicial Conference of the U.S. Courts should take another look at whether it is feasible to enact subject matter reform in the circuit court in Washington, D.C. As the discussion points out, past studies, like the 1990 *Report of the Federal Courts Study Committee* and the 1995 *Long Range Plan for Federal Courts*, have dealt with the issue in an incomplete fashion and without the perspective that the data in this book offers.[5] Consequently, the modern nature of the court's docket, membership, and jurisprudence not only makes the D.C. Circuit a special court in the

American judiciary, it also presents an opportunity for scholars, legislators, and judges to study the judicial experience of the D.C. Circuit and determine whether restructuring the circuit offers a viable alternative for reform as all federal courts try to meet the challenges of a litigious society in the twenty-first century.

Many of the book's conclusions in the pages that follow are derived from a historical, doctrinal, and an empirical analysis of only one regionally based court of appeals. There are other more specialized and nonregional judicial forums, such as the U.S. Court of Appeals for the Federal Circuit, that are not studied extensively in this book. Instead, the focus here has been on comprehending the judicial behavior and function of the D.C. Circuit, a court that is part of the regional design of the traditional middle tier of federal courts. Consequently, the court's history, along with many of its judicial opinions and the extralegal writings of its judges, has been inspected in order to achieve a partial understanding of the D.C. Circuit's political and legal significance in the American polity. Another rich source of analysis for the book has been the published and unpublished judicial workload statistics from the Administrative Office of the U.S. Courts. Moreover, my prior research on the judicial behavior of the D.C. Circuit has been instrumental in formulating my perspective about the court and its place in the federal judiciary.[6]

Regardless of my own efforts to study this very influential court of appeals, much more needs to be done in order to reach a full appreciation of the role that circuit courts will play in the next millennium. As the last chapter suggests, it is implausible to believe that in the future the structure and operation of the federal circuits will remain insulated from the effects of a burgeoning caseload or the impact of a dynamic legal and political environment. For example, if the U.S. Supreme Court continues to use its discretion to decide (or even consider) fewer appeals, circuit courts invariably will shoulder the political responsibility of decisively resolving the legal disputes of most federal litigants. As circuit courts become more significant policy-makers, there will always be opponents of particular courts who desire to alter judicial behavior for political reasons. Thoughtful proposals to restructure the circuit courts (as epitomized by the final report of the Commission on Structural Alternatives for the Federal Courts of Appeals issued in December of 1998) should be adopted only if there are compelling, nonpartisan reasons to do so. Scholars, therefore, need to pay more attention to the way in which external political forces affect circuit court jurisprudence and, in the end, federal court reform. Apart from reform, another area for research is exploring the method by which circuit courts set their agendas or how they substantively or procedurally decide cases that have a discernible impact on citizens. In addition, political scientists and law professors alike should work toward comprehending the diversity of circuit courts and how they interact with other judicial entities or different political institutions. In short, the types of research questions that can be posited are only limited by the ingenuity of those in the scholarly and legal communities who are willing to ask them. At the very least, I hope that this book provides an impetus for stimulating the interest of scholars who are willing to investigate in future research the extent to which circuit courts are an important source of final legal and political change.

# Acknowledgments

Although I take sole responsibility for what is said in the book, writing a manuscript is really a group endeavor and this book is no exception. I would like to thank Henry Abraham, Steven Finkel, and Glen Robinson and the rest of my colleagues, friends, and the library personnel at the University of Virginia for the time they generously spent in reading or supporting past or present versions of the manuscript. In particular, David O'Brien's efforts in assisting me at the beginning and throughout the research and writing of the book merit special praise, appreciation, and admiration. John Blakeman, Tim Collins, and Steve Tauber, along with my parents, Richard and Frances, and my son, Zachary, and daughter, Samantha, in various ways also made special contributions to the book and I would like to thank them as well. Several colleagues, students, and staff at the University of Akron, too numerous to mention, were always very supportive of my work, but special recognition must go to David Louscher who, as department chair, provided the type of academic support that is necessary to complete such a book. I would also like to thank the professional staff at the Administrative Office of the U.S. Courts, in Washington, D.C., for their kind and patient responses to my never-ending requests for judicial workload data. The executive editor, Henry Tom, and the rest of the staff at the Johns Hopkins University Press were an invaluable source of assistance in not only initially supporting the book, but in also getting it to press. I am grateful to the editors at the University of Virginia's *Journal of Law and Politics* for granting permission to reproduce some of the findings from my earlier research on the D.C. Circuit. Finally, the book could not have been written without the moral and logistical help of my wife, Diane, who saw the project through from the beginning and is very much a part of what is reflected in the pages that follow. It is to her that I dedicate this book, with much love, affection, and gratitude.

*Judicial Politics in the
D.C. Circuit Court*

# An Anomalous Court of "Great Authority"

Despite their importance as Article III constitutional courts, the federal circuit courts of appeals are described, paradoxically, as the courts that "nobody knows." Yet an increasing number of contemporary scholars observe that the United States Courts of Appeals, or, as they are popularly known, the circuit courts, perform a myriad of institutional functions that underscore their significance as political and legal institutions in the American republic. Originally perceived as judicial upstarts that threatened to usurp the United States Supreme Court's undisputed reputation as the "guardian of all constitutional claims," the intermediate tier of courts quickly evolved into judicial bodies that were "taken for granted as courts of great authority." As an integral part of the complex hierarchy that makes up the federal judiciary, circuit courts now generally superintend district courts, make national law, and act as the courts of last resort for most federal litigants.[1] In the process, they also are key sources of political power and legal policy change because they often define the scope of the law and invariably shape the contours of permissible social policy through their decision-making. On an institutional and political level, understanding the judicial role of the intermediate tier of federal courts should be a primary objective for laypersons, court watchers, and scholars alike.

One circuit court in particular, the U.S. Court of Appeals for the District of Columbia Circuit (D.C. Circuit), has emerged as a contemporary leader in regulatory legal and political change among the family of federal courts. Nearly a quarter of a century ago pundit Joseph Goulden, the author of the insightful *The Benchwarmers: The Private World of the Powerful Federal Judges*, perceptively noticed that the D.C. Circuit was having a substantial impact upon the emerging administrative state in Washington, D.C., in the 1970s. He identified two factors—the court's jurisdiction over regulatory appeals and its situs in the nation's capital—that accounted for the court's then-fledgling reputation as a "mini Supreme Court," a title intimating that the court is second only in importance to the highest federal court in the land.[2] While it is problematic to argue persuasively that the D.C. Circuit is generally more profound than any or all of the rest of courts in the middle tier, it is less controversial—and more accurate—to claim that it enjoys an unmatched reputation as a leader in determining the substance and content of administrative law.

In fact, the D.C. Circuit can be conceived as a special and unique court in the area of regulatory law, and this book will explore the political and legal reasons why it has earned that prestigious title. While some scholars maintain that the D.C. Circuit is the nation's "second most powerful court," this book does *not* make that claim. Rather, it simply asserts that the court's enduring influence as a quasi-specialized court in modern administrative law is derived from a fundamental political transformation in the court's jurisdiction, membership, and jurisprudence in criminal and administrative law after 1960. In addition, an underlying theme is that the D.C. Circuit's political significance stems from its judicial function as a de facto, limited subject matter court and not a generalist one (as all regionally based courts of appeals are, in theory). Understanding the true nature of the D.C. Circuit's role as a subject matter court assists in trying to formulate any coherent plan for judicial reform of circuit courts in the future. Moreover, it helps us to appreciate the constitutional significance of all courts of appeals organized under Article III, especially as courts of last resort and agents of political and legal change in America.[3]

Apart from the D.C. Circuit's political significance and its large impact on administrative law and the regulatory state, there are a number of separate if not inherent reasons why studying it is important. As it has been historically and is in modern times, the D.C. Circuit is a distinctive court in the federal judiciary. First, unlike other circuit courts, the D.C. Circuit is eminent as a consequence of its location at the seat of the national government. In speculating about the court's unique contribution to administrative law, legal scholar Paul Verkuil commented that "[location] is what the D.C. Circuit has, and that is where you begin. The facts are that this is Washington, and what we are talking about is the federal government in action, and the D.C. Circuit is bound to be at the center of activity."[4] Or, as former judge Abner Mikva tells it in considering why many feel that the D.C. Circuit is "the top of equals" among circuit courts, "It's mostly a matter of geography. [The court's] entire geographical jurisdiction is the 10 square miles that make up the District of Columbia, but that happens to be the 10 square miles which is also the seat of government. So almost all of the important governmental appeals are taken to our court. Seventy-five percent of our cases involve the government on one side or the other, and so we sort of frame these key government issues for the Supreme Court."[5] Its location and the fact that the lower court plays an integral part in setting the agenda of the Supreme Court in regulation cases give the D.C. Circuit its own institutional personality that immediately sets it apart from all of its sister courts.

There is more to the story than just simple logistics, however. Since the court is indigenous to the District of Columbia, it has been able (at different but over consecutive time periods) to extend its influence in both criminal and administrative law for the last quarter century. Its history shows that the inhabitants of the Washington community often sought the protection of the circuit court since it had "supreme court" jurisdiction over local criminal appeals in the 1960s. Yet, after 1970, it also became a central place for the adjudication of administrative agency appeals, which has not gone unnoticed by a multitude of special interest groups, lobbyists, and agencies that comprise and permeate the district's political infrastructure. The implications of the connection between the D.C. Circuit and its immediate political environment are evident considering that the federal bureaucracy in Washington, D.C., consists of fourteen cabinet-level departments and over sixty independent agencies having over two thousand governmental subunits.[6] Since Washington, D.C., is regionally at the vortex of politics in this country, it makes sense that the D.C. Circuit is an integral part of the American government. Its location naturally augments its judicial stature and influence over the citizens of this country in the first place.

Another explanation underscores its geographic situs and the consequences that flow from its relationship to the Supreme Court and the executive bureaucracy. Because the District of Columbia is not legally a geographic state, it has the advantage of being free from the political regionalism endemic to the judicial selection process in other circuit courts in the country. This is important because judges appointed to D.C. Circuit owe little political allegiance to presidents. As a nonstate, the district is not represented by senators who otherwise wield enormous institutional authority to blue-slip, or veto, the selection of judge. Consequently, judicial appointees of the D.C. Circuit tend to be nationalists who hail from all over the country with diverse educational, social, and political backgrounds. One legal commentator summarizes the distinct impact that the district's location has on the presidential appointing process, noting that "Over the years, in terms of the appointment process, presidents have been able to name judges on the D.C. Circuit with much greater freedom than they can in the other circuits. What you get is a tendency, I believe, to pull together people from all over the country who have expertise, talent and knowledge, but may not have the necessary political ties to be appointed from their states. These nationally selected judges come together in an exciting, 'hot' circuit, and spend their lives defining the law. That possibility for creative judicial selection simply does not exist in any other circuit: indeed, it can be found only in the United States Supreme Court."[7]

The nexus between geography and judicial selection illuminates why presidents appoint distinguished judges of exceptional merit to the circuit. Quite simply, more opportunities exist for presidents to make apolitical decisions about appointees who routinely come with few political liabilities. Not only does this win-win scenario increase presidential power, but it also allows presidents to make better choices that serve the country well. From one perspective, "Since appointments are made without senatorial prerogatives, the members of the D.C. Circuit are picked more on merit than [those of] other circuits." From another, the geographic uniqueness of the D.C. Circuit contributes to its judicial independence and, interestingly, gives its judges more room to disagree about the very public (and national) cases that come before the court on partisan grounds.[8] On balance, then, the court's location and judicial selection process combine to affect directly the quality of its judicial policy-making and, in the end, its political notoriety.

With the chance to fill judicial vacancies with high quality, nationally oriented judges, the D.C. Circuit has also gained a visible reputation for fostering the development of prospective United States Supreme Court justices, particularly in recent times. In the words of one pundit, "The D.C. Circuit has long been thought of as the second most powerful court in the land and a good breeding ground for the Supreme Court."[9] It is not happenstance, then, that one-third of the Supreme Court's membership in 1998 (Justices Antonin Scalia, Clarence Thomas, and Ruth Bader Ginsburg) consists of former judges of the D.C. Circuit; and, that one sitting D.C. Circuit judge (Douglas Ginsburg) and one former D.C. Circuit judge (Robert Bork), were nominated but not confirmed in the 1980s. Judges Patricia Wald and Laurence Silberman, along with former judges Abner Mikva and Kenneth Starr, have also been reported to be on the short list of nominees considered by Presidents George Bush and Bill Clinton in replacing Justices Thurgood Marshall, Byron White, or Harry Blackmun, all of whom have left the Court. It is little wonder, then, that a legal writer referred to the circuit as an "on-deck circle for high-court nominees," which helps make the Supreme Court justices "another inside-the-Beltway-bunch."[10] Notably, the high achievement of D.C. Circuit judges is consistent with historical trends; at least six judges have served on the Supreme Court or have held politically significant positions in the federal government.[11] Given its nomination and appointment track record, no doubt the D.C. Circuit stands out as one of the modern premier training grounds for fledgling United States Supreme Court justices, thus enlarging its influence.

Another distinctive aspect of the D.C. Circuit is its controversial nature, which draws attention from the national and local media. An analysis of the court's decision-making since 1960 demonstrates that it consistently makes headlines by ruling on cases that are politically significant. The strife it generates is intimately related to the political composition of the court and, of course, the nature of its docket and its location in Washington, D.C. Although in many cases its judges agree on case dispositions, it is still important to acknowledge that, with the ideological differences on the court, things are "not always sweetness and light" on the D.C. Circuit.[12] The tumultuous nature of the court's interpersonal relationships not only affects D.C. Circuit decision-making, but it is also an important clue to how the circuit acquired a special spot alongside the rest of the federal appeals courts. Even though this book inspects what the D.C. Circuit has done in its jurisprudence after 1960, it is critical to recognize that the court's internal disharmony is an integral aspect of its history, as the early decision of *Bush v. District of Columbia* (1893) attests.

From Judge Mikva's perspective, *Bush* is the first conspicuous display of the type of disunity that has become an important characteristic of the court's work over time. In *Bush* ". . . reasonable judges [became] unreasonably exercised about how to divine the meaning of the legislators." *Bush* involved whether a bar-room proprietor is subject to criminal prosecution for illegally selling liquor after the repeal and amendment of a statute permitting him to sell alcohol. In reversing Bush's conviction, the D.C. Circuit held that the legislature did not state an express legislative intention to revoke unexpired licenses issued under the previous liquor law; hence, Bush could not be criminally prosecuted under the law.[13] In commenting on *Bush*, Judge Mikva said:

> While the *Bush* case in 1893 was the first strong difference among the judges of the D.C. Circuit, it was far from the last. There are legends passed on from generations of judges and clerks about the sharp disagreements that existed during the Groner-Edgerton years, the Bazelon-Burger years, the Wright-Robb years, and all of the combinations since. When Robert Bork was going through his confirmation ordeal before the United States Senate, his tenure on this court was frequently described as if he were a key player in a maelstrom. He was, but that maelstrom was by no means limited to his tenure. Even to this day, some of the dissents are turgid and have ad hominem-ad feminem overtones.[14]

Many of the acute disagreements on the modern D.C. Circuit transpired between several legal titans on politically sensitive issues affecting criminal and administrative law. Judges David L. Bazelon and Warren Burger, for instance, found little to agree on in considering the proper scope of a criminal defendant's constitutional rights. Judges Patricia Wald and Robert Bork locked horns over the proper reach of the standing doctrine and the appropriate scope of judicial review pertaining to agency action.[15] In addition to the intracourt wrangling over hot-button issues of the day, some of the off-the-bench activities of the judges have, from time to time, caught the attention of the press.[16] Hence, the perception of animosity between D.C. Circuit judges, along with the court's inherent susceptibility to being unwittingly thrust into the national limelight, is not, in actuality, a historical oddity. Discord on the court—as roughly measured by the frequency of handing down nonunanimous judicial opinions—appears in as much as 20 percent of its published cases.[17]

Some of the judicial conflict on the bench boils over and spills onto the pages of journalistic accounts of the court's behavior. In 1991, for example, it became so turbulent in the court that the *New York Times* reported that Judge Laurence Silberman threatened to assault Judge Mikva over a particularly contentious affirmative action case. After the *New York Times* declined to publish Judge Silberman's version of the incident, the *Legal Times* picked up the story. The *Legal Times* version indicated that while Silberman denied threatening Mikva, he conceded that the brethren "were engaged in a quite spirited, indeed heated, discussion" in which Silberman said to Mikva that if "[Mikva] were ten years younger [he] would be tempted to punch [him] in the nose." But, as Silberman later rationalized, "Judge Mikva did not become ten years younger, our tempers receded, and we continued our discussion of the case." In the end, though, the event had important consequences since it raised questions about Silberman's judicial temperament and may have adversely affected his chances as a "short-list" candidate to fill a United States Supreme Court vacancy in the wake of Robert Bork's failed nomination.[18]

While the judicial politics of the D.C. Circuit helps to define the court's historical and political legacy, the court's modern reputation ultimately rests upon the enduring quality of its decisions. In this regard the D.C. Circuit has been characterized by the nature and scope of its criminal and administrative law policy-making. The court's influence over criminal and regulatory matters begins with its jurisdiction. As it will be seen, the court's power to hear certain cases has been strongly affected by external partisan considerations that were instrumental in establishing the court's authority over criminal and administrative law. Political scientist David O'Brien is correct, therefore, in claiming that the D.C. Circuit in the 1970s "became the second most important court in the land because it was given jurisdiction over health-and-safety and regulatory law." Another commentator familiar with the court reinforces this statement, noting that "as the federal government becomes more active and more intrusive, and more authority is given to agencies and departments, the D.C. Circuit takes on increasing significance as [a] court of last resort for most agency decisions."[19] Both views, to be sure, highlight that the court is a tour de force in administrative law.

Therefore, the D.C. Circuit is a special court because it acquired two distinct reputations after 1960. The first emerged from the court's liberal jurisprudence that expanded the individual rights of criminal defendants. The second is derived from the court's status as the premier judicial institution for deciding administrative appeals on a national scale. Significantly, in response to the court's judicial activism in criminal law in the 1960s, Congress politically transformed the court's jurisdiction in 1970, an event that had enormous implications for the court's future judicial role. As a result, the judicial politics of the D.C. Circuit is the point of departure for understanding the court's reputation in administrative law. Yet before examining the D.C. Circuit's political transformation, it is first essential to inspect the court's special genesis. From there it is possible to comprehend the manner in which its evolution and the aggregation of its power to hear certain appeals in criminal law in the district became the political impetus for taking it away.

## THE ANOMALOUS EVOLUTION OF THE D.C. CIRCUIT

From its beginning, the District of Columbia court system acquired a distinctive jurisdictional status that affected how courts in the district delivered justice in the nation's capital. Typically, in other jurisdictions, courts only had authority to hear cases applying federal or state law. Yet in the District of Columbia the federal appeals court was slated to be different because it immediately obtained the power to resolve questions of state law even though it was primarily a federal court. As a result, this hybrid or dual judicial function of what became the D.C. Circuit is the starting point for comprehending its controversial place in the American polity.

The special origin of the D.C. Circuit can be traced to the beginning of the nineteenth century, when Congress, in 1800, established the District of Columbia as the formal seat of the national government in the United States. Because the district was designated to symbolize national governmental authority, it was not legally considered a state. As a result, the district never assumed the type of sovereignty normally associated with statehood. Instead, at their inception the district's courts functioned in the hybrid capacity described earlier. Although this meant that the district's courts handled federal cases as a federal court situated in the nation's capital, it also conferred upon them the power to operate as state courts in the absence of regional courts, which dealt with disputes normally arising from everyday, local affairs.

The history of the D.C. Circuit reflects this uniqueness, a judicial trait that has substantially determined the nature and scope of the court's function over time. The beginning of the D.C. Circuit, in other words, results from the way in which the district's courts were created and developed over four general time periods. The first era, 1801–1863, is significant because it featured the development of the Circuit Court of the District of Columbia. In the second epoch, from 1863–1893, the Supreme Court of the District of Columbia operated. In the third period, from 1893–1948, the Court of Appeals of the District of Columbia was established and an independent federal judiciary began to develop. And, in 1948 and until the present time, the U.S. Court of Appeals for the District of Columbia emerged and continues today. With the partial exception of the last (and present) court, each court had the distinction of adjudicating federal *and* local cases, thereby causing at least one commentator to describe the historical progression of the district's court system as anomalous.[20]

### CIRCUIT COURT OF THE DISTRICT OF COLUMBIA

In 1801 the Circuit Court of the District of Columbia (Circuit Court) was created. In addition to its jurisdiction, probably the most distinguishing feature of the Circuit Court was its membership. Chief Judge William Kilty was famous for compiling "Kilty's Laws of Maryland," and Assistant Judge James Marshall (of Virginia) was the sibling of Chief Justice John Marshall of the United States Supreme Court. William Cranch also served as an assistant judge for fifty-four years, an accomplishment that may be surpassed only by the enduring fame he received as one of the first and foremost United States Supreme Court reporters. Apart from its membership, the Circuit Court had unique power. For example, in 1802 Congress empowered the Circuit Court's chief judge to convene a District Court of the United States which had the authority to act in a fashion that was analogous to the other United States District Courts. As a general matter it exercised trial jurisdiction in law and equity. Yet the Circuit Court functioned as a local and national judicial forum for litigants because it heard "all crimes and offences committed within [the] district, and of all cases in law and equity between parties, both or either of which shall be resident or be found within said district, and also of all actions or suits of a civil nature at common law or in equity, in which the United States shall be plaintiffs or complainants; and of all seizures on land or water, and all penalties and forfeitures made, arising or accruing under the laws of the United States."[21] Unquestionably, the dual local and nationalist character of the Circuit Court was an enduring quality of this and later District of Columbia courts. It was not until much later (after 1970) that the federal courts in the district stopped acting like local "state" courts, an event triggered by the enactment of the District of Columbia Court Reform and Criminal Procedure Act of 1970 (discussed in Chapter 2).

## SUPREME COURT OF THE DISTRICT OF COLUMBIA

Sixty-two years later, in 1863, the courts of the District of Columbia were reorganized. As part of that restructuring the Circuit Court was abolished and replaced by the Supreme Court of the District of Columbia. The impetus for court reform was the suspected disloyalty of the Circuit Court judges in the midst of the Civil War. The new Supreme Court of the District of Columbia, which succeeded to all the jurisdiction of the defunct Circuit Court, had four justices—David K. Cartter of Ohio, as chief justice; Abram B. Olin of New York, associate justice; George P. Fisher of Delaware, associate justice; and Andrew Wylie of the District of Columbia, associate justice—appointed by President Abraham Lincoln. Not only did the four have solid local reputations for integrity, but they were also nationally known for their allegiance to the Union.

The Lincoln appointments were controversial, however, since Congress permitted the president to appoint the justices in the same act that created the Supreme Court. Not only did the abolition of the Circuit Court and the appointment of new justices instill the perception that Lincoln had successfully "packed" the Supreme Court with loyalists, but it also may have been an unconstitutional violation of the separation of powers principle, since life-tenured Article III judges of the Circuit Court can only be removed on the grounds of misfeasance.

Moreover, although the Supreme Court of the District of Columbia possessed general jurisdiction in law and equity (like the Circuit Court it supplanted), it acted as an appellate court when it sat in General Term (a method of appeals similar to the one used in New York). Notably, too, the Supreme Court of the District of Columbia maintained the power to convene as a district court of the United States, which again gave it the type of jurisdiction enjoyed by the other United States district courts. Like its predecessors, though, its most defining characteristic was that it was essentially a local court that was dressed in a distinctly federal or national attire.[22]

## COURT OF APPEALS OF THE DISTRICT OF COLUMBIA

The aftermath of the Civil War brought an increase in population in the district and, concomitantly, a new burden for the district's Supreme Court in handling a burgeoning caseload. Congress responded by enacting court reform legislation designed to ease the workload pressure. Two laws were particularly significant. One, passed in 1870, created a new single-judge Police Court that relieved the district's Supreme Court of minor, nonfederal criminal jurisdiction that otherwise compelled it to hear local noncapital or infamous crimes cases. Only thirteen years later, in 1893, the legislature created another federal court called the Court of Appeals of the District of Columbia. The Court of Appeals was a three-member court having appellate jurisdiction taken from the district's Supreme Court. Significantly, too, the fledgling Court of Appeals' judgments were made subject to appellate review by the United States Supreme Court.[23]

## UNITED STATES COURT OF APPEALS FOR THE DISTRICT OF COLUMBIA CIRCUIT

Perhaps the most important aspect of the district's new Court of Appeals was that it was the immediate forerunner of the D.C. Circuit, the court under review. In 1934 its name was changed not only to reflect its growing national influence but also to try to distinguish it as a court that was *not* the exclusive source of jurisdiction over local matters in the district. The name change, in essence, was a legislative attempt to clarify the ambiguity of the new Court of Appeals relative to its local and national judicial functions. Prior to the alteration, the nature of the court was misconceived in that the previous title, Court of Appeals for the District of Columbia, suggested that the court was the exclusive appellate forum for cases arising in the District of Columbia. Even so, the new court, referred to as the United States Court of Appeals for the District of Columbia, nonetheless maintained its local and national jurisdiction.[24]

In 1948, the court's name was again modified to reflect its current title, the United States Court of Appeals for the District of Columbia Circuit (or, as it is most often referred to, "the D.C. Circuit"). While seemingly an innocuous change, it was significant because it formally incorporated the D.C. Circuit into the family of federal courts of appeals, or circuit courts, created by the 1891 Evarts Act. Notably then, after 1948 the D.C. Circuit became part of the middle tier of federal courts known as the U.S. Courts of Appeals. In this framework, the court hears appeals from the federal district courts (the principal trial courts) and simultaneously acts as a buffer to the federal appellate court of final resort, the U.S. Supreme Court.[25]

## "BY ACCIDENT RATHER THAN BY DESIGN?"

Even though the U.S. Court of Appeals for the District of Columbia assumed federal court status in the intermediate tier of the federal judiciary in 1948, it still retained its powers over local matters in the district. After 1948, the fact that the court heard local cases—those that would otherwise be handled in a comparable state appeals court—became increasingly significant in light of its emerging reputation in the 1960s as a liberal or activist bench that was allegedly too sympathetic to the rights of criminal defendants and perhaps the politically disadvantaged. As pundit Joseph Goulden once put it, however, the court's growth as a liberal court was historically more of an "accident rather than by design," primarily because the court in the 1930s and 1940s was considered by many lawyers to be a conservative, "so-so, do-nothing bench."[26] Indeed, Jeffrey Morris, a legal scholar who has examined the court's history, characterized the pre-1940s circuit as a "less important court with more a local than a national impact."[27]

Surely such a description of the court's work is a bit misleading (if not overstated) since the court made enduring decisions that, at times, basked in the glow of the national limelight. In the 1930s, for instance, the D.C. Circuit caught the public eye by affirming the conviction of Secretary of the Interior Albert B. Fall, a cabinet official who accepted a bribe of $100,000 from the president of an oil company seeking a lucrative lease arrangement with the United States government. The case gained notoriety because, apparently for the first time, a member of the president's cabinet was convicted of committing a criminal offense in his official capacity. Furthermore, in an important case that changed the legal standard pertaining to the proper charge that should be given to a jury in a larceny trial, the court grabbed national headlines as it helped to adjudicate the guilt of two men who sought to profit from the infamous and tragic Lindbergh child kidnapping and murder case. And, in the late 1930s and throughout the 1940s, a time when war clouds overseas threatened the stability of the American democracy, the D.C. Circuit was an integral part of the widely noticed disposition of a pair of criminal cases involving a Nazi sympathizer (author of a book titled *Spreading Germs of Hate*) who was convicted under the Foreign Agents Registration Act of 1938. One account of the court's work in those cases described the second D.C. Circuit appeal (and subsequent United States Supreme Court case) as a landmark construction of the act, if for nothing else than their historical importance.[28]

Nonetheless, as Goulden accurately portended, "things began changing" on the purportedly so-so, do-nothing bench when David Bazelon assumed his place on the D.C. Circuit in 1949. As will be discussed shortly, Judge Bazelon's impact upon the collegiality of the court, as well as his influence on the public image and jurisprudential significance in D.C. Circuit policy-making, cannot be overstated. As scholar Jeffrey Morris first suggested many years ago, Bazelon's sway over the judicial process was especially singular from the time he became chief judge of the court in 1962. Writing in 1972, for example, Morris characterized Bazelon as "a leading authority on mental health and the law," and a "deeply engaged civil libertarian," as well as "the author of some of the most influential opinions of the past twenty years in the areas of criminal procedure, loyalty-security, and administrative law."[29] While much of the scholarly literature substantially agrees with Morris's assessment, there is little doubt that Bazelon was the target of extensive criticism (if not vilification) mainly from conservatives, both on and off the court.

Not only did he have strained relations with some of his conservative brethren on the D.C. Circuit, who by at least one account thought Bazelon was "absolutely daft and so soft-hearted he should be a social worker, not a jurist," Bazelon reportedly antagonized many district court judges, who vehemently objected to being constantly overturned on appeal by the liberal-leaning "Bazelon Court." On the appeals court his principal nemesis and colleague was Judge Warren Burger. The two often locked horns on touchy political issues concerning whether the exclusionary rule applied to remove allegedly tainted evidence from a criminal trial or whether defendants had the option to plead insanity and escape prison incarceration by being treated at mental health facilities. The professional disagreement reportedly led Burger to belittle Bazelon to the point of referring to him as "poor Dave" and calling him "misguided" and "pathetic" because Bazelon was inclined to let criminal defendants out of jail.[30] And, most significantly, the liberal D.C. Circuit in the 1960s under Bazelon infuriated President Nixon, a self-proclaimed "law and order" chief executive, and political conservatives in Congress who strenuously disagreed with the scope and direction of circuit's policy-making in criminal law. Suffice it to say that Judge Bazelon's liberal propensities earned him both praise and scorn among a variety of court watchers, judges, scholars, and pundits who were aligned differently along the political spectrum.

Irrespective of the partisan reaction that the circuit generated among the legal profession and the press, it cannot be overemphasized that the judges on the D.C. Circuit could not have earned any sort of reputation, including a partisan one, without having the agenda opportunities to make legal and social policy. The flow of litigation, or the cases going to and from the district court, the circuit court, and the Supreme Court of the United States, is a key to understanding the nature of the court's agenda and decision-making as a policy-maker in the federal judiciary.[31] A systematic inspection of the workload statistics of all the federal circuit courts reveals several different litigation patterns affecting the judicial agenda of the D.C. Circuit in the 1960s. Figure 1 summarizes these trends.

The figure shows, for example, that the D.C. Circuit is singular in terms of its subject matter workload because on average it heard more criminal appeals, and fewer private civil appeals, than any other circuit court in the 1960s. While the circuit court agenda generally is defined by a dispropor-

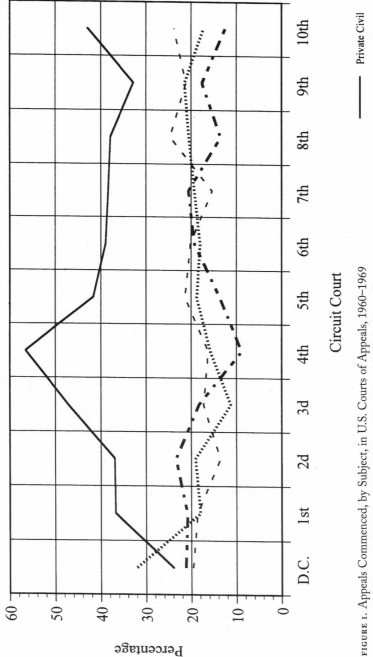

FIGURE 1. Appeals Commenced, by Subject, in U.S. Courts of Appeals, 1960–1969

Source: *Annual Report of the Director of the Administrative Office of the United States Courts,* from 1960 to 1969 (Table B-1).

Note: The category "Other," which includes bankruptcy, original proceedings, all other appeals, and District of Columbia appeals (from 1965 to 1969 only), is not reported. All data are based upon a twelve-month period ending June 30, as compiled by the Administrative Office of the U.S. Courts.

**TABLE I.** *Merit Terminations of Criminal Appeals, U.S. Courts of Appeals, 1960–1969*

| D.C. | 1st | 2d | 3d | 4th | 5th | 6th | 7th | 8th | 9th | 10th |
|------|-----|-----|-----|-----|-----|-----|-----|-----|-----|------|
| 10.4% | 1.4% | 6.8% | 2.3% | 3.8% | 9.7% | 4.9% | 3.8% | 3.0% | 8.6% | 3.7% |

SOURCE: *Annual Report of the Administrative Office of the U.S. Courts, 1960–1969* (Table B-1).

NOTE: "Merit terminations" are those "cases disposed of after hearing or submission" in Table B-1. All data are based upon the twelve-month period ending June 30, as compiled by the Administrative Office of the U.S. Courts.

tionate number of private civil appeals, the same cannot be said of the D.C. Circuit. In fact, the D.C. Circuit's docket primarily features criminal appeals. Specifically, 32.01 percent of the D.C. Circuit's docket is consumed by criminal appeals and 23.89 percent is taken up with private civil appeals. In comparison, for all circuits (excluding the D.C. Circuit) the average rate of criminal appeals is 18.19 percent and, for private civil appeals, the rate is 40.86 percent. But for the difference in criminal and private civil appeals, the judicial business of the D.C. Circuit is mostly comparable to what is on the docket of the remaining circuit courts. In particular, the D.C. Circuit heard on average 19.61 percent of U.S. civil and 21.24 percent of administrative appeals, whereas for all circuits (excluding the D.C. Circuit) the average is 19.05 percent (U.S. civil) and 16.82 percent (administrative).

Figure 1 clearly shows that the D.C. Circuit had more opportunities within its agenda space to make policy in criminal law. This finding is buttressed by Table 1, which reveals that the D.C. Circuit is also the top court in terms of disposing of criminal appeals on the merits. Specifically, the D.C. Circuit decided 10.4 percent of the 58.3 percent of the total criminal appeals heard on the merits in all the circuits from 1960 to 1969.[32] Only the Fifth (9.7 percent) and Ninth (8.6 percent) Circuits had a comparable number of criminal merit terminations during the 1960s. Table 1 summarizes the findings for all the circuit courts.

## CRIME, POLITICS, AND THE JUDICIAL ACTIVISM OF THE D.C. CIRCUIT

With a large proportion of criminal appeals on the docket, the D.C. Circuit was poised to assume its first significant national reputation as a liberal activist court that favored expanding the legal protections afforded to those accused of crimes in the district. Legal academicians and jurists agree that the D.C. Circuit's most lasting influence in the 1960s was its impact on criminal justice and, to a lesser extent, poverty law. Legal scholar Jeffrey Morris, for example, concluded that the court made its most pronounced mark in criminal justice "in insuring access of the poor to the judicial system, and in modifying the balance in civil cases in support of the claims of the poor." Likewise, in commenting upon the sway that the circuit court had as a court of last resort over local issues, former U.S. Supreme Court justice William J. Brennan, Jr., observed that "this special responsibility has had the greatest importance in the area of criminal law, since the jurisdiction of the court has permitted its use of supervisory powers in areas where other federal courts could intervene pursuant to constitutional command, or not at all."[33]

Much of the court's influence in criminal law stemmed from the jurisprudential outlook of D.C. Circuit Judge David L. Bazelon, once described by his colleague, Judge Abner J. Mikva, as the quintessential legal realist. After ascending to chief judge in 1962, Bazelon used his leadership to push the D.C. Circuit in an increasingly progressive direction in the areas of criminal responsibility, mental health law, juvenile rights, and bail reform. Unquestionably, this effort is entirely consistent with his general philosophy of criminal justice, which emphasizes openness, morality, liberalism, and a firm adherence to exercising correct judicial procedure.[34]

Notably, too, during this time progressive-minded jurists like David Bazelon, James Skelly Wright, Charles Fahy, Henry W. Edgerton, and Spottswood W. Robinson jelled into a solid voting bloc that consistently seized upon the agenda opportunities afforded them, thereby making the D.C. Circuit a bulwark for liberal criminal justice legal policy. For example, time and again throughout the 1960s the Bazelon court shaped the law of criminal responsibility by first deciding and then continually revisiting one of Bazelon's early seminal decisions, the famous *Durham v. United States* (1954) insanity case.[35] Although the decision was originally handed down by the D.C. Circuit in 1954, the court thereafter tried to apply the *Durham* insanity doctrine in an acceptable fashion to the recurring but myriad fact patterns of cases that routinely appeared on the court's criminal docket in the 1960s and early to mid-1970s. Prior to *Durham,* virtually all jurisdictions employed *M'Naghten's Case* (1843), a rule that evaluated an individual's criminal responsibility by inquiring whether the defendant knew the difference between right and wrong in respect to his act, as the governing legal standard.[36] The 1954 *Durham* rule—which supplanted the *M'Naghten* test of criminal responsibility in the district—is deceptively simple. It holds that "an accused is not criminally responsible if the unlawful act is the product of a mental disease or defect."[37] Yet its application to cases remained very problematic.

For instance, an immediate issue arose as to *who* (either the judge, jury, or a medical expert) was to decide if the defendant labored under a "mental disease or defect." Thereafter, juries and medical experts struggled to apply the language of the rule to insanity cases, leading to a reformulation of the rule in *McDonald v. United States* (1962) where, in a per curiam (an unsigned) en banc ruling, the court redefined "mental disease or defect" as "any abnormal condition of the mind which substantially affects mental or emotional processes and substantially impairs behavior controls."[38] Considering these problems, then, it is easy to see why the court finally overruled itself in *United States v. Brawner* (1972), which, in all likelihood, turned out to be an especially bitter pill for Bazelon to swallow.[39]

Nonetheless, perhaps it is best to judge *Durham* in light of the impact it had on the way mentally impaired defendants were treated in the criminal justice system during the time it was circuit precedent. "At least," one scholar asserted, *Durham* "not only redefined the test for criminal responsibility but also generated case law modifying the rules governing competence to stand trial and governing the commitment of mental patients." *Durham's* lasting legacy, in other words, lay in forcing the legal and medical professions to reconsider what the best approach was to using the insanity test or any other medical-legal rules dealing with the mentally ill.[40] Moreover, the ruling, its progeny, and the debate it stirred certainly enhanced the D.C. Circuit's growing reputation as an activist court. Commentators, legislators, interest groups, and court watchers alike both praised and condemned the opinion and the court that had produced it, making the D.C. Circuit a lightning rod for controversy and perhaps power in the 1960s.

While its subsequent cases in criminal law may not have been as significant as *Durham,* the D.C. Circuit produced many other activist decisions involving criminal responsibility and procedure, all of which increasingly exasperated conservatives and like-minded jurists. *Easter v. District of Columbia* (1966) was especially provocative since it made chronic alcoholism a defense to a criminal charge of public intoxication.[41] Although the decision drew accolades from those who were sympathetic to the plight of the mentally ill, its practical effects were disastrous for district treatment facilities, which could not handle the massive influx of new patients after the ruling. Nor was the case or the policy it engendered followed anywhere else in the nation. In fact, in 1968 the Supreme Court, in *Powell v. Texas,* had a chance to embrace it but declined.[42]

Similarly, in two other closely related cases, *Rouse v. Cameron* (1966) and *Lake v. Cameron* (1966), the D.C. Circuit showed its progressive tendencies when it wrote into law a "right to treatment" for criminal defendants who were involuntarily confined to mental institutions as a consequence of their mental disability. After an insanity acquittal on a dangerous weapons charge, the petitioner in *Rouse* was involuntarily confined to a mental hospital, as was the one in *Lake*. In *Lake*, however, the petitioner was an elderly woman suffering from brain disease who was not considered dangerous to anyone but herself. The most controversial aspect of these cases was that the writ of habeas corpus was successfully used by both defendants to challenge their involuntary confinement in mental hospitals.[43]

The impact and reaction to both cases was swift. As a result of *Rouse*, courts had to insure that defendants were receiving adequate treatment for their disabilities or, if they were not, explain the circumstances in detail. As a consequence of *Lake*, judges had to determine if there were any alternative forms of treatment on similar grounds. Both cases also had profound implications for permitting mentally ill defendants who were sometimes perceived to be criminally dangerous to employ, successfully, a writ of habeas corpus for their release.[44] Each ruling provoked the claim that the D.C. Circuit was more interested in pampering convicted felons than in punishing them.

The expansion of juvenile rights and bail reform also occupied the attention of the progressive D.C. Circuit in the 1960s. In spite of the belief that juveniles were a recurring source of crime in the district, the D.C. Circuit rendered a series of opinions aimed at securing better rehabilitative treatment of underage offenders. In addition, the court worked to give them expanded rights of representation, along with more due process protection at juvenile hearings. Bail practices in the district were also the target of D.C. Circuit jurisprudence, although much of the court's success in reform came as a result of the extrajudicial efforts and not through the court's political decision-making. In 1962, for example, at the prodding of Chief Judge Bazelon, an internal committee of the Judicial Conference of the District of Columbia was created to study the feasibility of changing the bail procedure in the district, including pretrial release on personal recognizance in lieu of posted bond. After receiving the recommendations of this committee (and that of the Junior Bar Association), the Circuit Conference launched the D.C. Bail Project in 1964, which subsequently released a substantial number of defendants on personal recognizance (on a trial basis) to see if it would work. It did, and the project's success was instrumental in the enactment of the Bail Reform Act of 1966, national legislation that facilitated the pretrial release of offenders who otherwise would have remained incarcerated because of their inability to post financial bond that insured their presence at trial.[45]

If that was not enough to earn the contempt of conservatives, the D.C. Circuit continued to march to its liberal tune by deciding cases that gave criminal defendants more protection in defending themselves at trial. In 1965 the court decided *Luck v. United States*, which severely limited the prosecution's ability to use prior convictions as a means to impeach a criminal defendant's credibility on the witness stand. Writing for the majority, Judge Carl McGowan construed D.C. Code Section 14-305 on the use of this type of evidence broadly. The ruling in *Luck* gave trial judges considerable discretion to admit or exclude prior convictions as evidence in a criminal case. Criminal defendants were also given greater rights in respect to being represented by counsel in the district when they could not afford one.[46]

For example, with *Blue v. United States* (1964), not only did the court constitutionalize an indigent's right to counsel at a preliminary hearing but, in dicta, the court suggested that the purpose of a preliminary hearing was for the defendant to conduct discovery on the charges and determine if probable cause exists to bind the accused over for trial.[47] In still other decisions, appointed counsel was extended to indigent defendants attending grand jury proceedings prior to indictment, and the right to an attorney was also provided for parolees in parole revocation hearings. And, in other cases, the circuit's liberal wing was not shy in its efforts to expand the applicability of the exclusionary rule, to guard against coerced confessions, and to insure that a defendant would get a speedy trial under the Constitution. But by adding these protections the D.C. Circuit increasingly provoked the ire of conservatives in Congress and the executive branch.[48] Perhaps typifying the discontent was the disgust expressed by Senate Minority Leader Hugh Scott, a Republican from Pennsylvania, who reportedly said after a bombing in a restroom at the United States Capitol that even if the perpetrators were caught and convicted, the D.C. Circuit "would find some way to get them out."[49]

## THE "SECOND MOST IMPORTANT" COURT IN CRIMINAL LAW?

Regardless of the short-term effect of its decisions, a more resilient quality of the D.C. Circuit's criminal judicial policy-making is that the United States Supreme Court more often than not did *not* disturb D.C. Circuit rulings. Because the D.C. Circuit was in part acting like a state supreme court, it had more agenda space to decide local criminal law appeals which, in turn, let it rule with the final authority of a court of last resort in the federal constitutional system. Political scientist J. Woodford Howard had it right when he once observed that "because [circuit court] decisions are final except when the Justices [of the United States Supreme Court] grant review, circuit courts are courts of last resort for the great mass of federal litigants."[50] This fact gave the D.C. Circuit considerable influence over criminal law policy in the district.

Needless to say, the substance of the D.C. Circuit's criminal law decisions assumes more importance in light of what happened to them on appeal. While it is difficult to determine the exact number of appeals heard by the Supreme Court, it is more feasible to analyze the grant and denial rate of certiorari petitions from the circuits in order to achieve a sense of the Supreme Court's posture toward D.C. Circuit criminal law appeals. But, even before looking at the findings it is important to note that intuitively one would think that there would be more denials (or affirmance of the circuit court position) of certiorari, simply because the historical relationship between the two courts has been characterized by deference in respect to D.C. Circuit local authority. In other words, because of the D.C. Circuit's hybrid federal-state jurisdiction, the Supreme Court tended to refrain, as a matter of judicial policy, from overruling the D.C. Circuit whenever the circuit court exercised its supervisory power over local criminal matters.[51]

This supervisory power was expressed as early as 1946 by the Supreme Court in *Fisher v. United States*, in which the Court left intact a D.C. Circuit affirmance of a petitioner's murder conviction in district court. In *Fisher*, a criminal defendant was sentenced to death for first-degree murder, an offense requiring a finding of premeditation. At issue was whether the defendant was entitled to an instruction permitting the jury to weigh evidence of the defendant's mental disabilities and therefore vitiate the capacity for premeditation. Since the settled law in the district clearly disallowed the instruction, the district court refused to give it, an act that became the basis for the appeal to the D.C. Circuit. By refusing to disturb the conviction, Justice Stanley Reed took notice that the law on the challenged jury instruction in the district was firmly established:

> The administration of criminal law in matters not affected by constitutional limitations or a general federal law is a matter peculiarly of local concern . . . Matters relating to law enforcement in the District are entrusted to the courts of the District. Our policy is not to interfere with the local rules of law which they fashion, save in exceptional situations where egregious error has been committed. Where the choice of the Court of Appeals of the District of Columbia in local matters between conflicting legal conclusions seems nicely balanced, we do not interfere. The policy of deferring to the District's courts on local law matters is reinforced here by the fact that the local law now challenged is long established and deeply rooted in the District.[52]

**TABLE 2.** *U.S. Supreme Court Certiorari Dispositions, U.S. Courts of Appeals, 1960–1969*

| Disposition | D.C. | 1st | 2d | 3d | 4th | 5th | 6th | 7th | 8th | 9th | 10th |
|---|---|---|---|---|---|---|---|---|---|---|---|
| Denials | 80.9% | 61.3% | 71.4% | 76.0% | 80.7% | 61.6% | 73.9% | 71.7% | 72.9% | 70.7% | 66.2% |
| Grants | 6.0% | 14.1% | 7.9% | 5.7% | 1.9% | 5.7% | 4.8% | 9.1% | 5.7% | 4.9% | 11.4% |
| Dismissals | .57% | — | .27% | .63% | .47% | 5.2% | .32% | .57% | — | .55% | 21.9% |

SOURCE: *Annual Report of the Administrative Office of the U.S. Courts,* from 1960 to 1969 (Table B-2).
NOTE: Percentages are derived by dividing the sum of criminal certiorari dispositions for each circuit for the ten-year period into the sum the criminal certiorari filings in that circuit for the same time period. The "total number of criminal certiorari filings" includes the ten-year sum of pending cases from the prior fiscal year. Percentages for each court do not equal 100 percent because the percentages relative to the pending cases from the current fiscal year are not presented in the table. All data are based upon the twelve-month period ending June 30, as compiled by the Administrative Office of the U.S. Courts.

It is rather unremarkable, then, that in later cases the D.C. Circuit employed its local supervisory power to make new criminal policy in those instances in which doing so would not offend extant statutory or constitutional provisions.[53]

Moreover, the Supreme Court's policy-making in criminal justice also made it more likely that it would affirm, rather than reverse, liberal outcomes from the D.C. Circuit in the 1960s. During this period the Supreme Court's criminal justice revolution in civil rights and liberties peaked under the leadership of Chief Justice Earl Warren, a liberal jurist. Thus, it was logical that the High Court probably affirmed a large proportion of appeals coming from the D.C. Circuit, since the court was reputed to be sympathetic to the rights of criminal defendants, and, consequently, that the rate at which certiorari was granted would also tend to be low while affirmances (denials) would be high.[54]

Table 2 confirms these hypotheses by summarizing the frequency with which the U.S. Supreme Court denied and granted certiorari in cases involving criminal appeals from the U.S. Courts of Appeals from 1960 to 1969. Just as it had been first in the number of criminal appeals it heard and disposed of on the merits, the D.C. Circuit had 80.94 percent of its criminal certiorari filings denied by the Supreme Court over the ten-year period, the highest ranking percentage of denials among circuit courts. In fact, as Table 2 makes evident, this rate is 8.98 percent over the average percentage for all circuit courts (71.96 percent, inclusive of the D.C. Circuit; for all circuits, the average grant rate is 6.61 percent). The Fourth Circuit had the next highest percentage (80.7 percent), followed by the Third (76.0 percent), Sixth (73.9 percent), and Eighth (72.9 percent) Circuits, respectively. Even though denial rates between the D.C. Circuit and the Fourth Circuit are virtually identical, the D.C. Circuit sent a far greater number of certiorari petitions to the High Court that were denied (565) than the Fourth Circuit (or any other court), thereby making the D.C. Circuit's denial rate more significant. Furthermore, the table demonstrates that D.C. Circuit criminal certiorari petitions were granted only 6.0 percent of the time in the 1960s. Four other circuits, the First (14.1 percent), Tenth (11.4 percent), Seventh (9.1 percent), and Second (7.9 percent), had higher grant rates. As with the denial rate, the grant rate of D.C. Circuit certiorari petitions is substantively more important because the Supreme Court granted from the D.C. Circuit a higher number of certiorari filings (42) than all of the other circuit courts, save one (i.e., the Second circuit, with 58 grants, or 7.9 percent). As a result, the Supreme Court granted a proportionately smaller number of certiorari petitions from the D.C. Circuit than any other court with a comparable number of grants.

The high denial and low grant rates of certiorari petitions in the D.C. Circuit suggest that the Supreme Court largely chose to let the appellate court make policy in criminal law in the 1960s. That decision was probably an ideological choice since both courts were liberal in their composition in the same period. One would, in fact, expect to see an opposite pattern—that is, low denial and high grant rates—only if the Supreme Court disapproved of what the lower court was doing with its criminal law decision-making. But Table 2 reveals a different finding, mainly because the Supreme Court generally condoned the type of policy decisions emanating from the D.C. Circuit in that area of jurisprudence. When considered together with the unencumbered exercise of local supervisory power by the D.C. Circuit, the Supreme Court's noninterference thus transformed the circuit court in Washington, D.C., into a court of last resort for litigants suing in the federal court in criminal appeals. This had profound implications for the nation because the Supreme Court implicitly *let* the D.C. Circuit's activism change the scope of criminal law policy by expanding the rights of the accused in a turbulent civil rights decade.

## CONCLUSION

From at least one perspective, the almost milk-toast bench characterizing the D.C. Circuit in the 1930s and 1940s emerged as a dominant force in criminal law in the 1960s under the activist, liberal leadership of Chief Judge David Bazelon. Bazelon's impact on the court's jurisprudence, though, is only part of the explanation as to why the court earned that controversial reputation. Indeed, a number of legal and political factors combined to produce it.

Perhaps the most important reason relates to the structure of the District of Columbia's judiciary and the nature of the court's agenda. As an anomalous bench, the D.C. Circuit acted in a dual judicial capacity. Although it heard cases involving federal law, it also decided local criminal law appeals. The unique, hybrid nature of the court's jurisdiction gave the D.C. Circuit the chance to seize its many agenda opportunities in criminal law, especially since at least one-third of its docket consisted of criminal appeals during a ten-year period. As a result, Bazelon's interest in exploring the legal frontiers of innovative criminal, mental health, and juvenile jurisprudence affected the court's liberal activism, much to the chagrin of politically opposed conservatives.

In fact, as Chapter 2 describes, the court's reputation in protecting the rights of the criminally accused provoked a political response that fundamentally altered the D.C. Circuit's jurisdiction after 1970. The conservative reaction stemmed from the direct impact that the D.C. Circuit had in the 1960s as an appellate court of last resort. Since the Warren Court condoned much of what the Bazelon Court was doing in its criminal law jurisprudence (by way of high denial and low grant rates of certiorari criminal appeals emanating from the D.C. Circuit), the D.C. Circuit became the final say in creating legal policy for most federal litigants in criminal law. Soon, however, the court's judicial function would change dramatically as President Richard Nixon's conception of a "law and order" society became a reality under the pretense of judicial reform. What the conservatives did not count on, however, was that the D.C. Circuit would be able to remain a liberal court, in spite of court reform.

# Mollycoddling Judges and the Politics of D.C. Circuit Court Reform

For many, the criminal process, while promising "Equal Justice Under Law," continues to deliver only "Justice For Those Who Can Afford It."
—JUDGE DAVID L. BAZELON OF THE D.C. CIRCUIT

I do not believe that regulation through judicial decision or statute of investigatory procedures should have as its purpose to remedy all the inequalities which may exist in our society as a result of social and economic and intellectual differences to the exclusion of all other purposes and values sought to be achieved in the criminal process.
—ATTORNEY GENERAL NICHOLAS deB. KATZENBACH

The D.C. Circuit's liberal activism in criminal law did not go unnoticed by court watchers and ideologically opposed critics. Detractors of the court believed that the circuit's lack of judicial restraint was the worst kind of judicial interventionism because it hampered the laudable efforts of law enforcement to put away criminals. Courts were increasingly blamed for the crime problem besetting the nation. The circuit court in Washington was, in particular, heavily criticized because of the perception that "the D.C. appeals court is what politicians have in mind when they rant about mollycoddling judges who dream up ingenious excuses to free criminals from jail."[1] Mollycoddling judges, therefore, and not the criminals, did more to victimize society through their judicial inclination to enlarge the constitutional protections afforded felons.

Judge David Bazelon did little in his opinions or off-the-bench activities to dispel the popular notion that D.C. Circuit judges were aligning themselves with the interests of violent offenders.[2] An extraordinary exchange of letters between Judge Bazelon and Attorney General Nicholas deB. Katzenbach in 1965 is illustrative. The private letters, which debated the merits of adopting the American Law Institute's (ALI) proposals to revise Model Code prearraignment procedures, were leaked to the press and published in the Washington, D.C., *Evening Star* in June of 1965. Once they were made public, the competing views of a liberal judge and a law-and-order attorney general were thrust before the public eye.

The letters disclosed two distinct perspectives on the best way to handle crime. From Judge Bazelon's standpoint, the ALI revisions discriminated against the poor by failing to give indigents appointed counsel during interrogation while, paradoxically, unjustly allowing retained counsel to be present. For Bazelon, this double standard epitomized unequal treatment under the law since "those who could afford it would have some support from counsel [whereas] the poor [would] have none." Katzenbach, in turn, responded by suggesting that inequality is an inevitable part of the criminal justice system. The attorney general argued that the elusive quest for absolute equality in court only worked to tread on innocent victims of crime unfairly since it impeded the police in trying to catch and convict criminals. In the end, for Katzenbach, "acquittal of the guilty in the name of equality of treatment may prevent our achieving other, more fundamental goals also contained in the ideal of equal justice." One of those "other, more fundamental" objectives was to deter crime and protect innocent citizens from random acts of crime.[3]

Although the merits of these positions remain debatable, at the time of publication the Bazelon-Katzenbach letters intensified the feeling that the American judiciary was too soft on criminals.[4] The judicial workload statistics of the Administrative Office of the U.S. Courts support that perception.[5] Clearly there was a sharp increase in crime which ultimately resulted in more criminal cases being commenced in appellate court. In 1960, for instance, 323 criminal cases were initiated in the circuit courts, whereas by the end of the decade, there were 2,508; hence, all circuit courts experienced a 302.6 percent increase in criminal case filings. A very similar increase occurred in the Washington circuit court. For 1960, in particular, 100 cases were filed and, in 1969, there were 497, representing an impressive 379 percent increase in criminal appeals.

Having more criminal cases on the docket fueled the criticism that the courts had too many agenda opportunities to create law favoring the interests of criminal defendants at the expense of society. The specific findings in Figure 2 regarding the percentage of criminal appeals commenced in the D.C. Circuit underscores that claim. Apart from the D.C. Circuit, the workload data indicates that 15.9 percent of the total circuit courts' dockets in 1960 consisted of criminal appeals, and, in 1969, it was 24.4 percent. But the percentage of criminal appeals commenced in the D.C. Circuit was considerably higher. In 1960, only 19.8 percent of its docket were criminal appeals. In 1969, that percentage rose to become nearly half (45.5 percent) of the D.C. Circuit docket.

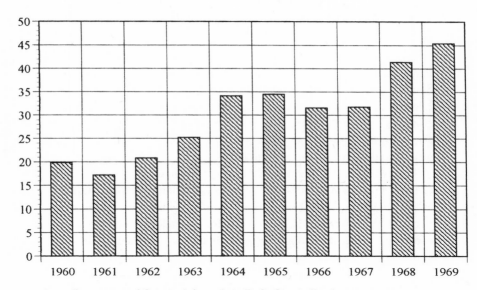

**FIGURE 2.** Percentage of Criminal Appeals in D.C. Circuit Docket, 1960–1969
Source: *Annual Report of the Director of the Administrative Office of the United States Courts,*
from 1960 to 1969 (Table B-1).
Note: All data are based upon a twelve-month period ending June 30, as compiled by the
Administrative Office of the U.S. Courts.

As criminal filings continued unabated in the 1960s, there was a corresponding rise in the number of pending criminal appeals as well. This was a disturbing trend, since a larger number of pending cases signified that more time was elapsing between arrest and trial. Critics found it easy to argue, therefore, that an elevated rate of pending appeals proved that criminal suspects were being given too many rights by the courts. Since the percentage of pending appeals increased by 487 percent in all circuit courts (and by 904.3 percent in the D.C. Circuit), it was difficult for defenders of the courts to sustain a convincing argument that the backlog of criminal cases was not due to the courts' lenience in punishing dangerous felons.

The high crime rate, along with an increased frequency of criminal case filings and pending appeals, galvanized the 1968 presidential race and ultimately became the impetus for changing how some liberal courts in America functioned in the 1960s. Led by its no-nonsense presidential nominee, Richard Nixon, the Republican party made the return to "law and order" its foremost domestic issue in the 1968 campaign and, from most accounts, with good political reason. Statistics confirmed that the crime rate in Washington was soaring, and presidential and congressional studies reinforced the popular notion that it was out of control. This, in turn, created the impression that the nation's capital was a city under siege and torn apart by an increasing amount of economic and racial disharmony. A report issued by the Advisory Panel Against Violence, a thirteen-member panel of legal experts led by Senator Joseph D. Tydings (D-Md., chair of the Senate Committee on the District of Columbia), exacerbated these fears by concluding that "armed crime [is] rampant in D.C." It is not surprising, therefore, that by the end of the 1960s the fear of street crime was the most pressing social issue of the day next to ending the Vietnam conflict.[6]

Perceiving a social mandate for change, Nixon used the politics of law and order as a platform to launch a frontal assault upon the federal judiciary in an effort to win the White House. Anti–Warren Court sentiment—or the belief that the U.S. Supreme Court and its liberal majority were lax on crime—continued to mount throughout the campaign. Since the Bazelon Court was perceived by many as a willing judicial accomplice to the Warren Court's due process revolution,[7] presidential nominee Richard Nixon was prompted to say in his August 1968 acceptance speech at the GOP Convention, "Let us always respect, as I do, our courts and those who serve on them, but let us also recognize that some of our courts in their decisions have gone too far in weakening the *peace forces* as against the criminal forces in this country" (emphasis added).[8] As a result, by the end of the decade the D.C. Circuit became the focus of a conservative movement to alter the political landscape and arm the so-called peace forces with more weapons to fight crime. As the D.C. Circuit was about to find out, the weapon of choice was congressional court reform legislation that clipped the liberal wings of the circuit court.

## THE D.C. CIRCUIT CRIME BILL

After winning the White House, the enactment of the District of Columbia Court Reform and Criminal Procedure Act of 1970, colloquially known as the D.C. Crime bill, gave President Nixon and conservatives more of a chance to claim victory in the political war against crime.[9] By any measure, it was also a stunning partisan success in the battle against liberal judicial politics. Ostensibly touted as the best means to insure swift and sure punishment of criminals in the district, the act curbed the D.C. Circuit's liberal tendencies by weakening its criminal law precedent and changing its jurisdiction to hear criminal appeals. Presumably recognizing that an effective means to fight crime was also to challenge liberal conceptions of justice, the Nixon Administration found a way to do so through the passage of the D.C. Crime bill in July 1970.

According to its principal sponsor, Senator Joseph D. Tydings (D-Md.), the D.C. Crime bill was supposed to fight crime *and* achieve court reform in the District of Columbia. Court reorganization generated little controversy in Congress because most representatives thought that the D.C. Court system was anachronistic at best. At worst, the consensus was that it could not deliver adequate criminal justice to the district due to a variety of problems caused by case backlog, delay, and general inefficiency. So no one really quarreled with the notion of fixing the D.C. courts, simply because doing so fit the rhetoric of improving the overall quality of the criminal justice system.

More controversial, though, were the crime components of the legislation. Besides dramatically restructuring the district's judiciary, the D.C. Crime bill featured several proposals that gave the police more resources to combat the soaring crime rate successfully. The new statute permitted "no-knock" police searches. A comprehensive police wiretapping procedure was authorized, and police were given new authority to detain criminal suspects in lieu of bail if they thought a suspect was dangerous to the community. More power was given to the courts as well; judges could sentence recidivists to life in prison. Because of these measures, Senator Sam J. Ervin (D-N.C.), a political conservative and chair of the Senate Subcommittee on Constitutional Rights, opposed the bill vigorously. Ervin argued that the bill's criminal provisions were too repressive for a democracy and "smack[ed] of a police state." The press took notice, and much of the ensuing debate in Congress and throughout the country centered on the constitutionality of certain parts of the legislation.[10]

Curiously, one aspect of the bill that has been de-emphasized is its conspicuous partisanship. That is unusual since the D.C. Circuit is routinely portrayed as an ideologically divided court of appeals. Furthermore, as suggested earlier, the results of D.C. Circuit criminal cases increasingly disturbed conservatives. Political considerations—especially those favoring a Nixon brand of law-and-order politics—must have been a part of the thinking of conservative strategists responsible for drafting the D.C. Crime bill. Nixon's Department of Justice, in fact, initially wrote the bill and forwarded it to Congress immediately after the 1968 presidential election.[11] As law professor Jeffrey Morris quipped, "Court reorganization was at least partially a vehicle for getting Bazelon and Wright's hands out of the criminal law–poverty law 'cookie jar.'" Pundit Joseph Goulden was even more direct, saying that the D.C. Crime bill was "attributable directly to hostility towards the Bazelon court by the Nixon Administration and congressional conservatives." After all, conservative critics generally thought liberal courts were responsible for exacerbating the district's crime problem. Since the D.C. Circuit was an increasingly progressive court in the 1960s, an underlying motivation for the bill's enactment must have been to curb the ideological direction of the court's output in criminal law appeals.[12]

A careful examination of the legislative history of the bill indicates that the judicial politics of the D.C. Circuit was on the mind of the legislature when it searched for a court reform rationale.[13] Beginning at least four months before the president signed the legislation into law, remarks made on the floor of the U.S. House of Representatives indicate that court reform was necessary because it would end the D.C. Circuit's jurisdiction over local criminal matters. For example, Representative Joel T. Broyhill (R-Va.) offered, "Another benefit of this proposal is that it will eliminate appellate review by the U.S. Court of Appeals. This court of appeals is notorious. Getting a conviction past Judge Bazelon and Judge Wright is like passing a ship between Scylla and Charybdis. Local offenders in the District are well aware of the proclivities for leniency by men on that court. In the new proposed system, they will appeal convictions to the District of Columbia Court of Appeals." On the same day Representative Thomas G. Abernethy (D-Miss.) voiced a similar sentiment, noting that court reform was essential because liberal rulings by the U.S. Supreme Court and the D.C. Circuit increased the time it took to dispose of criminal cases. This, for Representative Abernethy, thwarted any possibility of attaining swift criminal justice. In his view, the proposed legislation was wise since "under this court reorganization, decisions in the [new] superior court will be appealed to the District of Columbia Court of Appeals. Beyond that, cases may be reviewed by the Supreme Court. With rare exceptions, this new regimen bypasses the U.S. court of appeals. The elimination of this unnecessary layer of review and the attendant decrease in the opportunity for mischief by that court is more than sufficient grounds to adopt this legislation."

Admittedly, most legislators were not as candid as Representatives Broyhill and Abernethy in articulating their desire to end the liberal mischief of the D.C. Circuit. Most others echoed the sentiments of Senator Allen J. Ellender (D-La.), whose partisan motivations were apparent but couched in softer rhetoric. On the day the bill left the U.S. Senate, he remarked that court reorganization was beneficial because "in recent years our courts have been all too active and 'helpful' in striking down provisions in the law and procedures in our judicial and law-enforcement systems which in my opinion encouraged lawlessness."[14] In other words, liberal courts like the D.C. Circuit were the problem because they gratuitously cloaked criminals in protective garb called the Bill of Rights.

After the bill left Congress, on July 29, 1970, President Nixon signed it into law with most of its uncontroverted and dubious features intact. From any perspective, the legislation dramatically transformed the District of Columbia court system. Three local courts with trial jurisdiction—the Court of General Sessions, the Juvenile Court, and the District of Columbia Tax

Court—merged into a single court called the Superior Court of the District of Columbia. The Superior Court was given the power to hear cases in civil, criminal, domestic, probate, and tax law. More significantly, as a court of general jurisdiction the Superior Court not only assumed all of the local matters once heard by the federal district court, but it also had the authority to hear all civil and criminal matters in the district. Additionally, the bill transferred all local appeals to the District of Columbia Court of Appeals. As a result, the U.S. Court of Appeals (D.C. Circuit) could only adjudicate federal appeals, thus ending the D.C. Circuit's ability to function as a local "state supreme court" in criminal matters.[15] With the new legislation, the anomalous court of great authority was now politically transformed into an ordinary federal court of appeals, or so it seemed.

Conservatives accomplished court reform in other respects as well. The D.C. Crime bill created a circuit executive position to increase court efficiency in judicial administration. More judgeships were authorized, judicial salaries were increased, and judges received better retirement benefits. The delivery of legal services was enhanced through the institution of a comprehensive public defender system. The legislation devised a new juvenile code and the scope and responsibilities of the District of Columbia Bail Agency were expanded. In addition, significant changes were made in the laws affecting habeas corpus, paternity proceedings, and certain interlocutory appeals.[16]

The new law featured several crime-stopping initiatives as well, including some provisions specifically reversing or vitiating liberal D.C. Circuit precedent. The *Luck* doctrine, which gave judges wide authority over admitting or excluding prior conviction evidence at trial, was gutted since the legislation stripped judges of the power to keep from the jury a defendant's prior conviction for impeachment purposes. Prior to the change in the law, some in Congress criticized the *Luck* rule as unworkable. The D.C. Circuit, the critics argued, did not establish meaningful criteria for guiding trial court discretion in deciding whether or not to admit impeachment evidence. After much debate, Congress ultimately supported the view of law enforcement, which held that the D.C. Circuit's ruling in *Luck* impeded the prosecution of criminals who took the witness stand knowing that their past misfeasance could not be used against them at trial. Consequently, Section 133(a) of the new legislation (or, *D.C. Code* Section 14-305) removed judicial discretion as a means or an obstacle to exclude evidence. From then on, it permitted impeachment by proof of any felony conviction or any misdemeanor involving dishonesty or false statement under the statute. This provision was tantamount to a specific rejection of the *Luck* doctrine, a creative aspect of D.C. Circuit jurisprudence.[17]

The D.C. Crime bill also reversed prior law that did not compel the courts to take into account whether an offender was dangerous to the community in noncapital cases arising under the 1966 Bail Reform Act. The D.C. Crime bill's legislative history shows that some members of Congress chastised the D.C. Circuit for interpreting the Bail Act to mean that defendants could be released on bail even if they were a threat to the pubic safety. They supported their argument by referring to D.C. Circuit cases like *United States v. Leathers* (1969) and *United States v. Alston* (1969) which, in their view, increased the crime rate. In *Leathers,* the court narrowly construed the 1966 Bail Reform Act as creating a presumption in favor of releasing defendants on personal recognizance or upon the execution of an unsecured appearance bond; this implied that the imposition of a money bond was proper only when all other nonfinancial conditions had been found to be inadequate, thereby making it easier for a court to release a defendant on bail. With *Alston,* on the other hand, the court remanded to the district court on the grounds that the trial judge failed to consider fully the nonfinancial circumstances of the case concerning a determination to set a money bond instead of letting the defendant—who was charged with armed robbery—go free on personal recognizance.

The opinions were controversial because they stood for the dual principle that courts could not set a high bail bond or, conversely, that courts could not evaluate a person's violent propensities as part of a bail order. So Section 210 of the new crime bill (or, *D.C. Code* Section 23-1322) required that the judiciary take into account the threat a defendant posed to the community if they let him out on bail. It also gave judges a chance to detain in jail suspects alleged to have committed violent crimes for up to sixty days after a hearing. From a practical perspective, the new pretrial detention provisions were a significant step in helping to keep dangerous offenders off the streets. More importantly, from a political vantage point it also prevented the D.C. Circuit from being the court that put them there.[18]

Furthermore, under the new statute defendants who pled insanity as a defense bore the evidentiary burden of proving it, something the D.C. Circuit (and many other federal courts) had not required in its earlier cases. Under prior law, the government had the hardship of establishing a defendant's sanity in criminal cases that implicated an insanity defense. This principle virtually guaranteed an acquittal if the jury felt there was a reasonable doubt about the defendant's sanity.[19] Critics charged that the D.C. Circuit exacerbated the situation by deciding *Bolton v. Harris* (1968), a ruling by Judge Bazelon prohibiting the involuntary commitment of defendants who were acquitted on the grounds of insanity, unless the government could show by a preponderance of the evidence that they were mentally ill.

According to critics like the House Committee on the District of Columbia, *Bolton* let "psychopaths" secure acquittals from serious crimes by merely pleading insanity. The "result is a revolving door that ... allows defendants 'to have it both ways'—to escape both conviction and commitment to a hospital." Thus, by enacting Section 207(3)(6) (or, *D.C. Code* Section 24- 301[j] of the D.C. Crime bill), Congress shifted the burden of proof and transformed the issue of insanity into an affirmative defense. The change made the defendant (and not the government) prove insanity by a preponderance of the evidence, which virtually eliminated the possibility of allegedly insane defendants "having it both ways."[20]

Court-curbing legislative changes were made to the juvenile law as well. The new law constrained the ability of the D.C. Circuit to place severe procedural restrictions on the Juvenile Court's decisions to transfer juveniles to the district court for criminal prosecution as adults. Critics of the D.C. Circuit complained that the court made it too difficult to prosecute and punish violent or mentally disturbed juvenile offenders more harshly. For example, in the fall of 1969 the Senate Committee on the District of Columbia heard the testimony from Associate Deputy Attorney General Donald E. Santarelli, who squarely blamed the sharp increase in juvenile crime in the district on the D.C. Circuit. D.C. Circuit decisions like *Kent v. United States* (1968) and *Haziel v. United States* (1968) pampered juvenile felons since the court made it more difficult for prosecutors to secure a waiver of juvenile court jurisdiction, which had the effect of impeding the decisions to treat juvenile offenders as adults in criminal cases. At hearings before the U.S. Senate on the problem of crime in the United States, Santarelli thus testified that the D.C. Circuit was responsible for hindering adult prosecution of juveniles and this was, in the end, indicative of the court's propensity to favor the rights of juvenile offenders at society's expense.[21]

Therefore, the new juvenile code under the D.C. Crime bill provided that the transfer of juveniles (from juvenile court to criminal prosecution in adult court) must be ordered unless the judge ruled that there was a reasonable prospect for the offender's rehabilitation before reaching the age of the majority. The provision, along with the new code section lowering the age (from eighteen to sixteen) at which a juvenile could be charged as an adult for the commission of select violent crimes, limited the power of the judges on the D.C. Circuit to insulate youth offenders from adult prosecution in nonjuvenile courts in the district.[22]

Other "get-tough-on-crime" measures that indirectly affected the D.C. Circuit's approach to crime included the imposition of life terms for three-time violent felons, the enactment of new wiretapping provisions to battle organized crime, the authorization of "no-knock" searches (i.e., without a warrant, and without advance notice) when the police are confronted with the prospect of losing key evidence in a prosecution, and, significantly, granting a right to the government to file expedited appeals to the D.C. Court of Appeals in cases when the Superior Court ruled that evidence in a criminal trial would be suppressed.[23]

In retrospect, the D.C. Crime bill was a comprehensive effort to tip the scales of justice in favor of the police and against mollycoddling courts or judges who were allegedly pampering criminals. Even though it is, in the end, debatable whether it truly succeeded in its partisan objectives, there is little doubt that the law had an enormous effect on the D.C. Circuit's judicial role after 1970, since its jurisdiction was fundamentally altered. The eradication of the court's local criminal jurisdiction affected its agenda and the scope of its judicial policy-making. The magnitude of the agenda change and some of its implications are suggested through analysis of the court's post-1970 docket, covering a time when the court forged a new reputation as a leader in administrative, and not criminal, legal policy. Before specifically inspecting the court's docket, it is first imperative to comprehend the way that the external political environment was the impetus for creating it.

## THE 1970S ERA OF "BURGEONING REGULATION" AND SOCIAL REVOLUTION

By the early 1970s the economic regulatory politics epitomizing the post–New Deal era was replaced by an unprecedented period of social regulation which had begun a decade earlier. In the 1960s the civil rights movement, the Vietnam War, and a number of highly publicized episodes concerning the abuses of industrialism created a dynamic political climate for social change that lingered on for the next ten years. In addition to the civil strife caused by divisive issues like racial equality and the American intervention in the Indonesian War, a number of events arose in civic affairs that magnified the problems associated with nuclear fallout, pesticides, oil spills, auto safety, and consumer product safety. By the 1970s a deep distrust of government and a distinctly anticorporate bias emerged from an increasingly politicized citizenry that pressed for legislation that would improve the quality of life in America. Sensing that Americans were no longer complacent with the status quo, the government responded by churning out regulation aimed at promoting the public health, safety, and general welfare. In the first half of the decade, Congress wrote into law (mostly during 1970–75) far-reaching social legislation like the National Environmental Policy Act, the Clean Air Amendments, the Federal Water Pollution Control Act Amendments, the Endangered Species Act, the Occupational Safety and Health Act, the Consumer Product Safety Act, the Equal Employment Opportunity Act, the Noise Control Act, the Atomic Energy Act, and the Safe Drinking Water Act.[24]

The emergence of the new regulatory state in the 1970s had important consequences for the relationships among Congress, the courts, and agencies. First, since social administration inherently signifies the federal government's willingness to protect certain community values in absolutist terms and without regard to economic cost, it is understandable that Congress, as a driving "powerful engine of social regulation," enacted laws that defined the policy goal to be achieved in an elementary fashion. For example, the regulation *had* to fix water pollution because the problem itself was described simplistically; the water was either clean or dirty. Thus, the regulation was forced to make it clean, irrespective of cost. Yet this approach created more scientific and technological uncertainty, which in turn forced political institutions to confront the problems of progress head-on. These difficulties impelled *someone* to make controversial policy judgments about the best way to proceed in effectuating the broad social mandate instilled in the governing legislation. By political default, executive agencies were that "someone."[25]

Since agencies were delegated the responsibility to make substantive decisions about public policy, frontline bureaucrats increasingly used informal rule-making as the method of choice to make these determinations. Clearly, as administrative law experts Kenneth Davis and Richard Pierce believe, agency "rulemaking . . . emerge[d] as the dominant form of regulation in the 1970s." Not everyone welcomed this development since skeptics wondered if agencies—who might be either captured by clientele interests, incompetent, or unaccountable under the rule of law—could be trusted as the exclusive guardians to regulate in the public interest. Congress responded to the dilemma by enacting "action-forcing" legislation.

For legal scholar Robert Rabin, the passage of the Clean Air Amendments in 1970 (CAA) demonstrated that "a new congressional mood was evident—a willingness to go beyond the blank-check [legislative] delegation of the past." Pursuant to the statute, agencies were given the responsibility of promulgating specific air quality standards by a certain date or under a firm timetable. By setting deadlines and other procedural requirements for compliance, Congress signaled that it was going to take a more interventionist posture in assisting agencies to make policy. By the same token, it was also a means to convey the message that Congress did not believe that agencies could be exclusively trusted to regulate in the public interest. In this sense, Congress used its legislative power to forecast to the bureaucracy that the New Deal style of deferential judicial politics was increasingly becoming an anachronism. At the same time, though, Congress's new attitude toward agencies inadvertently provided the D.C. Circuit with the opportunity to superintend the administrative process more actively.[26]

The opportunity to engage in judicial activism arose because the D.C. Circuit, with its local criminal jurisdiction eliminated, quickly became the foremost judicial forum for adjudicating agency appeals. As Figure 3 illustrates, the number of criminal appeals that dominated the D.C. Circuit docket in the 1960s was replaced by a relatively equal number of regulatory cases in the 1970s. In general, the figure indicates that the rate of criminal appeal filings is inversely proportionate to the rate of administrative appeal filings. Specifically, the steep increase in administrative appeals began in 1971 and reached its zenith, with only a two year interruption (1976–78), in the last year of the decade. Conversely, following a brief two-year increase (1971–73), the rate of criminal appeals steadily diminished thereafter and reached its lowest point in the decade in 1979. The figure clearly implies that the void left in the docket after the court's local criminal jurisdiction was excised was replaced by an influx of administrative law appeals.[27]

These findings also imply that two external political events—the passage of the 1970 D.C. Circuit Crime bill and an era of burgeoning social regulation in the public interest—combined to alter the nature and composition of the D.C. Circuit's docket in the 1970s. As it will be discussed shortly, the change in the nature of the court's business had a profound impact on the court's judicial role in the future. Since the court's political composition did not substantially change in the 1970s, the political environment laid the foundation for establishing the court's new reputation as an aggressive, if not liberal, activist court in administrative, rather than criminal, law.

How that reputation emerged is clarified by Figures 4 and 5, which complete the portrait of the new D.C. Circuit's docket by indicating that the circuit court heard more administrative appeals than any other circuit court in the 1970s. The former table reveals that a little more than a third of its docket (33.98 percent) was devoted to their adjudication in the D.C. Circuit, whereas for the rest of the circuit courts, administrative appeal filings rank last. A comparison of the judicial business across the circuits also discloses that the D.C. Circuit's docket was very different in other ways as well. While all other circuit courts enjoyed a high rate of private civil appeals, the D.C. Circuit ranked last in that category (14.91 percent). In addition, unlike most other circuit courts, the D.C. Circuit heard a substantial proportion of U.S. civil cases (25.63 percent) throughout the decade. Notably, too, although the average number of criminal appeals filed in all circuits (24.65 percent) and in the D.C. Circuit appears comparable, the number of filings in the D.C. Circuit actually decreased 76.59 percent between 1970 to 1979, whereas the number of criminal appeals in all circuits rose 54.12 percent over the same time.

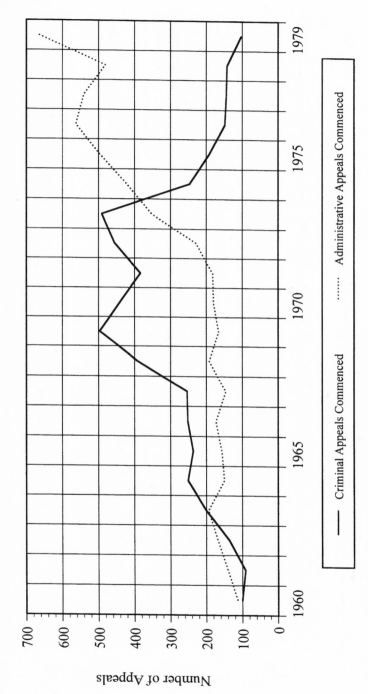

**FIGURE 3.** Number of Criminal and Administrative Appeals Commenced in D.C. Circuit, 1960–1979

Source: *Annual Report of the Director of the Administrative Office of the United States Courts*, from 1960 to 1979 (Table B-1).

Note: All data are based upon a twelve-month period ending June 30, as compiled by the Administrative Office of the U.S. Courts.

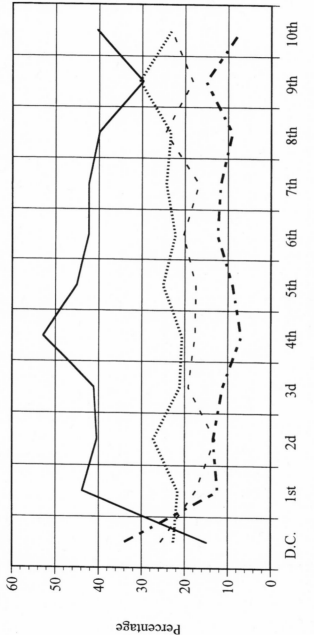

**FIGURE 4.** Appeals Commenced, by Subject, in U.S. Courts of Appeals, 1970–1979

Source: *Annual Report of the Director of the Administrative Office of the United States Courts,* from 1970 to 1979 (Table B-1).

Note: The category "Other," which includes bankruptcy, original proceedings, all other appeals, and District of Columbia appeals (from 1970 to 1971 only), is not reported. All data are based upon a twelve-month period ending June 30, as compiled by the Administrative Office of the U.S. Courts.

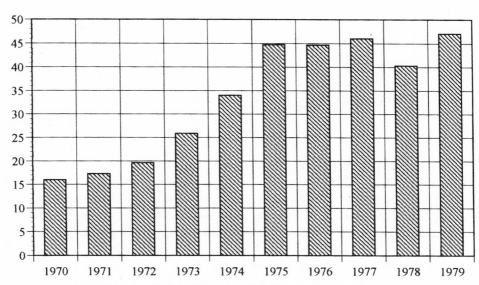

**FIGURE 5.** Percentage of Administrative Appeals in D.C. Circuit Docket, 1970–1979

Source: *Annual Report of the Director of the Administrative Office of the United States Courts,* from 1970 to 1979 (Table B-1).

Note: All data are based upon a twelve-month period ending June 30, as compiled by the Administrative Office of the U.S. Courts.

While Figure 4 shows that the point of departure for comprehending the D.C. Circuit's docket in the 1970s is the court's high number of appeals involving federal agencies and the U.S. government (a feature that distinguishes it from the rest of the circuits), Figure 5 is a visual summary of the court's annual administrative appeals docket. With the exception of 1978, when regulatory appeals constituted 40.32 percent of the D.C. Circuit workload, the percentage of appeals rose rapidly from 16.0 percent in 1970 to well over 40 percent in every year after 1975. In the last year of the decade nearly half (47.06 percent) of the docket is represented by agency appeals.

A number of factors combined to make the D.C. Circuit a cutting-edge regulatory forum in the 1970s. In addition to court reform and the onset of the public regulation era, Congress, through a variety of statutes, gave the D.C. Circuit exclusive jurisdiction over certain agency appeals. The court's liberal composition also made it an attractive forum for special interest groups to advocate broad social reform through litigation. D.C. Circuit rulings, which lowered the threshold of litigant standing and created a presumption of reviewability in agency litigation, only encouraged this type of organized behavior. Furthermore, the court's location in the District of Columbia facilitated agency litigation since the court was a convenient place to file appeals for most federal agencies, governmental parties, and special interest groups.[28] Naturally, the large concentration of regulatory appeals had important consequences for the nature and scope of the court's political jurisprudence. Partially as a result of the changes to the court's judicial business, the D.C. Circuit was now poised to assume a new judicial role in the family of federal courts.

## "GREATNESS THRUST UPON IT"

As the number of administrative appeals mounted on the court's docket, the D.C. Circuit quickly became an important check to preventing arbitrary agency action after 1970. While D.C. Circuit Judge Patricia Wald may be right in thinking that the court became a de facto administrative law court "not by grand design but by historical accident," it is probably more convincing to say that the D.C. Circuit had "greatness . . . thrust upon it in administrative law" for a variety of reasons.[29] All politically significant courts become great because of the way their judges apply the law. From this perspective, the D.C. Circuit's political transformation let the circuit judges seize the agenda opportunities it was given and make it into a court of great authority in administrative law.

First, the change in the docket caused the focus and emphasis of the circuit court's jurisprudence to change. In many ways, the agenda opportunities of the D.C. Circuit brought on by the social regulation era encouraged its judges to assume the role of faithful guardian of the public interest. In that capacity, D.C. Circuit judges were the first line of defense for legitimizing the policy choices of agencies. In essence, through judicial review, the D.C. Circuit wielded the legal authority to decide if agencies were making the *right* procedural or substantive choices in their rule-making. From this perspective, in the 1970s the D.C. Circuit was in the unique position to impel agencies to give the "Right Answer" in developing the solutions to technocratic regulatory problems.[30]

Accordingly, there is little doubt that the D.C. Circuit was at the forefront in altering the way courts approached the agency-court relationship in the public interest era. With landmark D.C. Circuit rulings like *Office of Communication of the United Church of Christ v. Federal Communications Commission* (1966) and its progeny, the circuit court was instrumental in ushering in a "less deferential" judicial attitude toward administrative agencies trying to make social policy. In *United Church of Christ*, the D.C. Circuit granted standing to two church groups and some citizens who objected to the FCC's decision to renew the broadcast license of a television station that allegedly discriminated against African Americans. By letting organizations and individuals, as nonparties to the original proceedings, become active participants in the regulatory hearing, the D.C. Circuit expanded access to the court *and* directly challenged the prior rule that agencies had the legislative authority to restrict the right of the public to be heard in regard to an important public policy issue. This sort of judicial temerity set the tone for the new public interest era by demonstrating that courts were reluctant to yield to the legal conclusions and policy statements of agencies who were operating on the basis of an implied delegation of legislative authority.[31]

Path-breaking decisions like *United Church of Christ* illustrated that a new, less deferential judicial attitude was taking hold of the D.C. Circuit, a posture that meant that the court was going to become an "aggressive senior partner" in regulation.[32] Two other events intensified the court's newfound moxie. The first relates to the court's membership and the second concerns the creativity of the judges' interpretation of the law. Throughout the 1970s, the D.C. Circuit bench consisted of several judicial all-stars who made adoption of the new judicial role much easier. A core group of unusually gifted judges—David Bazelon, J. Skelly Wright, Carl McGowan, Spottswood Robinson, Ed Tamm, Harold Leventhal, George MacKinnon, Roger Robb, and Malcolm Wilkey—served together in a time of rare natural court stability (i.e., when the membership remains the same over time) and clearly provided the type of judicial leadership that was necessary to scrutinize agencies closely. As a collective entity, the inherent talent of the court invariably shaped the ideological direction of regulatory politics in America in the 1970s because, from at least one perspective, "the skill with which they mastered and ultimately came to dominate [the field of administrative law] was breathtaking."[33] While the legal brilliance of the D.C. Circuit's bench was surely impressive, a more important contribution was the evolution of the so-called hard-look doctrine in the circuit. Since hard-look judicial review was really a function of the circuit's membership and a reflection of its ideological attitude toward public policy, it empowered the court to legislate judicially in such diverse areas as environmental protection, consumer safety, and energy regulation.

Although some scholars may disagree, hard-look judicial review originated from the pen of Judge Harold Leventhal, a prominent D.C. Circuit jurist. Ironically, Judge Leventhal conceptualized the doctrine as a decision-making "process [that] combines judicial supervision with a salutary principle of judicial restraint." In fact, he described hard-look review as a "doctrine of principled fairness."[34] In the landmark ruling of *Greater Boston Television Corporation v. Federal Communications Commission* (1970), he explained that the reviewing court had a significant role in guaranteeing that agencies acted reasonably when making policy decisions. Specifically, he emphasized:

> Its supervisory function calls on the court to intervene not merely in case of procedural inadequacies, or bypassing of the mandate in the legislative charter, but more broadly if the court becomes aware, especially from a combination of danger signals, that the agency has not really taken a "hard look" at the salient problems, and has not genuinely engaged in reasoned decision-making. If the agency has not shirked this fundamental task, however, the court exercises restraint and affirms the agency's action even though the court would on its own account have made different findings or adopted different standards. Nor will the court upset a decision because of errors that are not material, there being room for the doctrine of harmless error. If satisfied that the agency has taken a hard look at the issue with the use of reasons and standards, the court will uphold its findings, though of less than ideal clarity, if the agency's path may reasonably be discerned, though of course the court must not be left to guess as to the agency's findings or reasons.

Judge Leventhal thought that courts and agencies should work together as "partners" or "collaborative instrumentalities of justice" in the administrative process because both contributed to the salutary development of the "public interest."[35] Other legal experts, though, were not convinced and scoffed at the possibility that courts and agencies could become partners. Judge Henry Friendly, for example, sniffed, "There is little doubt who is considered to be the senior partner." But from Judge Leventhal's viewpoint, courts and agencies were "joint venturers" and not rivals in their pursuit of the greater regulatory good. Leventhal's colleague, Judge David Bazelon, agreed, at least in principle; that is, from his vantage point, this new partnership let the D.C. Circuit stand "on the threshold of a new era in the history of the long and fruitful collaboration of administrative agencies and reviewing courts."[36]

Even so, just as Judge Friendly intimated, the partnership between courts and agencies turned out to be quite one-sided, since the D.C. Circuit often used hard-look review as an unprincipled method to rebuff or reverse agency rule-making. The court's activism was fueled, in part, by the types of cases the court adjudicated. This was particularly true in regard to the construction of statutes aimed at broadly protecting consumers or the environment. In those areas, agencies enjoyed broad delegated authority to define the scope of public policy through rule promulgation.[37] As a result, all that stood in the way of a roving bureaucracy was the D.C. Circuit. From the court's standpoint, the newfound partnership was not a good enough reason to abdicate the judicial responsibility to hold agencies accountable. Accordingly, the hard-look doctrine directly empowered the court to curb agency excesses and, at the same time, ratify the social mandate through active judicial review.

Perhaps this is why political scientist David M. O'Brien commented, "the 'hard look' approach demands a great deal of judges and may provide a pretense for judicial activism rather than judicial self-restraint."[38] Ironically, but realistically, this assessment turns Judge Leventhal's rationale for creating it on its head. In other words, it was virtually impossible for the court to act with judicial restraint while superintending agencies. Instead of the doctrine being employed to curb agency discretion passively (as Judge Leventhal perhaps envisioned), the D.C. Circuit discovered that hard-look was an effective means to legislate judicially under the pretense of holding agencies accountable. Several D.C. Circuit cases illustrate this point well.

In *Calvert Cliffs Coordinating Committee, Inc. v. U.S. Atomic Energy Commission* (1971), the D.C. Circuit ruled that the National Environmental Policy Act (NEPA) compelled the Atomic Energy Commission (AEC) to incorporate the environmental impact of its decisions into its general rule-making and decisional processes. The court, speaking through Judge J. Skelly Wright, perceived that NEPA obliged the agency to carefully balance the effect that its regulation had on the environment. Since the AEC failed to weigh the importance of environmental factors, Judge Wright ruled that the court had a judicially enforceable duty to reverse the agency's substantive policy decision. For Judge Wright, the D.C. Circuit's "duty . . . was to see that important legislative purposes, heralded in the halls of Congress, were not lost or misdirected in the vast hallways of the federal bureaucracy." In short, the judicial role was designed to ensure that the substantive "promise of [the] legislation will become a reality."[39]

*Calvert Cliffs* is a landmark case because it indicated that the D.C. Circuit had unilaterally appointed itself the guardian of the public interest in certain policy areas, like environmental regulation. Perhaps the outer boundaries of the court's authority to rewrite the NEPA's substantive mandate was established by Judge Wright's opinion in *People Against Nuclear Energy v. United States Nuclear Regulatory Commission* (1982). In that case, the court held that the NRC had to perform a study to determine if restarting the Three Mile Island nuclear power plant posed a psychological threat that was significant enough to require that the agency prepare an environmental impact statement.[40] Judge Wright's rationale was perfectly consistent with the objectives of hard-look review since the doctrine's author, Judge Leventhal, conceded that it was intended to have a strong impact in the way agencies developed substantive policy. Since courts have a "role of review which [is] of major significance," Judge Leventhal believed that "in exercising this role, they have shared the public sense of urgency reflected in the new laws, and working within the framework of existing legal doctrine, have exerted a pervasive influence over the legislation's implementation."[41] Quite simply, hard-look review was the means by which the D.C. Circuit was given a license to lead in the modern administrative state that emerged in the 1970s.

Notably, the D.C. Circuit's assertive posture toward the resolution of regulatory appeals is not that unusual in light of the standard of judicial review that was employed to test the validity of social legislation. Hard-look review always triggered strict judicial review whenever the court perceived a "danger signal" in factual circumstances in which the agency failed to take its *own* hard-look at the basis for its policy decisions. As law school professor Samuel Estreicher observed, the court can discover danger signals in a variety of situations involving substantive and procedural questions of law.[42] The likely candidates for strict review included, for instance, cases in which an agency's substantive policy decision conflicted with either the first amendment or pro-competitive and environmental policies; situations in which the agency made procedural errors by inexplicably deviating from routine practice; or cases in which an agency failed to afford litigants procedural rights in administrative proceedings. Significantly, too, hard-look review was warranted when an agency acted informally (i.e., not on the record), which constituted the bulk of agency regulation.

As a judicial legislature, the D.C. Circuit was willing to take on the role of expert in select cases involving application of the hard-look doctrine. When acting in this capacity the court would question an agency's technical competence to promulgate a rule. Despite its generalist orientation as an Article III court, the D.C. Circuit apparently thought (at times) that it could do a better job in developing highly complex and technical social policy. As a result, the court did not see agency expertise as a cloak protecting the agency from being subjected to a probing form of judicial review. Sometimes, in fact, the D.C. Circuit seemed to perceive the concept of agency expertise as an impetus, not a constraint, for engaging in substantive judicial policy-making. As Judge Leventhal once explained, "technological and scientific issues do not free a court of the substantive review obligations contemplated by Congress, and the agency must make timely disclosure of its regulatory methodology and basis of decision, as well as respond to substantial criticisms raised by the regulated public." From Judge Leventhal's perspective, the court should not be intimidated by not having sufficient expertise in a policy area. If anything, it was more important that the court insured that the agency got it right in making policy. Judicial activism, by this reasoning, was justified because "the deference owed to an expert tribunal cannot be allowed to slip into judicial inertia."

A good illustration of the type of substantive review Judge Leventhal brought to a case is *Portland Cement Association v. Ruckelshaus* (1973). In *Portland Cement,* the D.C. Circuit held that the Environmental Protection Agency failed to adequately explain the standard it promulgated under the Clean Air Act in an effort to control emissions, or particulate matter, produced from kilns in Portland cement plants. After a lengthy review of the scientific and chemical processes that caused the pollutant, the D.C. Circuit concluded that the EPA did not show how the emission standard set by the statute was ever going to be technologically "achieved." In remanding the case the court stated, "While we remain diffident in approaching problems of this technical complexity, the necessity to review agency decisions, if it is to be more than a meaningless exercise, requires enough steeping in technical matters to determine whether the agency 'has exercised a reasoned discretion.'" Yet what is lost in the translation is the acknowledgment that it is very hard to discover at what point the court has engaged in "enough steeping" to know when the agency acted reasonably in making a decision. Nevertheless, in *Portland Cement* the court reached a liberal (i.e., pro-environmental) result by claiming that it could understand the scientific validity of the EPA's decision to promulgate a technically sophisticated emission standard.

Judge Leventhal's substantive version of hard look, however, was not without its detractors, even from within the D.C. Circuit. Judge Bazelon, in fact, sharply disagreed with Judge Leventhal on the proper scope and application of the hard-look doctrine. At the core of the debate was Judge Bazelon's insistence that judges were incompetent to assess the scientific and technical policy judgments of experts. In *Ethyl Corporation v. Environmental Protection Agency* (1976) Judge Bazelon explained, "In cases of great technological complexity, the best way for courts to guard against unreasonable or erroneous administrative decisions is not for the judges themselves to scrutinize the technical merits of each decision. Rather, it is to establish a decision-making process that assures a reasoned decision that can be held up to the scrutiny of the scientific community and the public."[43] Bazelon's "strict procedure ensures correct results" mode of hard-look review presupposed that judges only have an expertise in matters relating to the judicial process. This assumption meant that the hard-look doctrine was really only a procedural (and not a substantive) doctrine of judicial review in cases involving complex scientific matters.

From an esoteric viewpoint, Judge Bazelon's version of hard look is consistent with his conviction that judges were only one group of many participants in an "open" democratic process. Judge Bazelon, in fact, strongly felt that "even society's most technical decisions must be ventilated in a public forum with public input and participation." For Bazelon, then, "the court's role is rather to monitor the agency's decision-making process—to stand outside both the expert and political debate and to assure that all the issues are thoroughly ventilated." Clearly, Bazelon's conception of an "open decision-making process" motivated him to make agency rule-making more courtlike, which, in turn, made it more difficult for agencies to get their policy decisions approved in court. In this fashion, Bazelon's procedural hard-look principle was analogous to the more substantive version propounded by his colleague, Judge Leventhal.

Judge Bazelon's concurrence in *International Harvester Company v. Ruckelshaus* (1973) is illustrative. There, he argued that the EPA's decision to not grant a one-year suspension of the 1975 emission standards prescribed under the Clean Air Act was procedurally deficient because the petitioners were not given a *general* right of cross-examination during the EPA rule-making proceedings. This deficiency, for him, prevented the resolution of "complex questions [that] should be resolved in the crucible of debate through the clash of informed but opposing scientific and technological viewpoints." Although Judge Leventhal (in writing for the court) vacated the agency's decision on different grounds (i.e., because the EPA failed to adequately explain the underlying methodology of its decision to promulgate an emission standard pursuant to requirements of the Clean Air Act), he nonetheless agreed that there should be a *limited* right of confrontation. The scope of his disagreement with Judge Leventhal, then, is really only a matter of degree, and not principle. Therefore, "the battle within the D.C. Circuit [was] more apparent than real" since both judges agreed that it was necessary for the court to superintend aggressively agency conduct aggressively. In the end, the jurists only differed on the particular method by which the court could properly supervise the legal decisions of agencies.[44]

Even though Judge Bazelon's argument did not win the day in *International Harvester,* the D.C. Circuit routinely demonstrated its willingness to overturn agency policy decisions on procedural grounds. Indeed, the court earned the perhaps infamous distinction of employing the "procedural" hard-look doctrine as a means to enter into a dialogue with agencies about the proper method to make rules. This colloquy, mainly nourished through "hybrid rule-making," forced the agency to explain its rationale in making policy decisions by presenting sufficient facts, giving notice of the proposed rule, permitting the opportunity for debate, and responding adequately to public comment with a thorough investigation and due consideration of alternative options to the path ultimately chosen by the agency. In short, procedural hard look attempted to generate a "paper hearing" in informal rule-making cases. As a result, it legitimized the court's power to impose, unilaterally, procedural requirements upon agencies that went above and beyond those required by

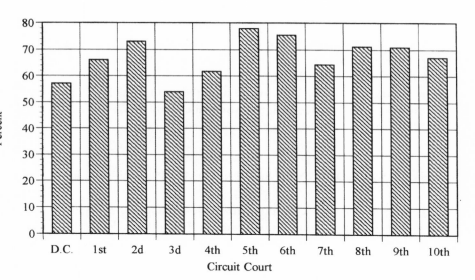

**FIGURE 6.** Affirmance Rate of Agency Appeals in U.S. Courts of Appeals, 1970–1979

Source: *Annual Report of the Director of the Administrative Office of the United States Courts,* from 1970 to 1979 (Table B-1).

Note: All data are based upon a twelve-month period ending June 30, as compiled by the Administrative Office of the U.S. Courts. "Affirmance of Agency Appeals" is the average percentage of affirmances, grants, or enforcements of agency petitions.

the minimum notice and comment provisions of the APA. Consequently, procedural hard look became increasingly associated with D.C. Circuit judicial activism in administrative law.[45]

An underlying premise of the competing versions of the hard-look doctrine is the idea that the court was extremely reluctant to give the bureaucracy unfettered control over the formulation of legal and public policy. The extent to which this judicial skepticism expressed itself in cases is suggested by Figure 6, a summary of merit terminations of agency appeals in the U.S. Courts of Appeals from 1970 to 1979. The table demonstrates that only two courts, the D.C. Circuit (57.06 percent) and the Third Circuit (53.98 percent), affirmed agencies at an average rate below 60 percent. Although the Third Circuit has a slightly lower percentage, it is important to observe that the D.C. Circuit had the lowest average deference rate among the courts with the largest number of agency affirmances, namely the D.C. Circuit, the Fifth Circuit, and the Ninth Circuit.[46] Among the courts, the D.C. Circuit was a leader in showing less judicial deference since both the Fifth (77.86 percent) and the Ninth (70.93 percent) Circuits, respectively, exhibited a much greater tendency to accede to agencies.

Figure 6 confirms that the D.C. Circuit made a significant contribution to administrative law through its activist application of hard-look review in the 1970s. Quite clearly the court questioned agency conduct regularly. And, although Congress was the first impetus to effectuate social regulatory reform through action-forcing legislation, in the end it rested with the D.C. Circuit to make (in Judge Wright's words in *Calvert Cliffs*) "the promise of legislation a reality," either substantively or procedurally.

## THE COURT OF FINAL SAY IN ADMINISTRATIVE LAW?

Whether Judge Wright's jurisprudential vision of administrative law would become real largely depended upon whether the highest federal court in the land condoned the D.C. Circuit's approach to regulatory decision-making. Since the liberal Warren Court was replaced by a moderate Court under the leadership of Warren Burger (Judge Bazelon's nemesis before Burger's elevation to the Supreme Court) in 1969, one would expect that the D.C. Circuit's activism in regulation would be met by some resistance from the U.S. Supreme Court, especially since the D.C. Circuit was ideologically incompatible (in membership) with the Supreme Court in the ensuing decade. Notably, too, even though the D.C. Crime bill had an impact on the lower court's jurisdiction, it failed to affect the court's liberal membership, which, in theory, would increase the possibility of intercourt friction. For all these reasons, it would be entirely plausible that D.C. Circuit rulings applying a hard-look approach would be scrutinized carefully by the High Court.

Nonetheless, key Supreme Court precedent at the beginning of the decade appeared to suggest that it paradoxically favored the type of rigorous judicial review that was regularly utilized by the lower federal appellate court. In *Citizens to Preserve Overton Park, Inc. v. Volpe* (1971), the Supreme Court held that all federal courts should perform a "thorough, probing, in-depth review" of agency decision-making. As suggested earlier, there is little doubt that the D.C. Circuit found it difficult to obey at least the spirit of that precedent with the development and application of the hard-look doctrine. Yet, the Supreme Court strongly implied in two later opinions that it did *not* approve of courts requiring agencies to adopt trial-like procedures during rule-making in the absence of a clear statutory mandate to do so.[47] Consequently, even though the Supreme Court appeared to condone a hard-look type of judicial review in regulatory appeals, it also seemed to say (but had not yet ruled upon) that it did not favor the sort of ad hoc, judicially imposed "hybrid" rule-making that the D.C. Circuit practiced when it engaged in its

**TABLE 3.** *U.S. Supreme Court Certiorari Dispositions, U.S. Courts of Appeals, 1970–1979*

| Disposition | D.C. | 1st | 2d | 3d | 4th | 5th | 6th | 7th | 8th | 9th | 10th |
|---|---|---|---|---|---|---|---|---|---|---|---|
| Denials | 60.0% | 60.5% | 69.4% | 73.8% | 68.8% | 65.2% | 55.5% | 74.8% | 51.8% | 48.9% | 78.0% |
| Grants | 19.3% | 10.5% | 7.5% | 7.1% | 11.3% | 11.2% | 7.3% | 3.6% | 23.2% | 7.2% | 4.9% |
| Dismissals | 1.4% | — | .60% | 1.6% | — | 1.8% | — | 1.4% | — | — | — |

SOURCE: *Annual Report of the Administrative Office of the U.S. Courts,* from 1970 to 1979 (Table B-2).
NOTE: Percentages are derived by dividing the sum of administrative certiorari dispositions for each circuit for the ten-year period into the sum of administrative certiorari filings in that circuit for the same time period. The sum of administrative certiorari filings includes the ten-year sum of pending cases from the prior fiscal year. Percentages for each court do not equal 100 percent because the percentages relative to the pending cases from the current fiscal year are not presented in the table. All data are based upon the twelve-month period ending June 30, as compiled by the Administrative Office of the U.S. Courts.

procedural hard-look review of agency decision-making under the leadership of Chief Judge David Bazelon.

Against this background, it is instructive to learn that judicial workload data from the Administrative Office of U.S. Courts reveals that the Supreme Court largely chose not to rubber-stamp D.C. Circuit activism in administrative law during the 1970s. Table 3, for instance, discloses that the courts had something of an uneasy relationship. It shows that certiorari petitions from D.C. Circuit regulatory appeals were granted more frequently (19.3 percent) and denied less frequently (60.0 percent) than those of most other U.S. Courts of Appeals from 1970 to 1979. Of the ten circuit courts, the D.C. Circuit had the second highest percentage (behind the Eighth Circuit) of regulatory appeals granted certiorari, thus suggesting that the Supreme Court disapproved of D.C. Circuit jurisprudence. That implication is buttressed by the data disclosing that the Supreme Court denied certiorari in D.C. Circuit regulatory appeals only 60.0 percent of the time. The D.C. Circuit accordingly had the third lowest percentage (ranking eighth) of certiorari denials among the ten circuit courts, indicating that the Supreme Court ratified much less of what the D.C. Circuit was doing in comparison with the rest of the intermediate tier.

Significantly, the high grant and low denial rates of certiorari petitions in regulatory appeals in the 1970s are patterns of judicial behavior in stark contrast to the one shown by the Supreme Court in the 1960s regarding D.C. Circuit criminal law jurisprudence. One obvious explanation for the disparity is political ideology. It will be recalled that Table 2 in Chapter 1 indicates that in the 1960s the liberal Warren Court implicitly approved of D.C. Circuit decision-making in criminal law with high denial (80.9 percent) and low grant (6.0 percent) rates. At that time, the D.C. Circuit's liberal majority produced the type of policy outcome that was favored by a liberal-leaning Supreme Court. But, as Table 3 reveals, the more conservative Burger Court was not as receptive to D.C. Circuit policy-making in administrative law in the 1970s. The D.C. Circuit's liberal membership was most likely the cause of the tension between the two courts, which also suggests that the Supreme Court at that time favored a more deferential judicial approach to regulation.

That the Supreme Court was less tolerant of the D.C. Circuit in the 1970s is also demonstrated by a significant case decided by the High Court in 1978. In *Vermont Yankee Nuclear Power Corporation v. Natural Resources Defense Council, Inc.* (1978), the Supreme Court abruptly curtailed the D.C. Circuit's persistent effort to expand the reach of procedural hard-look judicial review and hybrid rule-making. Specifically, *Vermont Yankee* concerned whether the Nuclear Regulatory Commission had to use procedures that were not required by the informal rule-making provisions of the Administrative Procedure Act in making a policy decision about the best method of atomic waste disposal and energy conservation in nuclear plant licensing proceedings.[48] In the underlying D.C. Circuit opinion, Judge Bazelon remanded to the agency for its failure to incorporate procedures that would have "thoroughly ventilated" the issues on whether the agency fulfilled its statutory requirements under the National Environmental Policy Act. The opinion is in many ways a classic restatement of his judicial philosophy. In his ruling, Judge Bazelon emphasized that the agency must provide the petitioners with a "genuine opportunity to participate" in the proceeding since doing so would air all the relevant issues and create the requisite dialogue between the government and the public about the range and feasibility of various waste disposal methods. After citing a number of procedures that the agency could have used to air the issues, Judge Bazelon held that the agency had acted arbitrarily and capriciously in not employing some of these procedures at the agency hearing.[49]

On appeal, a unanimous Supreme Court, in an opinion written by Justice William H. Rehnquist, reversed and remanded. In its ruling, the Court expressed its strong disapproval of Judge Bazelon's insistence that the agency had to use additional procedures during agency rule-making. Although Justice Rehnquist conceded that agencies had the option to use extra procedures under the APA, he also stated that the D.C. Circuit had no right to force the agency to do so. In the Court's view, the lower court "seriously misread or misapplied [the] statutory and decisional law cautioning reviewing courts against engrafting their own notions of proper procedures upon agencies entrusted with substantive functions by Congress." Rehnquist concluded that not only did Bazelon's "best procedures" approach threaten to make judicial review unpredictable, but it was precisely of the sort of "Monday morning quarterbacking" that wrongly converts all agency rule-making proceedings into full-blown trials. In sum, Judge Bazelon's decision to remand and delay the proceedings further "border[ed] on the Kafkaesque."[50]

## CONCLUSION

The practical effect of *Vermont Yankee* was that it ended only the internal debate on the D.C. Circuit between Judges Bazelon and Leventhal concerning the proper scope of procedural hard-look review. In light of the Supreme Court rejection of Judge Bazelon's "correct procedures" approach, the D.C. Circuit was forced in subsequent appeals to embrace a modified version of hard look that is arguably more in line with Judge Leventhal's substantive view. This underlying significance of *Vermont Yankee* transcends the actual disagreement between the judges on the circuit because it had the potential to nudge the court's policy-making in an even more progressive direction. As Judge Wright's 1982 opinion in *People Against Nuclear Energy v. United States Nuclear Regulatory Commission* aptly demonstrates, despite the harsh rhetoric of *Vermont Yankee* the court was not easily dissuaded from creatively protecting substantive values in certain cases.[51] D.C. Circuit liberalism in administrative law, it seems, could not be completely stopped through one restrictive Supreme Court precedent.

Therefore, despite *Vermont Yankee,* the development of hard-look review in the 1970s enabled the D.C. Circuit to become progressively a "mini Supreme Court" in D.C. Circuit administrative law cases that were not appealed to or overturned by the U.S. Supreme Court. Since the High Court denied certiorari an average of 60 percent of the time in regulatory cases from the D.C. Circuit (Table 3), as a federal circuit court it remained the court of last resort for a large proportion of litigants in regulation cases that had a national impact. Ironically, the court's new judicial role as the quintessential skeptic of the bureaucratic process is something that conservatives opposing the court in the late 1960s could have not reasonably foreseen. In fact, by trying to stop D.C. Circuit liberalism in criminal law with the D.C. Circuit Crime bill, conservatives could only blame themselves for creating the agenda opportunities that the D.C. Circuit would aggressively seize in its administrative law cases later on. While the 1970 D.C. Crime bill probably tempered the court's lack of judicial restraint in criminal law, conservatives learned in hindsight that changing the court's jurisdiction was not enough to solve the problem of D.C. Circuit judicial activism. Short of a radical change in court's composition, the liberal judges of the D.C. Circuit demonstrated that it would continue to apply a liberal judicial philosophy to regulation cases that now consumed close to half of the court's docket by 1979.

In a related sense, *Vermont Yankee* reinforces the important effect that the judicial selection process has on the ideological direction of legal policy. After all, *Vermont Yankee* was decided by the Burger Court, a Supreme Court that was much different in membership from its predecessor, the Warren Court. Had the D.C. Circuit bench been conservative instead of liberal in its membership in 1978, *Vermont Yankee* might have been differently decided. From this perspective, *Vermont Yankee* indirectly suggests how the membership of the High Court affects the extent to which circuit courts can make final judgments about the scope of regulatory policy. Whether the Supreme Court would continue to challenge the lower court's authority to make administrative law policy is a legal question that resurfaced in the 1980s as well. A key difference, though, is that the political composition of the D.C. Circuit's bench was about to change with the election of President Ronald Reagan. Therefore, in the 1980s, the main issue was not so much whether the High Court would actively superintend the lower circuit court in Washington, D.C. Rather, it was whether the judicial politics of the D.C. Circuit would divide the court on key issues of administrative law.

# Judicial Politics in the D.C. Circuit Court

Judges are not experts in the field, and are not part of either political branch of the Government. Courts must, in some cases, reconcile competing political interests, but not on the basis of the judges' personal policy preferences. In contrast, an agency to which Congress has delegated policymaking responsibilities may, within the limits of that delegation, properly rely upon the incumbent administration's views of wise policy to inform its judgments. While agencies are not directly accountable to the people, the Chief Executive is, and it is entirely appropriate for this political branch of the Government to make such policy choices—resolving the competing interests which Congress itself either inadvertently did not resolve, or intentionally left to be resolved by the agency charged with the administration of the statute in light of everyday realities.

—JUSTICE JOHN PAUL STEVENS

Like Justice John Paul Stevens in *Chevron U.S.A. Inc. v. Natural Resources Defense Council, Inc.* (1984), Judge Harry T. Edwards of the D.C. Circuit once implied that courts are aloof from politics. Critics, who claim otherwise, he asserted, are guilty of perpetuating "a myth that grossly distorts the role of courts in our system of government and tends to undermine the public confidence in the judicial process." Issues of "great political importance" are not part of a court's agenda, his included. Instead, courts like his merely construe statutes, review administrative action, and superintend district courts. From Judge Edwards's perspective, ideology is not a source of judicial conflict or policy-making, particularly in his circuit, simply because its judges agree in a majority of cases. For him, this is clear proof that the rule of law is a powerful constraint upon discretion and protects judicial decision-making from becoming too politically result oriented.[1]

While Judge Edwards may be right in some respects, he certainly underestimates the impact that politics has on circuit courts. That partisan considerations are a part of the judicial function is even acknowledged by some of his colleagues; they have been inclined to dismiss Edwards's musing as mythmaking. As Judge Abner Mikva said of his own court, "Pick a controversial subject in our democracy, and you can find at least two points of view expressed by judges of the D.C. Circuit." The divergent viewpoints to which Mikva refers result from the diverse attitudes and policy preferences of judges who make the law in a distinctly political style of American government. Ironically, that is why a frustrated Judge Edwards later lamented that "politicking will replace the thoughtful dialogue that should characterize a court" if D.C. Circuit judges continued to manipulate the en banc process and overturn the thoughtful decisions of D.C. Circuit panels.[2]

All of this is not lost upon students of the courts. Despite the enduring myth that courts are apolitical, the reality is that they are political institutions.[3] Precisely because of its liberal policy-making in criminal law in the 1960s, in 1970 conservatives from Congress and the executive branch curbed the D.C. Circuit by stripping it of its local jurisdiction to adjudicate criminal appeals and overturning ideologically disfavored precedent. While the 1970 D.C. Crime bill surely accomplished its immediate objective, its long-term effect is more significant because it politically transformed the court's agenda at a time when the court's composition remained predominately liberal. This change, in turn, permitted the D.C. Circuit to emerge as a de facto national administrative law court with great policy-making influence. Therefore, political ideology, and not historical accident, is responsible for letting the D.C. Circuit earn its second reputation as a key court superintending national regulation in the 1970s.[4]

But, whether the D.C. Circuit could remain an activist, liberal court in the future was suddenly cast into doubt by 1980. The 1978 *Vermont Yankee* ruling and the high grant and low denial rates of certiorari in administrative appeals in the 1970s were signs indicating that the D.C. Circuit and the U.S. Supreme Court might have an uneasy political relationship in the new decade. Moreover, Ronald Reagan was just elected president of the United States. From one perspective, the prospect of new Reagan appointments to the D.C. Circuit jeopardized the natural court stability that characterized the liberal court from 1970 to 1979. From another, the appointments also held the promise of letting the circuit become more conservative. Either way, the judicial selection process was destined to be a key variable for understanding the judicial politics of the D.C. Circuit and the institutional relationship between the U.S. Supreme Court and the circuit court in the 1980s.

As the political events unfolded, it became apparent that President Reagan was going to have a number of opportunities to change the D.C. Circuit's membership. This, of course, had a considerable impact on the nature of D.C. Circuit administrative law jurisprudence. As the D.C. Circuit became more conservative in the 1980s, each new judge began to reexamine precedent and directly challenge the liberal majority's hold on the court in administrative law. Although there are many examples of judicial conflict in the

D.C. Circuit, two of the most tumultuous and politically significant illustrations involved cases raising issues of justiciability and judicial deference to agencies.[5] Since both areas generated differing viewpoints on topics like litigant access to courts, separation of powers, and statutory construction, they touched upon issues of law that invariably polarize ideologically opposed jurists on a bench. They also affected circuit court agenda-setting and the parameters of legal policy change associated with judicial control of bureaucracies. Accordingly, this chapter analyzes how political ideology influenced the court's access and judicial deference policy-making during a time of increasing conservatism.

## MADE IN HIS OWN IMAGE?
## RONALD REAGAN, DEREGULATION,
## AND THE D.C. CIRCUIT

Deregulation is a philosophy of governmental control that works to relax, suspend, delay, or rescind existing regulatory requirements. Its purpose is to stop expansion of regulatory growth and minimize governmental interference in economic affairs so that competitive market forces have a chance to flourish. Although some claim that deregulation began in earnest before 1980, almost single-handedly Ronald Reagan revitalized it as a sustained political movement that pushed for sweeping regulatory and fiscal reform. In his first term President Reagan signed Executive Order 1281, a proclamation freezing all existing regulations from the Carter administration. He also established a Task Force on Regulatory Relief and the Executive Office of Management and Budget. The task force tried to disable additional regulatory initiatives while the OMB was given preclearance authority, through cost-benefit analysis, to review the merits of any prospective regulation. Moreover, President Reagan aggressively used appointment power under Article II of the Constitution as an ideological tool to select cabinet and administration officials who faithfully shared his vision of limited government. The appointing strategy was effective since his executive appointees often possessed a singular zeal for deregulation and exhibited a palpable hostility to bloated government. In sum, Reagan's executive leadership provided the spark to downsize the bureaucracy and sharply limit any attempt by Congress to implement a pro-regulatory legislative agenda.

Initially the Reagan mandate faced little political opposition because Congress generally acceded to the president's attempt to reshape the American landscape in his own political image. After 1980, Congress enacted major legislation deregulating the transportation and banking industries. Other businesses were also affected by deregulation. Congressional indifference to enacting social regulation with potentially adverse economic consequences was replaced by an attentiveness to the costs and benefits of undertaking any new regulatory proposals. Economic security at home and abroad became a paramount legislative concern and affected the scope and ideological direction of congressional legislation. Even so, at times Congress found the political will to resist deregulation by conspicuously adhering to the type of social legislative mandate with which it was preoccupied in the 1970s. Certain enactments, like health, safety, and environmental legislation, were often politically protected from being cut by the deregulatory ax. Nevertheless, for the most part Congress seemed to march to the president's drumbeat of deregulatory politics.[6]

As Figure 7 suggests, it was only a matter of time before the D.C. Circuit would begin to adjudicate a flurry of regulatory disputes arising from the new Reagan era of conservatism. Even more so than the data pertaining to the D.C. Circuit's docket in 1970s (see Figure 4 in Chapter 2), Figure 7 confirms that regulatory case filings in the D.C. Circuit in the 1980s rose to the point at which administrative appeals dominated the court's business. The figure also shows that the court's docket remained very distinct from those of the rest of the circuit courts. Whereas a majority of circuit courts averaged nearly 50 percent or more of private civil appeals case filings, the D.C. Circuit maintained only an average rate of 15.99 percent throughout the decade. Moreover, while criminal case filings averaged about 15 percent in most circuit courts, they represented only 6.17 percent of the D.C. Circuit's docket. More significantly, the federal government had a strong presence in the D.C. Circuit, since three-fourths of the D.C. Circuit case filings (75.27 percent) consisted of U.S. civil and administrative appeals. Remarkably, nearly half, or 44.76 percent, of its business concerned regulatory appeals (an increase of 10.73 percent from the 1970s average rate), while almost one-third, or 30.51 percent, were U.S. civil appeals. All other courts of appeals had substantially fewer case filings in either of those two latter categories of appeals, thus continuing to distinguish the D.C. Circuit as the foremost judicial situs for adjudicating regulation cases.

Figure 7 implies that deregulation only spawned more appellate litigation in administrative law in the D.C. Circuit. Yet even though the court's regulatory docket remained constant, as the country became more conservative, so too did the D.C. Circuit. In fact, from 1980 to 1987 the D.C. Circuit was recast as a court in flux when several new judges were appointed to the bench. From 1982 to 1987 eight new judges were added to the suddenly conservative court; that is, President Reagan appointed Robert Bork (1982), Antonin Scalia (1982), Kenneth Starr (1983), Laurence Silberman (1985), James Buckley (1985),

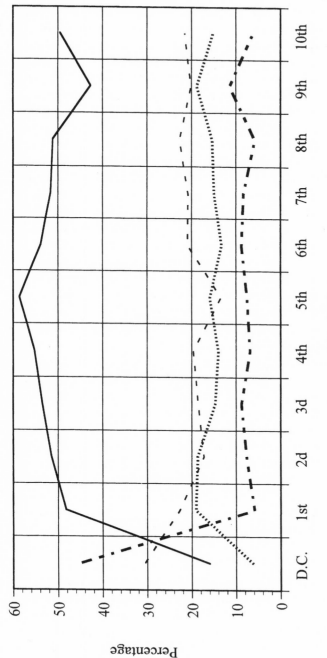

FIGURE 7. Appeals Commenced, by Subject, in U.S. Courts of Appeals, 1980–1989
Source: *Annual Report of the Director of the Administrative Office of the United States Courts,*
from 1980 to 1989 (Table B-1).

Note: The category "Other," which includes bankruptcy, original proceedings, is not
reported. All data are based upon a twelve-month period ending June 30, as compiled by
the Administrative Office of the U.S. Courts. "U.S. Civil" includes reported data under
"U.S. Civil," "Other U.S. Civil," "Prisoner Petitions," and "U.S. Prisoner Petitions."
"Private Civil" includes "Private Civil," "Other Private Civil," and "Private Prisoner
Petitions."

Stephen Williams (1986), Douglas Ginsburg (1986), and David Sentelle (1987) to the Washington circuit court. With the new appointments, the solid grip that the liberal majority had maintained since the 1960s (and strengthened by President Carter's four appointments of Patricia Wald [1979], Abner Mikva [1979], Harry T. Edwards [1980], and Ruth Bader Ginsburg [1980]) began to loosen as President Reagan exercised his constitutional prerogative to alter the court's composition. While the Carter appointments probably had the effect of staving off the conservative attempt to revamp the judiciary initially, any hope that liberals had in sustaining a majority on the D.C. Circuit were quickly dashed as President Reagan seized the opportunity to make three key membership changes—Robert Bork, Antonin Scalia, and Kenneth Starr—to the court shortly after President Carter left office. Each appointment was instrumental in permitting conservatives to gain a strong foothold and shift the balance of power on the court incrementally to the right. As it turned out, the new appointments were a harbinger to a new challenge facing the D.C. Circuit. As a court in transition it would soon discover that it had the unenviable task of superintending an administration bent on deregulation, even though the D.C. Circuit's liberal majority was equally committed to sustaining the pro-regulatory philosophy established in the 1970s.[7]

An inevitable consequence of this dilemma was that it compelled the D.C. Circuit to reassess past precedent that facilitated litigant access to the court. In the 1970s the D.C. Circuit often encouraged access with its liberal interpretations of jurisdictional and procedural doctrines (i.e., standing, ripeness, and mootness) which ordinarily let parties challenge allegedly arbitrary agency conduct in court. But with more conservatives on the bench, the D.C. Circuit began to restrict on-the-merits review and slowly shut the courthouse door. Consequently, the issue of justiciability increasingly divided liberals and conservatives because the court's "access policy-making"—such as whether a party has standing to sue—was fast becoming the focus of a pitched ideological battle over volatile political issues generally revolving around separation of powers and court deference to agencies' analysis.[8]

## STANDING ON IDEOLOGICAL PRINCIPLES IN THE D.C. CIRCUIT

The legal and political implications of litigant access to a court are important, considering that courts are not self-starters. Litigants must bring cases to judicial forums to have their cases heard. In this sense, they are requesting permission to seek the remedies available through the judicial process in order to have any possibility of receiving specific justice. But it should not be forgotten that the instigation of a lawsuit has profound policy implications since parties also sue to achieve legal policy change that goes well beyond achieving a favorable result. Courts may be the best, and sometimes the last, public policy venue that people have in influencing the ideological direction of law or social policy.[9] As a result, litigant access to a court is the linchpin in determining whether a party fulfills the promise of achieving individual justice or broader public policy objectives.

One procedural doctrine that greatly influences litigant access and the ideological direction of public policy is the doctrine of standing. Litigant standing is one of several threshold issues that could be raised in a circuit court appeal. Another is if there is a political question in the case. If so, a court may abstain from deciding it if it feels that the dispute is one that is best resolved by Congress or the executive branch. Or, the doctrines of mootness and ripeness may affect the prospect of having on-the-merits review. Whereas mootness prevents a lawsuit because the case is brought too early or too late, ripeness generally bars an action when it is prematurely litigated. The doctrine of standing, on the other hand, mandates that the litigant prove an injury to a legally protected interest and that all other remedies for asserting the claim have been exhausted.[10]

Despite the subtle differences between them, each threshold issue alternatively precludes or stimulates the need for hearing the merits of an appeal. The court's decision in this regard is an exercise of discretion, which makes the ruling on litigant standing attitudinal in scope and very political. It is also strategic. Denying standing to a litigant allows courts to avoid ruling on issues that they may not want to tackle for political reasons. Or, conversely, granting standing permits courts to reach the merits informally and effectuate a particular policy result under the pretense of not caring about the substance of an appeal. Overall, by acting strategically, courts apply the legal rules of litigant standing either to limit or expand their agenda space and prospectively influence legal policy. So conceived, the standing doctrine is really "nothing more than a convenient tool to avoid uncomfortable issues or to disguise a surreptitious ruling on the merits."[11] It is thus a significant clue to understanding the judicial decisions affecting circuit court agenda-setting. Or, as the 1980s litigation involving "corporate average fuel efficiency standards" attests, it provides key insight about the judicial politics of the D.C. Circuit at a time when the court's membership was in transition.

## CAFE AND THE POLITICAL MANIPULATION OF ENERGY REGULATION IN THE D.C. CIRCUIT

The appellate litigation surrounding "corporate average fuel efficiency standards" (or CAFE standards) began with President Gerald Ford's reaction to the 1973 energy crisis. In response to an OPEC oil embargo, President Ford signed the Energy Policy Conservation Act (EPCA) in an effort to reduce America's dependence on foreign oil. The law had several effects. First, it generally increased the president's power to react to an energy crisis by letting the executive directly control flow of domestic energy supplies. Second, it optimized the use of the nation's energy resources by expanding the Federal Energy Administration's power to regulate energy production by using alternative fuels. The legislation also created a national oil reserve to protect against any interruption of delivery caused by unexpected foreign events (such as an oil embargo). And, finally, it imposed federal price controls over domestic oil, which, by far, was its most controversial provision.

Notably, in spite of its emphasis on promoting energy conservation, the law was politically volatile. In the U.S. Senate, Senator Henry Bellmon (R-Okla.) referred to the legislation as the "Energy Hash Act," while Senator John Tower (R-Tex.) called it the "Cold Homes and Dark Factories Act" or the "Energy Dependence Act." A third Republican, Dewey F. Bartlett (Okla.), thought the final version of the bill was a "hackneyed nostrum, conjured up by the nation's Congress of energy alchemists." The tepid reaction of the U.S. Senate to the act is measured by the fact that only thirteen of the twenty-five Senate conferees actually signed the conference report before it was sent to the president.[12]

One important aspect of the legislation concerned its attempt to conserve energy by imposing fuel efficiency requirements upon car manufacturers. This rather overlooked and relatively noncontroversial aspect of the law had a profound effect on the auto industry and, in hindsight, the D.C. Circuit's interpretation of the standing doctrine in the 1980s and the iron rectangle (i.e., subcommittees, interest groups, agencies, and courts) of administrative law. This is best understood by first considering Title III of the EPCA, a provision requiring car manufacturers to meet mandatory fuel economy standards applying to new cars domestically built or imported into the United States for any model year after 1977.[13]

Overall, the CAFE standards impelled the car industry to make passenger vehicles (including light trucks and vans) more fuel efficient. For any model year after 1977, manufacturers had to produce cars averaging a fuel economy of 18 MPG in 1978, 19 MPG in 1979, 20 MPG in 1980, and 27.5 MPG in 1985 and thereafter. From 1981 to 1984, the EPCA directed the secretary of transportation to set standards of average fuel economy that maximized progress toward the 1985 standard, but which also could be adjusted downward to 26 MPG, if necessary. Subject to congressional approval, the secretary also had discretion to set stricter standards for model years after 1985. In addition, two agencies, the National Highway Transportation Safety Administration (NHTSA) and the Environmental Protection Agency, assisted in implementing the CAFE provisions by generally establishing the methods, calculations, and testing procedures that were needed to make CAFE a reality. Both agencies were imbued with enough statutory discretion to influence the CAFE ratings procedurally or substantively.

A critical part of the law concerned its power to impose sanctions on the car manufacturers if they failed to comply with CAFE. Even so, the law had an important loophole that became the basis for subsequent D.C. Circuit litigation. Although car companies were heavily penalized for the failure to comply with CAFE, the fines for noncompliance could be avoided if the manufacturer accumulated enough "credits" during any year in which the average fuel economy exceeded the standard in a given model year. For instance, the EPCA set penalties at 5 dollars per 10 MPG for every tenth mile by which a manufacturer's average failed to meet the standard, multiplied by the number of cars produced by that company. Specifically, credits were earned in the same amount as the penalty to be incurred, as applied to any year in which the average fuel economy was greater than the standard for that year. In addition, the credits could be applied forward a year or backward a year against any penalty that was assessed for noncompliance. In essence, then, building up enough credits allowed recalcitrant car companies to evade paying some or even all of the penalties incurred as a consequence of *not* meeting the required CAFE level. Despite the possibility of being manipulated, the credit scheme reflected Congress's altruistic intent to give car makers enough malleability and financial incentive to comply with CAFE. The built-in flexibility gave car companies the option to apply earned credits either backward or forward for a period up to three model years.

Even though the CAFE standards were hailed by consumer groups, they were repudiated by auto manufacturers as being much too costly and unprofitable. All "big three" domestic car companies—General Motors Corporation, Ford Motor Company, and Chrysler Corporation—opposed the bill and lobbied hard against it. In particular, the big three pressed for some regulatory method that would allow car manufacturers to elude adherence to the CAFE standards, especially in President Reagan's first term. In the short-term, the strategy worked. Both GM and Ford convinced the government to modify the CAFE standards in a favorable way. In fact, as a result of the changes, a cozy arrangement emerged between business and government wherein more CAFE credits were aggregated (thus reducing the level of compliance), which let GM and Ford substantially offset any fines they had to pay for failing to stick to the CAFE requirements.[14]

Against this background, the D.C. Circuit found itself in the middle of an ongoing dispute between the consumer industry and the federal government concerning the enforceability and scope of CAFE. From 1980 to 1992, at least eleven different CAFE cases were litigated in the D.C. Circuit. Of the eleven, in eight cases (73 percent) a justiciability challenge was raised. Of those eight cases, seven appeals (88 percent) concerned an issue of whether a litigant had standing to bring the lawsuit.[15] Two cases in particular became the focus of the judicial politics of the D.C. Circuit. *Center for Auto Safety v. NHTSA* (1986)(*CAS I*) and *Center for Auto Safety v. Thomas* (1986)(*CAS II*) not only divided the court, but also stirred the most debate within the legal community and had a pronounced impact on social policy.[16]

The first case, *CAS I*, concerned a panel decision involving four consumer advocacy groups who objected to the NHTSA's rule lowering the CAFE standards applying to Ford's light trucks for certain model years. In a 2-1 decision, with two Reagan appointees disagreeing on the outcome (Judge James Buckley siding with the majority and Judge Antonin Scalia dissenting), Judge Harry T. Edwards (a Carter appointee) rejected the government's contention that the groups lacked standing. In the opinion, Judge Edwards thought that reducing the CAFE standards thwarted the petitioners' ability to buy fuel-efficient vehicles. Consequently, the court held that the alleged injury was an Article III case or controversy worthy of judicial intervention since the NHTSA's rule-making caused a harm redressable by a court. Moreover, Judge Edwards noted that the EPCA contained a provision favoring a grant of standing to persons "aggrieved" by adverse agency rule-making. Judge Edwards, in following congressional intent, therefore granted court access. The result made sense, he argued, because to do otherwise would improperly limit judicial review on prudential grounds (i.e., as a matter of judicial self-restraint).[17]

D.C. Circuit Judge Antonin Scalia, a Reagan appointee, disagreed and registered a dissent in *CAS I*. Scalia contended that the petitioners did not identify the specific kinds of light trucks that were allegedly in short supply because of the agency's rule-making. As a result, the pleadings insufficiently omitted a pertinent allegation of particular harm that was traceable to the agency's rule-making. Since, in Scalia's view, the basis for the purported injury was too speculative and hypothetical, the court could not properly intervene in the appeal. For Scalia, the case was not justiciable.[18]

The decision granting standing in *CAS I* led to a second D.C. Circuit panel opinion approximately six months later. Although the parties (and their arguments) were slightly different, *CAS II* was virtually an identical challenge to the representational standing of the same petitioners litigating the first case. In *CAS II*, though, certain consumer organizations sought to invalidate an EPA rule granting GM and Ford a CAFE "adjustment factor" for passenger cars manufactured in the 1980 model year and thereafter. The car makers asserted that a retroactive adjustment was needed to compensate them because the EPA's testing procedures, which were initially used to measure fuel efficiency in 1975, had changed. The difference in testing, they asserted, caused the measured fuel economy levels to be lower than what they should have been under the original procedures.

The consumer groups countered that the rule was unfair since it greatly rewarded GM and Ford for their past misfeasance in not originally complying with the CAFE standards. They pointed out that the car makers, in fact, petitioned the agency to initiate rule-making at a time when they faced the prospect of paying millions of dollars of CAFE penalties. For the petitioners, the new EPA rule had the unconscionable effect of subsidizing the domestic auto industry's illegal conduct, since it gave GM and Ford more CAFE credits to use to offset the huge losses they incurred in past fines.

On the basis of CAS I, a unanimous D.C. Circuit panel in CAS II (consisting of two Carter appointees, Judges Patricia Wald and Ruth B. Ginsburg, and one Reagan appointee, Judge Robert Bork) held that the groups had standing because the EPA's decision to grant more CAFE credits to GM and Ford injured consumers. The injury, the court stated, was legally cognizable because the rule's effect was to obviate any financial incentive to produce more fuel-efficient vehicles.[19] Although the substance of the panel decision on justiciability was rather routine, it is exceptional for its tumultuous implications.

For example, Judge Bork, a conservative appointee, only concurred in the result and wrote separately to indicate that the ruling in CAS I, as precedent, compelled him to do so.[20] In addition, within two months of CAS II the D.C. Circuit, convening en banc, vacated the panel's opinion and agreed to revisit CAS II before another en banc court later. When the entire court membership actually reheard the case, the partisanship of the judges shone through. In a divided en banc, per curiam 5-5 opinion, the D.C. Circuit conceded that it could not agree how to resolve the question of the petitioner's standing and reinstated the prior panel decision of CAS II. One camp, consisting of Democratic appointees (Judges Patricia Wald, Harry Edwards, Spottswood Robinson, Abner Mikva, and Ruth Bader Ginsburg), voted to grant it. The other, all Republican appointees (Judges James Buckley, Kenneth Starr, Douglas Ginsburg, Stephen Williams, and Laurence Silberman), voted to deny it.[21]

The differing judicial postures on the justiciability question emanated from each bloc's political manipulation of the underlying law governing the dispute. Judge Wald, in representing the views of the Democratic appointees and engaging in a "liberal" standing inquiry, asserted that the groups had standing because the EPA's rule-making harmed the groups as consumers.[22] In particular, she saw an economic injury because the agency rules meant that there were fewer fuel-efficient cars available for consumers, and then only at higher prices. The injury, she also maintained, was traceable to the EPA's action since the EPCA's credit provisions provide little incentive for car manufacturers to make fuel-efficient cars. Moreover, there was redressability since the court had the power to invalidate the rule, thereby eliminating the credits and restoring the financial impetus to make fuel-efficient cars. Judge Wald concluded that Congress clearly intended for car manufacturers to be punished with financial penalties if they did not conform to the CAFE standards. For the liberal bloc, affording access to the consumers best effectuated congressional intent and sent a strong message to the car industry that CAFE noncompliance was not a viable legal option.

Although they could not all agree on whether there was a legally defined injury, in writing for the Republican appointees Judge Buckley expressed the politically conservative consensus that the petitioners lacked standing because there was no traceability or redressability. He argued that the credit provisions did not provide any real impetus for car makers to produce fuel-efficient cars. The incentive to do so was absent since it was technologically impractical to manufacture the cars in a timely manner; as a result, the injury was too tenuously linked to the enactment of the EPA rule. Nor could the court, if it chose to intervene, rectify any potential harm that might result. Notably, the bloc also disagreed that Congress, by law, intended that standing had to be granted. For Judge Buckley, the legislative record was inconclusive at best. Since legislative intent on access was absent, Judge Buckley reasoned that there was no obligation to hear the dispute on the merits.

The deadlock of the *en banc* court in *CAS II* is important for a number of reasons. In general, the failure of the court to agree strained intracourt relationships and affected social policy relating to energy conservation. But there were specific consequences, too. D.C. Circuit judicial policy, which mandated that a prior panel opinion remain intact until a majority, en banc court overturns it later, required that the full court reinstate the *CAS II* panel decision, which it did. Yet, in an extraordinary display of disharmony, the panel ruling was restored *on the condition* that it could not be used as controlling precedent. The judges went out of their way to insure that none of the separate opinions addressing the per curiam judgment were dispositive in later cases. Ironically, the consensus reached by the court on the inapplicability of future precedent presaged more disagreement on the issue, thereby increasing further dissension on the D.C. Circuit.

Confusion reigned again shortly after the *CAS II* panel decision was reinstated when the court reconvened en banc again and reversed itself for a second time. This time the court proclaimed that the preceding en banc determination and reinstatement were faulty due to the split decision on the standing issue. In its ruling, the court corrected itself by saying that it improperly acted on the merits because it was equally divided on the issue of standing. Hence the court vacated the *CAS II* decision and *changed* the original outcome on the merits by denying all (instead of just part) of the petition for review concerning the validity of the EPA's rule.[23]

The effect of the new holding was not only profound but consistent with the ideological preferences of a majority of the D.C. Circuit in 1988. In addition to contributing to the instability of the law, it clearly helped GM and Ford achieve a conservative policy result. Since the court's decision upheld the CAFE rule, the judicial opinion also let the car manufacturers apply more CAFE credits to their outstanding penalty liability. One report estimated that the adjustments reduced GM's liability in the 1984 model year from $629.8 million to $508.7 million (a $121.1 million benefit) and, conversely, increased GM's net credit surplus for the 1981 and 1982 model years to $462.4 million from $274.2 million (a $188.2 million benefit). Ford, too, benefitted since it reaped an estimated savings totaling approximately $245 million. Overall, the court's affirmance of the agency rule gave an aggregate windfall to both car manufacturers of about $554.3 million.[24]

*CAS I* and *CAS II* unequivocally revealed that the judges' voting behavior was divided along party lines. D.C. Circuit judicial politics, therefore, greatly shaped legal and policy outcomes at a time when the court's membership began to change rapidly. Between the two and a half year period that the cases were decided, the D.C. Circuit was in the midst of ending its transformation in membership from a liberal to a conservative court: that is, between March 1986 (the date *CAS I* was first argued) and September 1988 (the time *CAS II* finally ended), the majority of Democratic-appointed judges (including senior judges) became a minority. By the end of *CAS II*, the number of Republican-appointed judges in active service (6) and senior service (2) thus outnumbered their Democratic counterparts (5 in active and 1 in senior service). Consequently, the outcome of *CAS II* depended upon the addition of one judge, David Sentelle, who joined the rest of the Republican wing in vacating the May 17, 1988, judgment that previously left the court in a 5-5 tie on the standing issue. Judge Sentelle's participation, therefore, was the difference in giving the car makers a key victory in a public policy dispute involving energy conservation.[25]

To be sure, the judges who were sitting on the D.C. Circuit's bench at the time the CAFE cases were litigated led to the conservative outcome of *CAS II*. As a new majority of Republican appointees united on the court, it acted to reverse the decision-making of a liberal panel that, from the conservative's viewpoint, improperly granted standing. The political preferences of the judges controlling the court determined the ideological direction of the court's jurisprudence. Whereas the liberals on the bench supported open access to the court, the conservative jurists preferred to restrict it through adherence to judicial restraint and separation of powers analysis.[26] In other words, as one student of the judicial process observed, "The various approaches to standing reflect a fundamental difference in ideology among the . . . judges. At one end of the spectrum are jurists favoring liberal standing requirements that allow most plaintiffs in through the courthouse door. These jurists generally require a low threshold of injury and causation, preferring to rule on the merits rather than dismiss a claim on the pleadings without discovery. At the other end of the spectrum are jurists who exercise restraint in granting standing, closely scrutinizing not only the extent of the asserted injury but also the direct causal link between the injury and the relevant government action."[27] In the CAFE cases, then, judicial attitudes and the political composition of the bench were quite significant in ascertaining if a litigant had the legal ability to maintain an appeal in the middle tier of federal courts in the 1980s.

From this perspective, the politicalization of the standing doctrine (along with the partisan manipulation of the en banc process) explains litigant access where a faithful and consistent adherence to legal principles (e.g., *CAS I* precedent) probably should have. Next, the CAFE cases also show that the D.C. Circuit's decisions on the threshold question have an enormous impact on public policy and, in particular, the financial fortunes of the car manufacturers at the time the cases were handed down. The D.C. Circuit, already operating as a de facto specialized court in the adjudication of regulatory appeals after 1970, exercised its judicial authority to trump Congress's implied intention to provide *most* litigants with access to a federal appeals court in the event legal mistakes were made at the district court or agency level. In this way the court, and not Congress, substantially shaped regulatory policy since the D.C. Circuit, in essence, surreptitiously ruled on the merits of the CAFE appeal when it ultimately denied standing.

The judicial politics of the D.C. Circuit, therefore, not only strains collegial relationships by creating internal conflict on the bench, it also underscores how circuit courts refine their agenda space through its access policy-making decisions in administrative law appeals. This is an especially important point since Congress gives little discretion to the circuit courts to set their policy agendas through case selection. Thus it is quite meaningful to learn the extent to which the D.C. Circuit builds its agenda politically in spite of its inherently limited jurisdiction, especially since liberals and conservatives tend to fundamentally disagree on the access issue. In sum, ideological considerations and, to perhaps a lesser extent, the law play an instrumental role in affecting the court's CAFE jurisprudence and social policy.[28]

# JUDICIAL DEFERENCE TO AGENCIES AND THE
# JUDICIAL POLITICS OF THE D.C. CIRCUIT

Although the issues of justiciability and litigant access are important aspects of the D.C. Circuit's judicial politics, a more fundamental question relates to the political nature of its on-the-merits review. On-the-merits review in regulatory cases is central because it registers a level of deference that necessarily affects judicial policy-making. Often a court's ruling is intimately aligned with a judicial attitude about whether it is proper for the court to upset an agency's ruling in a constitutional democracy governed by a separation of powers principle.

Like the access policy-making rulings, the ideological dynamics underlying the court's decision to defer has profound dimensions. By deferring to an agency, the court acknowledges that it is suitable for *agencies* to make policy and related legal judgments about congressional intent which is, most times, unclear at best with ambiguous statutes. Conversely, by *not* deferring the court denies an agency's delegated authority to make what it believes is the superior policy choice under the circumstances. Therefore, ideological considerations—as expressed through the attitudes and biases of judges, the politics of the judicial selection process, and the external political environment—combine to impact judicial deference since the decision retaining or relinquishing judicial power to bureaucrats strikes at the very core of the judicial function in a constitutional democracy.

The social science and legal literature consistently suggests that political ideology is critical to understanding the occasionally volatile relationship between courts and agencies. Contemporary thinking about judicial control of agencies is conceptually rooted in the New Deal, a politically dynamic time when courts assessed the constitutionality of progressive regulation and defined the scope of the nondelegation doctrine. The New Deal period was a defining moment in administrative law since it necessitated an ongoing assessment of whether courts ought to facilitate or impede its progress.[29] A brief summary of the divergent political philosophies of the New Deal period thus aids in framing the basic issue of whether courts should actively police agency decisions. It also discloses how the law is keenly associated with political considerations that ultimately affect judicial behavior in the modern administrative state.

## NEW DEAL POLITICS, THE APA,
## AND JUDICIAL CONTROL OF BUREAUCRACIES

In the 1930s, New Dealers, or liberals, advocated progressive reform *and* judicial restraint because they thought that disrupting agency policy initiatives thwarted the goal of allowing government to assist its citizens. A central premise of the liberal doctrine was the strong faith in "government by the experts" (an idea borrowed from the Progressive movement), or the belief that agency expertise is best utilized to secure the common good or "public interest." Pro-regulatory New Dealers thus supported broad delegation of legislative power to agencies because they perceived that agencies had enough technical expertise to solve complex problems of public policy. Concomitantly, liberals favored a strong presidency: in fact, scholars speculate that this element of the New Deal ideology is more in line with parliamentary government, because a strong presidency is mostly presumed. As a result, giving legislative power to the executive is a central feature that illuminates the philosophy underlying an expansive, regulatory state.

Conservatives, though, objected to the creation of a proactive bureaucracy since they believed that government must be subordinate to the rule of law, an argument principally supported by Alfred Dicey, an English liberal reformer. Dicey asserted that individual freedom, along with the preservation of private property rights, could only be realized under a government of laws, not men. For conservatives, the specter of big government threatened individual property rights and, in the end, liberty itself. From this perspective anti–New Dealers concluded that an administrative state inherently fails to promote the public interest (as liberals thought) because the interests of private property owners are unduly compromised by more governmental interference. Additionally, anti–New Deal conservatives were convinced that only Congress can legitimately make law under the U.S. Constitution. Consequently, any delegation of legislative authority to an agency was not only bad policy, but also unconstitutional. In light of their principal contentions, it is not that surprising that conservatives wanted a larger role for the judiciary, since courts, through an aggressive exercise of the power of judicial review, had the institutional capability to safeguard private property.[30]

The New Deal debate over the judicial control of agencies, which raged until 1937, was part of a much larger concern about the political legitimacy of social Darwinism, laissez-faire capitalism, and, ultimately, the New Deal itself. Before then, a conservative United States Supreme Court routinely invalidated key New Deal legislation on a variety of constitutional grounds, including the so-called nondelegation doctrine. This principle, which holds that Congress cannot delegate its legislative power to agencies under the U.S. Constitution, is a key element of administrative law that prevents government from taking a more active role in managing the economy. To be sure, the use of this doctrine by an unelected, life-tenured branch of government was quite controversial since it crippled any bureaucratic attempt to bring the country out of the depths of the Great Depression. Accordingly, shortly after announcing his intentions to give every American a new deal from government, President Franklin Roosevelt, in his second term, took the disingenuous political risk in 1937 of trying to pack the Court with justices who would support his innovative but sweeping economic program.[31]

Although the Court-packing plan was never implemented, it provided the impetus for avoiding a constitutional crisis because the Supreme Court unexpectedly chose to reverse its prior antiregulatory course and *reject* the economic conservativism of the past in a bevy of landmark cases decided in 1937. With *West Coast Hotel Co. v. Parrish* (upholding state minimum-wage law), *National Labor Relations Board v. Jones & Laughlin Steel Corporation* (upholding the National Labor Relations Act), *Helvering v. Davis* (upholding old-age tax and benefit provisions of the Social Security Act), and *Steward Machine Company v. Davis* (upholding unemployment provisions of the Social Security Act), the Court's "switch in time that saved nine" had the dual effect of preserving the Court's institutional legitimacy as well as laying the basis for further expansion of the modern administrative state.[32]

Significantly, the doctrinal reversal occurred at a time when President Roosevelt had the opportunity to make a number of new judicial appointments which, in the end, reconstituted the Court's membership. The turnover in judicial personnel worked to negate the hold that the "four-horsemen-of-conservative-reaction" (Justices Willis Van Devanter, James C. McReynolds, George Sutherland, and Pierce Butler) had on the Court. These justices were the principal group of jurists who successfully impeded New Deal progress (often with the help of Justice Owen J. Roberts and Chief Justice Charles E. Hughes, both of whom in time began to support the president's program). President Roosevelt, in fact, had the good fortune to fill the High Court with at least nine new justices after June of 1937. FDR's first appointment, Hugo L. Black, was especially significant for two reasons: he was a loyal supporter of the New Deal and he replaced the oldest member (in age and judicial service) of the four-horsemen bloc, Justice Van Devanter. Notably, the new appointees—Justices Stanley F. Reed, Felix Frankfurter, William O. Douglas, Frank Murphy, James F. Byrnes, Harlan F. Stone, Robert H. Jackson, and Wiley B. Rutledge—all shared the president's vision of the New Deal and its underlying ideological principles of governmental authority.[33] At least symbolically, then, and for some scholars in fact, the new bench repelled the conservative attempt to dismantle the New Deal through litigation, thus ratifying Roosevelt's conception of positive government. With the New Deal essentially legitimated, the nature of the debate between conservatives and New Deal liberals subtly changed as well, largely because conservatives realized that a new political strategy might be more effective in diminishing further support for regulation.

Thus, as one scholar of the New Deal period observed, "Toward the end of the New Deal era, the focus of American administrative law began to change. It became generally accepted that administrative decision-making is constitutionally legitimate, even if administrators tended to function free from governmental constraints. The central question became not *when* administrators could decide matters but *how* they should decide matters."[34] Instead of trying to prevent regulation altogether, which was the old line of attack, conservatives now tried to pick it apart by asserting that agency decision-making was procedurally flawed and fundamentally unfair. The conservative plan featured a sustained effort by the organized bar, the American Bar Association (ABA), to weaken the viability of the pro-regulatory state by portraying the administrative process as "over-judicialized." Interestingly, even though the ABA's objective was in line with a conservative view opposing economic regulation on substantive (i.e., ideological) grounds, the ABA's methodology in achieving it was different because it advocated procedural reform of agency decisional processes. While the ABA's procedural assault on agencies predated the Supreme Court's 1937 *West Coast* pronouncement, the shrill timbre (replete with anti-Marxist rhetoric) characterizing the tenor of the ABA movement did not take hold until late 1938, the year that Harvard Law School Dean Roscoe Pound assumed the chair of the ABA's Special Committee on Administrative Law.[35]

Dean Pound took control of the committee at a time of rising skepticism about the procedural competence of agencies and the wisdom of limited court review. Tales of bureaucratic mismanagement were all too common, and Dean Pound seized the moment by using the committee to launch a polemic attack against what he called "administrative absolutism." In Pound's view, agencies were almost tyrannical, as agency discretion was virtually unbridled and largely unchecked by courts. Consequently, for Pound and much of the legal profession he represented, the process by which bureaucracies made decisions had to be reformed, which implied that the judiciary had to have enough specific statutory authority to review (and limit) agency discretion. To complete that objective, the chair used the *ABA Final Report of the Committee,* published in 1938, to "indict" the administrative process. The report lists, for example, "ten tendencies" of suspect administrative action, such as the inclination to make decisions without a hearing or the tendency to disregard jurisdictional limits. Not surprisingly, the *ABA Report* became the basis for new legislation sponsored by reform-minded congressmen, Senator Marvel Mills Logan (D-Ky.) and Representative Francis Eugene Walter (D-Pa.), to "fix" administrative procedure.[36]

The Walter-Logan legislation, sometimes referred to as "the high water mark of judicialization" and "blatantly political," failed to become law when

Congress was unable to override President Roosevelt's veto of the legislation. Not surprisingly, the bill generated plenty of its own discord within and apart from the legal profession. Attorney General Robert Jackson questioned it, the New York City Bar Association denounced it, and academicians criticized it. In 1939, the controversy prompted additional investigation into the question of whether regulatory reform was actually needed. The new pathbreaking study was in fact undertaken at the behest of the president himself, who instructed the attorney general to commission individuals to examine thoroughly the necessity for procedural reform of administrative law. It culminated in the *Final Report of the Attorney General's Committee on Administrative Procedure (Final Report)*, which some call "the best study of federal administrative procedure ever prepared." Few would deny, therefore, that it is the most influential treatise on administrative law ever written. Not only did the *Final Report* assuage the passion of the conservative critique, it also became the foundation for passing the federal Administrative Procedure Act of 1946 (APA), the statutory model for modern administrative law.[37]

Like the debate that preceded it, the APA reflected competing political views vying for supremacy in the New Deal era. Specifically, the legislation was the result of an accord forged between liberal, pro-regulatory New Dealers and conservative, antiregulation Diceyans. As political scientist Martin Shapiro described it, "The very fight over administrative law which culminated in the APA was a fight between conservatives and liberals. Conservatives wanted as big a role for the regular courts as possible because they thought of courts as protectors of private property. Liberal New Dealers wanted as small a judicial role as possible because they saw the courts as blocking liberal congressional and especially presidential programs. The APA is . . . a complex bundle of compromise between the two positions."[38] A key element of the agreement, though, centered upon the distinction the APA created between two agency functions, adjudication and rule-making.

Specifically, in terms of administrative adjudication, the APA mandates that agencies employ fairly elaborate and trial-like procedures "on a record" during the process of making specific decisions. This requirement was more in line with the conservative or Diceyan axiom that private disputes affecting the interests of particular individuals should be adjudicated in a formal setting, like the one typically conducted in a court proceeding. Conversely, rule-making under the APA was more informal and less courtlike. Valid rule-making only required giving proper notice of the rule and its effect. While in the process of making a rule the agency must: give advance notice that a rule is being promulgated; provide an opportunity for the public to comment upon the rule's content; and give a concise, general statement of what the agency is trying to accomplish with the rule. The rule-making provision was liberal in scope because agencies had the flexibility to make a rule independently under a broad grant of delegated legislative authority.[39]

Consequently, the APA adjudication and rule-making requirements only codified what agencies were already doing by 1946. The practical reality underlying the administrative process, in other words, dictated what went into the APA. For example, adjudication was designed to be more formal in scope because agencies routinely acted like quasi-judicial bodies when resolving actual cases prior to the APA's enactment. Likewise, rule-making was less informal because it had to be: that is, agencies realized—long before the APA was passed—that the successful administration of agency programs is best accomplished if they acted quasi-legislatively through frequent rule-making. Invariably, the APA distinction between adjudication and rule-making emanated from a decision to adopt (if not ratify) the standards of practice that agencies already developed by 1946 in response to their ongoing attempt to carry out the New Deal's legislative mandate.

Moreover, the right to judicial review of alleged agency misconduct under the APA was broadly defined. Yet the intensity or scope of review that a court applied in a case depended upon the type of agency action that was challenged. Pursuant to the APA, courts were instructed to undertake a relatively strict review of agency adjudication under a "substantial evidence" test. Requiring substantial evidence made it likely that courts would uphold an agency's decision if there was something *substantial* in the formal record supporting the agency's decision. For rule-making, however, the scope of review was less rigid. Under the APA, judicial review of agency rule-making was not accomplished through substantial evidence, but rather under an "arbitrary and capricious" standard. Unlike substantial evidence, the alternative scope of review greatly reduced the chance of upsetting whatever the agency did, since a court only reversed if the agency acted arbitrarily and capriciously in promulgating the rule.

The APA judicial review provisions are thus the basis for comprehending the judicial attitude toward agencies in the post-APA era, at least until 1970. Although conservatives were pleased with the stricter standard of review for adjudication, they won that small victory by conceding some political ground with respect to the standard governing judicial review of rule-making. Since rule-making does not require the creation of a record, courts applying the APA ordinarily deferred to the agency fact-finding that purportedly justified the policy decision to make the rule. In this sense, as Martin Shapiro wryly notes, the arbitrary and capricious test is tantamount to a "lunacy test" because courts do not reverse unless the bureaucratic decision is crazy. For these reasons, the compromise essentially favored New Deal liberals pressing for a more restrictive judicial role. Courts deferred to agencies more under the

APA, and it really did not matter that much if the type of proceeding was called "rule-making" or an "adjudication."[40]

The judicial pragmatism toward applying the APA in cases minimized, perhaps even obliterated, any meaningful analytical distinction that might have been important to the liberals and conservatives who were engaged in the New Deal debate concerning the proper scope of judicial control over agencies. After 1946, for example, courts increasingly assumed a more deferential posture in reviewing agency action, which continued the past trend of acceding to agency decision-making. Since agencies had more leeway to interpret the law, courts thus implicitly conceded that agencies were true "experts" in making difficult policy choices in the regulatory context.

Moreover, since informal agency actions (i.e., actions that did not technically involve either rule-making or an adjudication) were the mainstay for agency practice after 1946, courts had even more incentive to defer to administrative decisions. In hindsight, the APA accomplished Congress's goal of encouraging agencies to use less adjudication in their decisions while simultaneously restricting the courts from unduly interfering with agency policy-making. Courts deferred more, simply because the APA omitted reference to (and therefore did not specifically establish) a standard of judicial review pertaining to informal agency conduct. As many of the policy judgments made by agencies' experts were informally made through rules, courts found it easier to yield to agencies in light of the APA's silence on the issue.

With these latter points in mind, the APA's ineffectiveness as a judicial constraint on agency behavior had important consequences. While the APA of 1946 helped to facilitate a new age of judicial deference by implicitly encouraging agency rule-making, the "hands off" attitude of the courts only lasted in earnest until 1970. All courts, including the D.C. Circuit, soon challenged the rule-making assumptions of post–New Deal judicial deference. The basis for the new judicial attitude was derived from an unintended effect of the APA, which was to invite courts to superintend agency processes with increased vigor as a result of the APA's ambiguity.[41] Clearly, the D.C. Circuit accepted the offer by developing the doctrine of hard-look review in the 1970s. This had implications in the next decade as well, since forcing agencies to take a hard look at what they were doing significantly laid the basis for permitting the court to assert its judicial will whenever the core substantive values of the regulatory period were threatened by deregulation.

## THE D.C. CIRCUIT AS THE "TRUSTEE FOR THE GHOSTS OF CONGRESSES PAST"

Appreciation of the law and politics of the New Deal is a prerequisite for grasping the general modern approach that courts follow in superintending bureaucracies through judicial review. At least until 1970, perhaps the New Deal's most instrumental impact on courts was the APA itself because the APA created legal standards that reduced courts to rubber stamps of agency policy directives. In light of court reform and an unprecedented era of social regulation, the D.C. Circuit used hard-look review to take advantage of its numerous agenda opportunities and to control agency discretion more closely in the 1970s, a turn of political events that helped to signal the demise of the quiescent days of judicial deference to agencies.[42] The court's activism, however, was not entirely confined to the 1970s era, as the court's behavior over the next ten years reveals.

With hard-look judicial review firmly established, the D.C. Circuit certainly had the discretion to remain faithful to some or all of the pro-regulatory objectives of the 1970s. In theory, the D.C. Circuit analyzed the merits of deregulation appeals in the 1980s from at least three different judicial review perspectives: New Deal deference, procedural hard look, and substantive hard look.[43] Of course, *Greater Boston* was still on the books and its main principle—substantive hard-look review, the style of judicial questioning introduced by Judge Leventhal—was still a viable option for the liberal brethren to utilize if the political circumstances demanded it. Consequently, the court still retained the judicial authority to remain a harsh critic of agency conduct in select cases that challenged some of the fundamental values of the era of burgeoning regulation.

Early in the decade the D.C. Circuit demonstrated that it would not be shy in invoking hard-look review substantively. In *National Lime Association v. Environmental Protection Agency* (1980), for instance, the D.C. Circuit ruled on the legality of the EPA's new source performance standards (NSPS) enacted for the lime industry under the Clean Air Act. The standards were designed to limit the amount of particulate, or pollution, emitted in the exhaust gas from lime-manufacturing plants. Petitioners challenged the new rules by arguing that the EPA based its rule-making on faulty test data that belied the agency's conclusion that the pollution standards were "achievable" under the technological standards existing at the time. Although the D.C. Circuit agreed and remanded the case, it did so only after subjecting the agency's decision-making processes to a fairly strict version of hard-look judicial review. Specifically, the court remanded on the basis that the agency failed to support its factual conclusion that the new performance standards were achievable *even though* the agency purportedly explained its rationale when it made the rule.

If for no other reason, *National Lime* is significant because the court did not accept the agency's explanation that the pollution standards were achievable. Even though the agency presumably weighed the issue carefully in its policy evaluation of the rule, the court insisted that something more than a "reasoned" explanation was required before an agency's judgment was sanctioned by the court. The substantive nature of the judicial inquiry, along with its implications for affecting the ideological direction of public policy, was conspicuous in Judge Wald's description of the court's application of the standard of review to the case facts. Specifically, Judge Wald explained:

> Both decisions reviewing the NSPS and those reviewing other administrative determinations under the Clean Air Act evince a concern that variables be accounted for, that the representativeness of test conditions be ascertained, that the validity of tests be assured, and the statistical significance of results determined. Collectively, these concerns have sometimes been expressed as a need for "reasoned decision-making" and sometimes as a need for adequate "methodology." However expressed, *these more substantive concerns* have been coupled with a requirement that assumptions be stated, that process be revealed, that the rejection of alternate theories or abandonment of alternate courses of action be explained and that the rationale for the ultimate decision be set forth in a manner which permits the public to exercise its statutory prerogative of comment and the courts to exercise their statutory responsibility upon review [emphasis added].

Judge Wald's analysis (especially in outlining certain danger signals triggering heightened judicial review) arguably equates *agency reasonableness* with *substantive reasonableness*, as defined by the court. This made the court's reasoning analogous to Judge Leventhal's substantive version of hard look outlined in the landmark *Greater Boston* ruling. Even though the court asserted that the heightened level of review was "neither more rigorous nor more deferential than the standard applied" in earlier cases, *National Lime* strongly suggested that the D.C. Circuit was still committed to reaching politically substantive results through hard-look judicial review. In this sense, it was an indication that the court's activism in administrative law was not going to end completely with the dawning of a new deregulatory age.[44]

The famous air bags case reinforces this claim.[45] The origin of the controversy, which culminated in the D.C. Circuit opinion in *State Farm Mutual Automobile Insurance Company v. Department of Transportation* (1982), is traced to the American preoccupation with consumer safety in 1966. At the source of the litigation was The National Traffic and Motor Vehicle Safety Act (Safety Act), which empowered the Department of Transportation (DOT) to promulgate national motor vehicle safety standards. In order to fulfill its statutory mandate in 1967, the DOT issued Federal Motor Vehicle Safety Standard 208, which required that all cars sold in the United States be equipped with manual seat belts. The agency soon discovered, however, that the rule did little to increase traffic safety, since drivers and passengers often chose not to "buckle up."

This oversight prompted the agency to consider next using a "passive occupant restraint system" in 1969 (and afterward). Passive restraints, like automatic seat belts or air bags, were thought to be foolproof because they protected the occupants of a vehicle without requiring the voluntary participation of drivers or passengers. After voluminous rule-making proceedings and a court challenge in the Sixth Circuit testing the proposed system's legality, in 1972 the DOT revised Standard 208, which mandated that all new cars be installed with passive restraints by the fall of 1975. The revised rule was met with intense political and public resistance, later compelling the secretary of transportation to postpone in 1975 and then suspend in 1976 the rule in the last days of President Gerald Ford's administration.

After reviewing the issue, the new Carter administration quickly reversed course. Brock Adams, the secretary of transportation, promulgated a new, mandatory passive restraint resolution, which modified Standard 208. The new rule impelled installation of passive restraints in new cars by the 1984 model year. Although the agency's decision to do so was upheld on appeal by the D.C. Circuit in *Pacific Legal Foundation v. Department of Transportation* (1979), Ronald Reagan's election to the presidency in the following year caused the agency to change its policy again. In January of 1981 Reagan's secretary of transportation, Andrew Lewis, initiated a new round of rule-making which resulted in another new rule, Notice 25, rescinding modified Standard 208. Conceived as a political response and seen by many as a whimsical shift in consumer-safety policy, Notice 25 created a firestorm of controversy that soon engulfed the D.C. Circuit. Since the abrupt reversal of the passive restraint policy smacked of blatant partisanship, the new conservative administration had to defend the rescission politically, and then legally, in the D.C. Circuit.

Officially, the agency offered two principal reasons for its course of action. First, in studying the issue the agency predicted that there would be only a minimal increase in using automatic seat belts under modified Standard 208. Pursuant to the modified Standard, cars had to be equipped with either detachable automatic belts or air bags. In creating the rule, the NHTSA reasoned that it was relatively certain that detachable belts would be installed over air bags, thus defeating the essential purpose of having a passive restraint system that cured drivers' failures to attach them. The second and more significant reason, though, was traditional cost-benefit analysis. The agency thought that the safety benefits of having the modified Standard in place outweighed the economic cost of its application *only if* there was a marked increase in the use of seat belts. Yet this was unlikely, because the belts could be disabled at will. Such pessimism, it seems, was premised upon the intuition that fewer people would take advantage of the belts if they were detachable. Thus manual belts were just as effective as the ones mandated by the rule, thereby making the modified Standard superfluous. Neither rationale, however, placated representatives of the insurance industry, who sought judicial review of the agency's rescission of the rule in the D.C. Circuit in 1981.

In *State Farm* the D.C. Circuit adjudicated the novel legal question of whether rescission (rather than promulgation) of an agency's rule was "arbitrary and capricious" under the substantive sections of the Safety Act and the informal rule-making provisions of the Administrative Procedure Act. In writing for a unanimous court, Judge Abner Mikva remanded the case on the grounds that a sudden reversal of policy was a danger signal that alerted the court that Congress's "commitment to the concept of automatic crash protection devises" was being overlooked by the agency. Specifically, Judge Mikva held that the agency did not present any evidence that seat belt usage would not increase and result in fewer safety benefits. Also, it inexplicably failed to consider the possibility that air bags might be a viable alternative to using automatic detachable belts as a passive restraint device. Finding no clear and convincing reasons (a strict burden of civil proof) for upsetting congressional intent, the D.C. Circuit concluded that NHTSA failed to explain its recission adequately.

One of the main reasons *State Farm* is important is that the Supreme Court affirmed the D.C. Circuit's decision in a ruling that is widely regarded among scholars as a modern endorsement of the hard-look doctrine. Even though the Supreme Court in *Motor Vehicle Manufacturers Association of the United States v. State Farm Mutual Automobile Insurance Company* (1983) held that the circuit court wrongly intensified the scope of judicial review (in light of Judge Mikva's interpretation of the Safety Act's legislative history and purpose), the Court held that the D.C. Circuit correctly reasoned that the NHTSA acted arbitrarily and capriciously in rescinding the rule. In the words of Justice Byron White, this interpretation of the lower circuit court's opinion meant that *Vermont Yankee* was not a "talisman under which any agency decision [is] by definition unimpeachable."[46] Some of the D.C. Circuit's more liberal-minded judges apparently agreed, as the reasoning in *International Ladies' Garment Workers' Union v. Donovan* (1983) indicates.

In *International,* the secretary of labor lifted labor restrictions on the practice of so-called homework in the knitted outerwear industry, an action challenged by knitted outerwear manufacturers, manufacturers' associations, labor unions, and state labor law enforcement officials objecting to the rescission. Judge Harry T. Edwards, in writing for the appellate court, remanded and held that the secretary's action was arbitrary and capricious because the agency did not explore alternative rationales that might have obviated the need for rescission. The court also found that the agency's justification concerning the removal of the homework restriction was lacking in other respects as well. The secretary argued that lifting the homework restriction would lead to better enforcement of labor laws and increase employment opportunities in the knitwear industry. The court disagreed, referring to these rationales as "unreasoned" and "completely inadequate." Significantly, Judge Edwards candidly acknowledged that the politics of making law in a time of deregulation have an impact on the court's decision-making processes. In his concluding remarks he stated, "We recognize that a new administration may try to effectuate new philosophies that have been implicitly endorsed by the democratic processes. Nonetheless, it is axiomatic that the leaders of every administration are required to adhere to the dictates of statutes that are also products of democratic decisionmaking. Unless officials of the Executive Branch can convince Congress to change the statutes they find objectionable, their duty is to implement the statutory mandates in a rational manner."[47] The unstated premise of Judge Edwards's remarks was that the D.C. Circuit at times will *enforce* a social regulatory mandate even if the executive or Congress had elected not to do so for political reasons. By remaining faithful to congressional intent expressed in prior regulation, *International* (along with *State Farm* and *National Lime*) demonstrates the court's willingness to act like a "trustee for the ghosts of Congresses past," a political task assumed by liberal D.C. Circuit jurists who knew their clout was fading as they receded into minority status during the mid-1980s.[48] The extent to which political ideology, however, let the court aggressively curtail agency conduct was called into question by an important decision issued from the United States Supreme Court in 1984.

### THE "*CHEVRON* TWO-STEP" AND THE POLITICAL IDEOLOGY OF MODERN NEW DEAL JUDGING

With its membership in flux but with substantive hard-look judicial review still intact, the U.S. Supreme Court decided *Chevron U.S.A., Inc. v. Natural Resources Defense Council, Inc.* (1984), a ruling that had the potential to erase the D.C. Circuit's ability to act as a trustee for Congresses past. The Supreme Court's opinion resulted from a review of a D.C. Circuit panel decision. In *Natural Resources Defense Council, Inc. v. Gorsuch* (1982), the petitioners objected to the EPA's policy of allowing the states (through a permit program) to meet the Clean Air Act's mandate by treating pollution-emitting devises in industrial plants as coming from a single, stationary source. If for no other reason, the agency's decision was controversial because it represented a shift in environmental policy, albeit one that was consistent with conservative deregulatory objectives favoring business.[49]

Business benefitted (and the environment perhaps suffered) for two simple reasons: more money and less regulation. By classifying all pollution-emitting devises in an industrial plant as emanating from a single source, the new rule legally treated the entire plant as being encased in a single pollution "bubble" that hypothetically surrounded the plant. The distinction is important because it meant that less compliance with the Clean Air Act was necessary since there were fewer devises in the plant that had to meet the standards imposed by law. As a result, management was not pressured as much to monitor the pollution the plant spewed out into the atmosphere; and, of course, less regulatory compliance also substantially reduced the plant's operating costs. Hence, from a business perspective the EPA's new policy made plenty of economic and practical sense since it cut costs and significantly decreased the amount of government red tape.

The environmental group initiating the litigation saw things differently and perceived the bubble policy as a threat to the environment. It challenged the EPA's new rule in circuit court where, on appeal, the D.C. Circuit reversed the agency's rule-making. In writing for a unanimous court Judge Ruth Bader Ginsburg reasoned that the bubble policy was flawed since it conflicted with the CAA's regulatory mandate to clean the air. Judge Ginsburg stated that the EPA's pre-existing policy revealed a congressional intent to *improve,* and not just maintain, a certain level of air quality in America. By abruptly reversing course and authorizing the states to adopt a policy that slashed business costs at the expense of creating more pollution and a dirtier environment, the court concluded that the EPA shirked its main responsibility to enforce the clean air statute in a manner intended by Congress.

The U.S. Supreme Court, however, disagreed and reversed the D.C. Circuit in a landmark ruling that allegedly established a new principle of judicial deference for statutory construction cases, prompting one scholar to proclaim that it "marked a significant transformation in the Supreme Court's jurisprudence of deference."[50] In *Chevron U.S.A. Inc. v. Natural Resources Defense Council, Inc.* (1984), Justice John Paul Stevens held in a unanimous opinion that the circuit court wrongly usurped the EPA's quasi-legislative discretion to initiate and apply the bubble policy through its rule-making. The D.C. Circuit, wrote Stevens, "misconceived the nature of its [judicial] role in reviewing the regulation at issue." The lower court made the mistake, he said, of substituting its own view for that of the agency by concluding that the CAA was ambiguous on basic issue of whether the bubble concept applied to state permit programs. From the Court's perspective, the uncertainty about the statute or its meaning should have compelled the lower court to accede to the agency's policy-making, and certainly not challenge it. In the Court's estimation, the D.C. Circuit did not assess whether the agency's policy choice was *reasonable* in light of the statute's inconclusiveness. As a result, the High Court reversed and allowed the EPA to apply its new policy without any further judicial interference.

Unquestionably, the Supreme Court's holding in *Chevron* is in stark contrast to the *State Farm* decision and more reminiscent of *Vermont Yankee*, in which the Court upbraided the D.C. Circuit for acting like judicial legislators when it overturned an agency's policy decision. In *Chevron* Justice Stevens stressed that the agency's political decision ought to be left alone by the upstart circuit court. Like a parent scolding a child for a misdeed, Justice Stevens reminded the D.C. Circuit of its apolitical responsibilities as a federal circuit court:

> Judges are not experts in the field, and are not part of either political branch of the Government. Courts must, in some cases, reconcile competing political interests, but not on the basis of the judges' personal policy preferences. In contrast, an agency to which Congress has delegated policymaking responsibilities may, within the limits of that delegation, properly rely upon the incumbent administration's views of wise policy to inform its judgments. While agencies are not directly accountable to the people, the Chief Executive is, and it is entirely appropriate for this political branch of the Government to make such policy choices—resolving the competing interests which Congress itself inadvertently did not resolve, or intentionally left to be resolved by the agency charged with the administration of the statute in light of everyday realities.[51]

In *Chevron* Justice Stevens suggested that judges have a legal responsibility to put aside their own policy preferences and defer to agencies so long as the statutory intent is unclear *and* the agency does not overstep the bounds of its delegated authority by making an unreasonable policy choice. Consequently, with *Chevron* the Supreme Court upheld the agency and reinforced the myth that courts are apolitical institutions in the American system of justice.

The myth is perpetuated since, in theory, *Chevron* severely limits the judicial role by compelling courts to ask two questions in evaluating whether agencies properly interpreted the law and made policy. The first prong of the test mandates that courts ascertain if Congress "directly spoke to the precise issue" in the statute under review. If so, then the court must follow Congress's intent and automatically defer to the agency's judgment. Yet, if the intent is vague (as it is in most instances), under the second part of the test courts must yield to the agency's interpretation of the statute *if* the agency's decision is reasonable. While the test seems clear enough, its application in cases is far more problematic because of its inherent ambiguity. While the *"Chevron* two-step" purports to command judicial deference to agencies in many instances, a court's political discretion can adeptly convert the test into an anti-deference policy-making tool. Although the scholarship on the issue is ambivalent at best, a thoughtful reading of the test makes it very dubious whether *Chevron*—as a binding precedent—does little to constrain a court's power to engage in substantive judicial review from *either side* of the political spectrum.[52]

This irony results because *Chevron* has had the unintended effects of inviting courts to legislate judicially and exacerbating the political differences between opposing ideological judges on circuit courts like the D.C. Circuit. Irrespective of whether the court is construing a statute or not, conservative and liberal judges interpret the law in a way that often reflects their partisan preferences and personal biases. Yet the political conflict emerging in statutory construction cases is probably more significant under *Chevron* because the decision to defer invariably reflects an ideological attitude about what the court's role should be in checking agency discretion. For this reason specific outcomes in appeals become contingent upon the judicial inclination, or reluctance, to interpret the law *independently* of an agency's *legal* view. When seen in this light, modern conceptions about judicial deference are strikingly similar to the arguments made by New Deal liberals and antiregulatory conservatives in the 1930s. To be sure, as a legal deference principle *Chevron* cannot restrain a judge's temptation to manipulate the law and reach specific case results that reflect distinctly personal political attitudes. Just like the way liberals and conservatives disagreed over the legitimacy of the New Deal, "modern" New Deal judges are similarly tempted to use individual notions of democratic theory or separation of powers' analysis as a basis for controlling agencies in the ongoing political struggle between courts and bureaucracies.[53]

The point of departure for analyzing this modern approach is whether the judge believes that legislature has the power under the U.S. Constitution to give away some of its law-making authority to an executive agency. To illustrate, a contemporary New Deal liberal judge might defer to an agency in an appeal because the judge believes it is entirely proper for Congress to delegate legislative power to executive bureaucrats.[54] Without that authority, agencies cannot exercise the requisite discretion to make legislative policy judgments as experts in the field. Like an argument that might be made by a traditional New Deal supporter, the modern liberal judge claims that a "proper" conception of democratic theory impels that the court exercise judicial restraint in reviewing agency action. Conversely, a modern anti–New Deal conservative judge reasons that it is the court's duty to exercise legal judgment independently from the extralegal views of bureaucrats. For this conservative judge, democratic theory in the New Deal sense commands that courts keep agencies accountable, especially since the former has a constitutional obligation to "say what the law is." By definition, then, the agency's decision carries less presumptive weight since it is only proper for courts, and not agencies, to assume the role of judge in a democracy in the first place. In this fashion, respect for democratic and separation of powers principles legitimizes the active use of judicial discretion to trump an agency's legal conclusion, which can only be regarded by the modern anti–New Deal judge as the illicit by-product of improperly delegated legislative power.

Evidence of the modern New Deal judicial attitude is found in the viewpoints of D.C. Circuit judges who used *Chevron* in deciding administrative law appeals after 1984. While divergent, the political differences among D.C. Circuit judges surfaced whenever they tried to use either step of the *Chevron* test. Even so, as Judge Starr suggests, *Chevron*'s step one is an especially convenient tool to achieve specific policy results because it is a "primary battleground" for testing the validity of agency legal conclusions in appeals. Put otherwise, when judges try to ascertain if Congress "directly spoke to the precise issue" (i.e., in determining if Congress's intent in drafting the law is clear), they invariably must make a subjective evaluation about what the words of the statute mean or say. In doing so, *Chevron*'s step one encourages unprincipled judging simply as a result of the judicial preoccupation to interpret ambiguous statutes through elusive searches for congressional intent. Liberal or conservative ideology, therefore, can easily drive policy outcomes when judges have the discretion to determine a statute's meaning.

Conservative jurists, like Judge Starr for example, first look to the plain meaning of a statute because "Congress's intent controls, and not the agency's." Since a statute embodies the collective wisdom of the legislature, Starr asserts that judges should not resort to legislative history to glean an intent, since doing so only invites creative judging and possibly the usurpation of either the legislative or executive prerogative. Starr argues, for instance, that the will of the legislature *and* the president is ignored if a court consults extralegal material like legislative history. Often, he notes, the president typically signs legislation without referring to the circumstances surrounding the enactment. Thus, if courts use legislative history, they diminish the role of the executive because the judiciary is interpreting the law differently from the way the president construed it when he signed it into law. Significantly, in an analogous fashion to the old New Deal conservative, Starr's approach implies less judicial deference to agencies (under the pretext of judicial restraint and not using legislative history) because it is premised on the idea that courts, and not bureaucracies, are the best and final arbiter of what the law says.

Yet more liberal jurists, like Judge Abner Mikva, for instance, believe that courts should defer more readily to an agency's interpretation of an ambiguous statute unless an agency oversteps its delegated responsibility by trying to rewrite the statute through its decision-making. Not only does Mikva think that Congress has the option of passing a law later that would correct an erroneous construction of the statute by the court, Mikva claims a generalist judiciary is not in a position to supplant the view of an expert agency with its own policy determination. Moreover, Mikva states that congressional intent is not often discoverable by simply looking at the words of a statute. As a result, courts must consult legislative history to discern intent when the statute's meaning is unclear. Using this philosophy makes it far less likely that the court will legislate judicially because it will instead try to follow what Congress meant in enacting the law. Ironically, Judge Mikva rejects the plain meaning approach for precisely the same reason that Judge Starr embraces it: that using this approach judges have a greater tendency to write their own policy preferences into law. Consequently, Judge Mikva's thinking is identical to the old-style, liberal New Deal view because the court exercises judicial restraint (through an activist pretext of using extralegal sources in determining a statute's meaning) toward agency conduct and is quite willing to give an agency the first shot at making a valid legal judgment about a policy issue.

Even in light of these intriguing arguments it is still probably an overgeneralization to claim that judges of a particular ideological persuasion are irrevocably committed to deferring more (or less) to agencies solely as a result of the judges' political beliefs. It is important to not lose sight of the reality that modern liberal and conservative judges have the discretion to manipulate outcomes under *Chevron*'s step one, regardless of whether the court actually defers to the agency in a specific decision. As Justice Antonin Scalia reminds us, "policy evaluation is . . . part of the traditional judicial toolkit that is used in applying the first step of *Chevron*—the step that determines, *before* deferring to agency judgment, whether the law is indeed ambiguous."[55] While Judge Mikva's judicial philosophy, for instance, is at first blush more deferential to agencies, it can also lead to unprincipled results, since a liberal judge has the power to make the critical determination that a statute is vague when its words may in fact be fairly clear. If a judicial opinion penned by Judge Mikva does not defer to the agency, or even when the ruling yields to the agency's decision, it is difficult to know to what extent political ideology is a causal factor in determining the case's outcome. Even if judges are acting politically in their decision-making, it does not automatically follow that the court always (or never) defers to agencies.

Consequently, under step one, the main objective is not really to ascertain whether a particular judicial philosophy is used to command more or less deference to agencies in an absolute sense (i.e., in all cases). More critical to the analysis is accepting that even judges sharing opposing political ideologies can similarly manipulate the law to get the result they want by saying that the statute is (or is not) ambiguous. Having different approaches to construing statutes only exacerbates the potentiality of disagreement on a court over cases that are politically sensitive. But they do not, in all likelihood, cause more or less deference in every situation. While it is certain that the political attitudes of judges figure into increased judicial conflict and less stability in statutory construction case law, it is too much to claim that a modern liberal judge always defers and a modern conservative jurist routinely does not. It misses the point to assert otherwise because in all cases political ideology may not be the tail wagging the dog of judicial deference to agencies and commanding a Pavlovian response.

Not surprisingly, an identical point can be made about step two of the *Chevron* test. Even if it is presumed that jurists with discordant political attitudes can agree upon the meaning of congressional intent in a specific statute, since judges are mortal and politically diverse they still often differ on the basic issue of whether an agency's statutory construction is "reasonable." A variety of legal and nonlegal factors can influence the court's decision-making process and surely affect the political result the court reaches. But to say that modern liberal judges automatically defer to only reasonable agency outcomes is not very helpful. Similarly, claiming that modern conservative jurists reverse only unreasonable agency decisions is also a gross overstatement. Overall, the lack of certainty inevitably associated with interpreting either prong of the *Chevron* principle merely gives judges an opportunity to achieve personal policy objectives while pretending to apply the law in a neutral and principled fashion. But it does not *require* that court outcomes fall neatly on either side of the political spectrum in every agency case.

With these comments in mind it is not surprising that the evidence is less than clear as to whether *Chevron* has had a deference effect in the D.C. Circuit. If anything, the results are mixed since the court has inconsistently applied *Chevron* to regulatory appeals. Under *Chevron,* using either prong of the test, sometimes the court defers and sometimes it does not.[56] Even so, while scholars disagree on *Chevron's* impact, Figures 8 and 9 combine to suggest that the D.C. Circuit is still very much the quintessential skeptic toward agencies that it was in the 1970s *and* that *Chevron* has done little to change that judicial cynicism.[57]

Although part of the data applies to a time period before *Chevron* was decided, Figure 8 shows that the D.C. Circuit affirmed agencies (on average) only 55.65 percent in the 1980s, a D.C. Circuit rate of judicial deference that is even below the one of 57.06 percent that the court posted in the 1970s (as Figure 6 in Chapter 2 indicates). The rate is far beneath the percentage

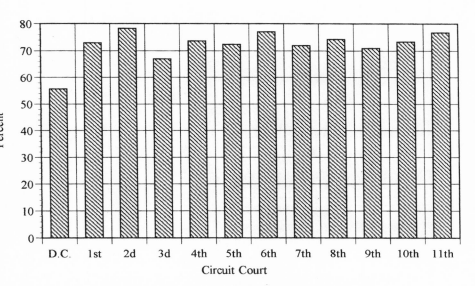

FIGURE 8. Affirmance Rate of Agency Appeals in U.S. Courts of Appeals, 1980–1989

Source: *Annual Report of the Director of the Administrative Office of the United States Courts,* from 1980 to 1989 (Table B-1).

Note: All data are based upon a twelve-month period ending June 30, as compiled by the Administrative Office of the U.S. Courts. "Affirmation Rate of Agency Appeals" is the average percentage of affirmances, grants, or enforcements of agency petitions.

observed in other circuit courts as well. With the exception of the Third Circuit (66.92 percent), all other courts of appeals registered an affirmance rate of 70 percent or more, thus suggesting more judicial deference to agencies. But, if circuit courts are acting in the traditional New Deal sense, the data should show less judicial deference since the courts in the 1980s gradually turned to the right through the presidential appointing process.[58] Only the D.C. Circuit seems to fit that paradigm well since the court grew more conservative and its affirmance rate is quite low.

Figure 9, on the other hand, summarizes the affirmance rate of each circuit court before and after *Chevron* was decided in an effort to discern more precisely what impact the case has on circuit courts. While Figure 9 is by no means conclusive, it nonetheless provides some indicia that *Chevron*, as a legal precedent constraining circuit court behavior, *may* have led to more judicial deference in nine of twelve circuit courts.[59] Only three courts—the D.C., Eighth, and Ninth Circuits—exhibited a lower affirmance rate from 1985 to 1989, the period immediately following the 1984 *Chevron* ruling. Of those three courts, the D.C. Circuit had the lowest affirmance rate of agency

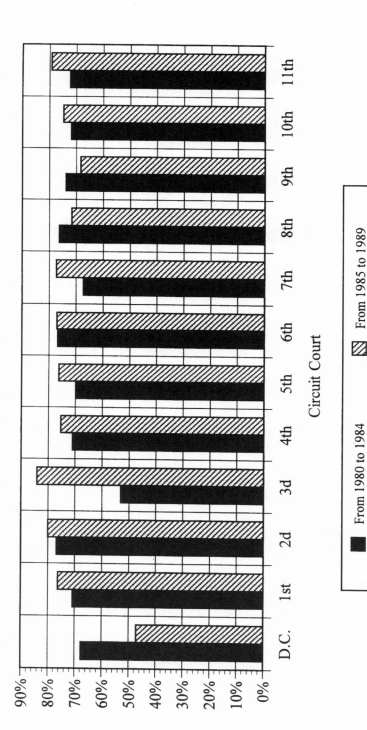

FIGURE 9. Affirmance Rate of Agency Appeals in U.S. Courts of Appeals before and after *Chevron*, 1980–1989

Source: *Annual Report of the Director of the Administrative Office of the United States Courts*, from 1980 to 1989 (Table B-1).

Note: All data are based upon a twelve-month period ending June 30, as compiled by the Administrative Office of the U.S. Courts. "Affirmation Rate of Agency Appeals" refers to the average percentage of affirmances, grants, or enforcements of agency petitions.

appeals (47.22 percent), whereas the Eighth (71.75 percent) and Ninth (68.34 percent) Circuits boasted a much higher average rate. With the primary exception of the findings pertaining to the D.C. Circuit, the results raise a question about whether traditional New Deal politics is still influencing the modern judicial politics of the circuit courts generally, or just in the D.C. Circuit. It also suggests *Chevron* is a legal factor limiting most, but not all, circuit courts.

Overall, Figures 8 and 9 provide descriptive support for the claim that the D.C. Circuit is a unique court because of its commitment to take a hard look at agency decisions. As with the evidence pertaining to the access policy-making cases, they also raise a similar inference that a circuit court's legal response to agency decisions is the product of a complex interaction of a number of diverse ideological and legal considerations that may singularly or together contribute to the court's decision to defer. Some of those factors may include, for example, the political composition of a panel deciding a case, the ideological direction of the agency policy under review, controlling Supreme Court precedent, or the Administrative Procedure Act provisions affecting rule-making and adjudication. Indeed, even the presence of "danger signals" associated with the D.C. Circuit's hard-look doctrine conceivably has an impact on judicial deference.[60] Scholars, in other words, should continue to research this issue in an effort to comprehend more fully the complexity of judicial behavior in the middle tier of courts.

## CONCLUSION

By now it should be fairly clear that much of what the D.C. Circuit does in the federal judiciary is strongly influenced by political considerations. While the mythology of judging casts a long shadow over common perceptions of what courts do in theory, in reality circuit courts routinely face the prospect that their judicial function may be directly influenced by internal or external political forces, a fact that invariably reflects the full range of agenda opportunities and judicial philosophies that come to dominate a court's style of jurisprudence over time. After having its power to adjudicate local criminal appeals diminished by court reform in the 1970s, the court experienced another political change in the 1980s that fundamentally altered its bench and the tenor of its judicial politics in a new era of deregulation. Whereas earlier court reform allowed the D.C. Circuit to redefine its judicial role and become a leader in administrative law through hard-look judicial review, Reagan's appointments to the D.C. Circuit polarized the liberal and conservative blocs on the court and brought into sharp relief the question of litigant access and judicial deference to agencies, two key issues in regulatory law.

The political struggle encompassing the court's work on both issues had a profound effect on judicial collegiality and the ideological direction of legal policy change in America in the 1980s. The D.C. Circuit was a court in ideological flux; the political differences of its judges conspicuously showed in opinions issued in the CAFE cases and exposed the deep level of disagreement that divided the bench on the question of litigant access. The increasing conservatism of the D.C. Circuit progressively restricted on-the-merits judicial review of regulation cases and, as the CAFE litigation illustrates, gave a victory to big business in the battle over energy regulation. The different judicial philosophies of D.C. Circuit liberals and conservatives also increasingly characterized the court's approach to controlling agency discretion in some familiar and not-so-familiar ways. Not only was the court willing to use substantive hard-look review at times and act as a trustee for ghosts of Congresses past, it also proved that its judges could politically manipulate the law under the *Chevron* deference principle and *still* remain a quintessential skeptic of agency action during a time of deregulation. Perhaps a primary lesson to be learned from the 1980s D.C. Circuit is that the judicial politics of the court did not diminish its capacity to assert its judicial will over agencies trying to fulfill their own statutory missions under broad grants of delegated legislative authority. As it did in the 1970s, the D.C. Circuit demonstrated that it would actively control agency discretion in cases presented to the court in the 1980s, notwithstanding *Chevron* or the political turmoil from within.

Even so, the decisions of the D.C. Circuit are not *solely* the product of judicial politics. Empirical analyses of the court's access decisions and its approach to judicial deference to agencies' cases reported in detail elsewhere indicate that judicial behavior is more complex than that and is accordingly affected by a variety of nonideological factors. Social scientists studying courts sometimes fall into the trap of believing that political considerations exclusively drive court outcomes.[61] This may not be true. Political ideology is an important, but not an omnipotent, element in affecting D.C. Circuit policymaking. Quite simply, the law counts, too. Yet, making that admission does not take away from the basic point that circuit courts are political institutions and, as the next chapter outlines, a key source of *final* legal policy change.

# The Judicial Politics of En Banc Review and the Finality of D.C. Circuit Court Decisions

Traditionally in our courts of appeals, the *en banc* process has been utilized to test the correctness of new precedents, as soon as they are issued. What is novel in our circuit right now, perhaps more than in any other circuit, is the increasing resort to *en bancs* to overrule venerable, heretofore respected circuit precedents. The shift is plainly a symptom of the rapidly changing makeup of the court.

—D.C. CIRCUIT JUDGE PATRICIA WALD, IN 1986

As the federal government becomes more active and more intrusive, and more authority is given to agencies and departments, the D.C. Circuit takes on increasing significance as court of last resort for most agency decisions.

—ARTHUR E. BONFIELD, CHAIR OF THE AMERICAN BAR ASSOCIATION SECTION ON ADMINISTRATIVE LAW, IN 1987

By 1987 the D.C. Circuit had gone a long way in establishing itself as the nation's de facto administrative law court. In less than twenty years, the D.C. Circuit was transformed from a liberal court that was sympathetic to the rights of criminals and the politically disadvantaged to a conservative judiciary that routinely challenged agencies and the presumption that bureaucracies are constitutionally empowered to make law. The change provided the impetus for allowing the D.C. Circuit to emerge as a leader of administrative law and solidify its growing prominence as a quintessential skeptic of agency action in the modern post–New Deal state. As a quasi-specialized court, it secured a formidable place as the "federal government's primary administrative law court" by insisting that agencies account for their policy decisions.[1] In the process, the circuit court defined the boundaries of legal regulation and shaped public policy.

Whether the court truly could assume a dominant place in administrative law, however, ultimately depended upon whether its rulings were binding as final, controlling principles of law in the regulatory state. Legal disputes that are heard in a circuit court are conclusively settled when a final judgment is entered and it remains intact after subsequent appeal. Typically cases are randomly assigned to a panel of three judges for adjudication. As a result, only two types of supplemental judicial review procedures threaten the resilience of otherwise authoritative panel decisions: (1) en banc, or full-court review in the same circuit court that renders the underlying panel decision; and (2) an appeal that is heard by the Supreme Court of the United States. In en banc review, a majority of circuit court judges agree to meet as one full court to determine if an initial panel decision is correct.[2] The second means for changing a panel decision (or, in some instances, a final ruling issued from an en banc court) is external to the circuit court: that is, the Supreme Court of the United States takes the case on appeal and then decides if the circuit court's ruling is legally sound. While en banc review and appeal to the Supreme Court are distinct judicial conventions, both still involve the use of discretion that is political. More importantly, since the Supreme Court does not superintend federal lower courts closely, the exercise of political discretion makes circuit en banc and Supreme Court review especially controversial since courts of appeals are courts of last resort in as many as 99 percent of the cases they rule upon.[3]

## THE HIERARCHICAL MODEL RECONSIDERED

The degree to which circuit courts are the final word in formulating legal policy is a topic that has received some attention from public law and legal scholars. A few social scientists, for example, describe the politics of federal appellate review in terms of a hierarchical model. Drawing from postulates of principal-agency law, the theory posits that the Supreme Court of the United States, as a principal, has a dominant but fiduciary relationship to the U.S. Courts of Appeals, the agent. As fiduciaries, the courts enjoy a close affinity that is usually characterized by lower court obedience (as agent) to the doctrinal pronouncements of the Supreme Court (as principal). Pursuant to this model of judicial behavior, circuit courts by and large remain "relatively faithful agents of their principal, the Supreme Court."[4]

Although the hierarchical model may be in part an accurate account of the intercourt relationship, it still overlooks the prominent *political* role that circuit courts play in setting the agenda of the Supreme Court in specific areas of public policy. Akin to what can be referred to as issue percolation, the "framing and staging function" of circuit courts is a key aspect of the intermediate tier function, since cases heard at the lower level become, in essence, policy cues for the High Court. According to D.C. Circuit Judge Wald, this appellate behavior has special relevance in the D.C. Circuit, because frequently reviewing agency cases lets the court act as "the watchdog of agency consistency and fidelity to statutory intent." As a result, the court's "unique role is in identifying and framing the major issues for High Court resolution," which, in her view, is the court's "distinctive contribution to administrative law." If one acknowledges, rather than ignores, the significance of the D.C. Circuit playing "the role of Supreme Court agenda-setter on administrative law issues," it is easy to see that circuit court obedience is more of an illusion than a reality since the lower court greatly assists in formulating any regulatory doctrine that the Supreme Court makes through its oversight.[5] Carried to its logical conclusion, perhaps it is even more correct to assert that the Supreme Court is acting more like the agent and less like the principal in establishing regulatory policy emanating from the D.C. Circuit, which, of course, calls into question some of the implicit assumptions of the hierarchical model.

Since it fails to address the circuit courts' ability to frame key legal issues for the U.S. Supreme Court, the hierarchical model also diminishes the extent to which the circuit court en banc process contributes to the judicial politics of the court and, in the end, its agenda-setting capacity. This is not to say that the model completely dismisses the notion that circuit courts are significant policy-makers in their own right. Indeed, political scientists Donald Songer, Jeffrey Segal, and Charles Cameron report that the agency relationship existing between courts is sometimes marred by the circuit courts' inclination to express their own policy preferences in law and depart from the policy mandates dictated by the principal.[6] Hence, although they infer that circuit courts are relatively docile entities that follow the lead of the Supreme Court, they still realize that circuit courts exert some judicial independence.

This is an important concession, because circuit courts do not have their decisions, en banc or otherwise, upset on appeal a majority of the time. Although it is an infrequent aspect of judicial decision-making, the en banc process is nonetheless a critical element of circuit court independence as well, especially in consideration of the framing and staging function. For instance, if the Supreme Court refuses to hear the last judgment of an en banc court, then the circuit court has made a significant step in developing policy by adjudicating the merits of a specific appeal that deals with a particular area of the law. More importantly, few would dispute that the en banc ruling has more clout (either as a legal precedent or statement of policy), since the court issuing it spoke as one collective entity instead of as a single panel of three judges.

Despite its deficiencies, however, the hierarchical model correctly implies that the nature and scope of appellate review of circuit court decisions is, by definition, highly political. Naturally the judicial politics of a court has an impact on collegiality on the bench and, for this reason, factors into the strategic calculations of judges when they try to garner support for their legal positions in cases. In any profession or business enterprise, the rewards of being a fine colleague are only offset by the risks of being a poor one. The same is true in circuit courts; a judge sitting on a panel, for example, must always persuade at least one other judge to join the legal rationale of choice in order to form a majority. The failure to do so means the loss of an ally and unwittingly thrusts the judge into the isolated role of being an obstructionist or a dissenter, a circumstance that may compromise the respect of peers and invite additional judicial scrutiny by a higher court on appeal.[7]

The importance of maintaining collegial relationships is even more obvious when the full court decides to meet en banc for the purpose of revisiting the legality of a panel outcome. Unless they are reversed by an en banc rehearing, most times the panel outcome sets the legal principle and controls the ideological direction of policy for the indeterminate future. Consequently, sitting en banc has the inherent tendency to intensify internal conflict on the bench in those circumstances in which the judges who decided the scrutinized panel ruling thought that they had reached the right result originally. In addition, since granting en banc review is at bottom an exercise of raw judicial discretion, the decision to meet as one can be politically manipulated by a majority of result-oriented judges in active service. This abuse of the en banc process only exacerbates discord on the court and invariably threatens the rule of law because legal precedent, which was already settled by the panel ruling, might abruptly change. Clearly, the prospect of politically motivated judges misusing the en banc process is suspect in that it supports the claim that circuit courts should not waste precious judicial resources by convening as a full court.

For these reasons, the hierarchical model underestimates the manner in which courts in the middle tier are frontline actors that create legal change and social policy in America. As such it is an incomplete explanation for judicial behavior because it fails to account for the agenda-setting role of circuit courts and the important place that en banc review has in generating political conflict and final decrees of social policy. Furthermore, if applied to the D.C. Circuit, the model undervalues the special contribution that the court makes to administrative law and regulation after 1970. Since it is an extraordinary procedure that is internal to circuit court decisional processes, the judicial politics of en banc review in the D.C. Circuit is discussed next in the context of its origin and application as an appellate procedure. As will be seen shortly, it has always been historically a key element of D.C. Circuit jurisprudence. Accordingly, it is a contentious point of departure for understanding the court and the finality of circuit court review in more contemporary times.

# EN BANC REVIEW IN THE FEDERAL CIRCUIT COURTS

The existence of en banc jurisdiction in the federal circuit courts is the result of a historical accident. Except for in the United States Supreme Court, sitting en banc was never contemplated to be part of Article III jurisprudence, either in theory or in practice. Instead, panel decision-making is more of a traditional part of the federal circuit courts' judicial function. The convention of hearing cases in panels originated with the Judiciary Act of 1789, which established the Supreme Court, thirteen district courts, and three circuit courts. While the district courts were staffed by a single district judge, the circuit courts had no judges of their own. Having both original and appellate jurisdiction, circuit courts were staffed by panels of two Supreme Court justices riding circuit and a judge of the district where the court session was held.[8]

Subsequent to the Judiciary Act, the decisional processes of circuit courts were shaped by key political events and congressional legislation originally aimed at reducing the burgeoning caseload that consumed the courts as the nation grew. The period from 1865 to 1891 was especially tumultuous as the federal judiciary underwent fundamental revision. As the political, social, and economic dynamics of the country intensified, court reform became imperative as the social upheaval brought on by the Civil War and Reconstruction caused the federal courts' dockets to swell. Congress reacted by altering the basic organization of the judiciary, which in turn naturally affected circuit courts. For example, Congress passed the Judiciary Act of 1875, which conferred diversity and federal court jurisdiction to the courts. That reform effort principally failed, though, because the 1875 legislation had the effect of increasing, rather than diminishing, the caseload.[9]

As a result, additional legislation was enacted to rectify the caseload crisis and the overall problem of judicial inefficiency. Congress established the Evarts Act of 1891 and the Judicial Code of 1911, both of which tried to streamline the federal judiciary. The new laws indirectly challenged the presumption of panel decision-making in the circuit courts. Along with inaugurating the principle of discretionary review by writ of certiorari in the U.S. Supreme Court, the Evarts Act created an intermediate tier of new circuit courts of appeals, which heard cases in the nine existing circuits. The original circuit courts, which were not abolished by the act, had their appellate jurisdiction eliminated. This had the effect of making them into federal trial courts (along with the district courts). The new circuit courts of appeals, composed of only three judges per court, assumed the appellate jurisdiction of the "old" circuit courts, which heard cases by three-judge panels.[10] While the Evarts Act did not directly speak to the propriety of en banc review, it helped to lay the foundation for it, especially in light of Congress's next reform effort, the Judicial Code of 1911.

The Judicial Code was the impetus for sharpening the debate about the wisdom of maintaining panel decision-making at the expense of its en banc counterpart. The code produced an ambiguity as to whether courts of appeals could do business with three judges or more. The problem centered on the reconciling of vague provisions of the relevant statutes. Although the Judicial Code ended the old circuit courts, it carried forward the Evarts Act's three-judge panel requirement. This created ambiguity in how the courts should hear cases—by panel or en banc—since Section 117 of the code established three-judge courts while its companion provision, Section 118, created more than three judgeships for the Second, Seventh, and Eighth Circuits. Since some circuit courts had more than three judges, it was unclear whether the circuit courts with extra judgeships should be restricted to hearing cases only by panel or, conversely, whether full-court consideration was also permissible. The situation was confused further because Congress added more courts and judgeships after 1911 in an effort to resolve the caseload crisis that was, at that time, continuing to disrupt judicial operations.[11]

## TEXTILE MILLS AND THE SALUBRIOUS QUALITY OF EN BANC REVIEW

With the enactment of the Evarts Act and Judicial Code, the federal courts had to solve a problem of statutory construction by ascertaining if en banc review was feasible in the light of the tradition favoring panel decision-making. In *Lang's Estate v. Commissioner* (1938), for example, the Ninth Circuit flatly asserted that en banc review was precluded under Section 117 of the Judicial Code because the provision plainly restricted the size of the court to just three judges. For this reason, the court said it was impossible for a court to hear cases by a larger number of judges. The court found support for its position in the Evarts Act (from which Section 117 of the Judicial Code was derived) since Section 2 of the Evarts Act, like Section 117, fixed the number of judges in the circuit courts at three. The Ninth Circuit reasoned, therefore, that the court is "not enlarged to a four-judge or five or more judge court because there are now more circuit judges competent to participate in its sessions." Significantly, too, for reasons of judicial economy the circuit court felt it was better not to permit en banc sittings because they would lead to the "embarrassment of an evenly divided court" in courts with an even number of judges. Furthermore, en banc review would paradoxically create more work for the bench when Congress actually intended to reduce the workload of the judiciary by authorizing more judgeships.[12]

The Third Circuit disagreed with the common-sense appeal of the Ninth

Circuit's position. In *Commissioner v. Textile Mills Securities Corporation* (1940), the lower court found that the Judicial Code gave authority to the circuit courts to sit en banc. After examining the legislative history of Sections 117 and 118, the court stated that Section 118, as revised by Congress in 1912, amended Section 117 by implication. This meant that the size of the circuit courts having more than three judges (i.e., the Second, Seventh, and Eighth Circuits) automatically increased to a number equaling the maximum number of judges authorized by law.

Notably, in its decision the court analyzed an amendment to Section 118 of the Judicial Code because it answered the critical question of whether judges acted in an ex officio capacity in circuit courts with more than three judges. This issue, the court reasoned, was important because the Judicial Code, upon its effective date, abolished the existing circuit courts. If the judges, who now had no court to sit on, were intended by Congress to be ex officio judges (and therefore could serve "by virtue of the office"), then it made sense that they must sit on the three-judge circuit courts of appeals created by Section 117. Consequently, the Third Circuit held that Congress intended that the size of the circuit court should expand to the number of judges allowed by law.

The Third Circuit's construction of the law had at least two main benefits. First, it eliminated the conflict between Sections 117 and 118. Second, it permitted the enlarged circuit to make internal rules of procedure that authorized the court to sit en banc whenever necessary. This discretion, the court implied, is an inherent power of the court, especially in light of the amendatory act's silence on the issue.[13] As it turned out, most of the Third Circuit's rationale was vindicated when the appeal was reviewed in the nation's highest court.

In *Textile Mills Securities Corporation v. Commissioner* (1941), the United States Supreme Court confronted the intercircuit conflict by examining the legality of the Third Circuit's decision to convene en banc in a tax appeal. In writing for the majority of the Court, Justice William O. Douglas resolved the contradiction created in Sections 117 and 118 by giving each provision a flexible interpretation in light of the facts. This construction, he explained, "makes for more effective judicial administration. Conflicts within a circuit will be avoided. Finality of decision in the circuit courts of appeal will be promoted. Those considerations are especially important in view of the fact that in our federal judicial system these courts are the courts of last resort in the run of ordinary cases. Such consideration are, of course, not for us to weigh in case Congress had devised a system where the judges of a court are prohibited from sitting *en banc*. But where, as here, the case on the statute is not foreclosed, they aid in tipping the scales in favor of the more practicable interpretation."[14] The Court therefore concluded that Section 118 only required that the size of a court of appeals could not fall below the number of authorized judgeships for the court. Accordingly, Section 117 did not defeat that purpose of Section 118 and, significantly, en banc review was held to be an acceptable judicial procedure.

In 1948, Congress recognized the importance of *Textile Mills* by codifying its holding and making full-court review an option. Even so, there is little evidence to suggest that circuit courts invoked it any more frequently than when they decided cases in panels. Indeed, the 1948 legislation actually discouraged regular use of en banc review by mandating that courts of appeals employ three-judge panels unless a hearing en banc was ordered by a majority of judges in active service. Even though Congress and the Supreme Court were united in thinking that en banc review was legitimate, the law expressed a preference for maintaining the circuit court tradition of adjudicating cases by panel. En banc sittings, therefore, became merely an exceptional form of judicial review, at least in theory.[15]

## WESTERN PACIFIC, AMERICAN-FOREIGN STEAMSHIP, AND CIRCUIT COURT INTEGRITY

In spite of resolving the immediate concern of whether full-court review was permissible, the 1948 legislation did not prevent further litigation about the scope of en banc review or its legitimacy. One case in particular had enormous implications in determining the efficacy of en banc review as a judicial procedure. In *Western Pacific Railroad Corporation v. Western Pacific Railroad Company* (1953), petitioners (a corporation and its stockholders) sued other corporations on the grounds of unjust enrichment. After the district court denied them relief, they unsuccessfully appealed to the Ninth Circuit. At that point the petitioners requested a rehearing en banc, but that motion was also denied. On appeal at the United States Supreme Court, the petitioners challenged the circuit's refusal to grant an en banc hearing on the grounds that Section 46(c) of the Judicial Code (of the 1948 legislation) gave litigants an unrestricted right to have full-court review upon demand.

While the Court found in the petitioners' favor on different grounds, it still rejected their argument that the judiciary had a duty to grant en banc hearings at will pursuant to the statute. While acknowledging that circuit courts enjoy "a wide latitude of discretion" in deciding when to sit en banc, the Court held that the lower court erred by summarily denying petitioners' request for a rehearing without an explanation. Petitioning for a rehearing, the Court reasoned, allows litigants to participate in the judicial process vicariously through their attorney. Through this holding the Court indirectly said that en banc proceedings serve the important purpose of allowing counsel to play a critical role in helping courts decide if certain cases merit special attention.[16]

The ruling in *Western Pacific* had the impact of giving appellate courts substantial authority to devise internal en banc review procedures, so long as the court's rules clearly state what the requirements are for re-petitioning the court for further review. Although the case could be interpreted as a limitation on circuit court discretion, it really expanded the judges' freedom to create almost idiosyncratic en banc procedures. Most importantly, the ruling did not impose any meaningful restrictions upon *litigants*. In fact, by permitting parties to suggest en banc review at virtually any time during the adversarial proceedings, it encouraged active litigant participation and made counsel a vital aspect of full-court, appellate review. Not surprisingly, circuit courts responded to *Western Pacific* by promulgating a variety of internal written rules and standards governing en banc review which aided in institutionalizing it as a viable but potentially disruptive tool of judicial procedure for both the bench and bar.

*Western Pacific* had other consequences as well. First, there was a sharp increase in en banc cases in the circuit courts after 1953. From 1949 to 1953, fewer than fifteen cases were disposed en banc on average per year. But, from 1954 to 1964, the rate tripled to fifty-one. A second effect concerned the diversification of circuit courts' en banc procedures. After the decision, individual circuit courts developed their own set of en banc rules, which transformed full-court review into a capricious appellate practice.[17]

In light of this latter difficulty, in 1967 Rule 35(a) of the Federal Rules of Appellate Procedure (FRAP) attempted to bring uniformity to circuit court en banc practice by prescribing that a majority of circuit judges in regular active service can hear (or rehear) an appeal en banc. The rule, though, states that full-court consideration is not ordinarily favored and will not be granted unless "consideration by the full court is necessary to secure or maintain uniformity of its decisions," or "the proceeding involves a question of exceptional importance."[18] In emphasizing that en banc review is the exception and not the rule in circuit court decision-making, Rule 35(a) incorporates some of the basic principles established by the Supreme Court in *United States v. American-Foreign Steamship Corporation* (1960), a case discussing whether retired judges may participate in en banc proceedings under Section 46(c).

In *American-Foreign*, the Supreme Court held that a retired circuit judge is ineligible to participate in an en banc proceeding because Section 46(c) requires that only active circuit judges have the right to convene en banc. Throughout the opinion the Court extolled en banc proceedings as promoting three salubrious values of judicial administration and fairness: (1) judicial efficiency, (2) the finality of circuit court decision-making, and (3) the resolution of intracircuit conflicts. The Supreme Court also observed that the main benefit of having en banc courts is that they foster circuit court integrity by letting a majority of judges work toward achieving uniformity in their decision-making. Even so, with these concepts in mind the Court emphasized that en banc courts should not be held unless "extraordinary circumstances exist that call for [an] authoritative consideration and decision by those charged with the administration and development of the law of the circuit." In this fashion the underlying policy of Section 46(c) is expressed because active circuit court judges can "determine the major doctrinal trends of the future."[19]

Like earlier Supreme Court cases addressing the issue, *American-Foreign* reiterated the principal advantages of en banc proceedings. One benefit is that full-court review cultivates the judicial legitimacy of circuit court decisions by restricting the procedure to "extraordinary circumstances." For this reason, en banc sittings are more consistent with the traditional circuit court practice of favoring panel adjudication. Second, en banc review works well to resolve intracircuit conflicts, an aspect of decision-making that naturally encourages stability in law. Third, resolving conflicts advances the finality of decision-making and allows circuit courts to fulfill their institutional responsibility to make consistent circuit precedent that endures over time. Fourth, en banc decisions express a court's collective judgment, which commands litigant respect and the ability of society to order its legal expectations fairly. And fifth, in close cases en banc review ventilates all of the complex issues in a circuit court proceeding before the appeal is heard by the Supreme Court, which of course allows the High Court to perform its own appellate function more competently.[20]

## THE POLITICS OF EN BANC REVIEW IN THE D.C. CIRCUIT

This historical description of en banc review in the federal judiciary indicates that it is idealized as a valued component of circuit court judicial administration. If the practice is not abused, it is an attractive procedure because it tends to make the law more predictable in the intermediate tier. It also has the subtle effect of permitting circuit court judges to debate the merits of complex disputes and formulate policy positions that either remain final law in the circuit or, ultimately, become a legal principle or cue for the Supreme Court to use if there is an appeal.

However, the en banc process is, in practice, very problematic at times. In the 1980s, for instance, the D.C. Circuit exposed the underbelly of full-court review by politically abusing it and creating the impression that achieving the policy preferences of judges was a higher priority than making good law. Even so, the problems generated by the unprincipled behavior of the D.C. Circuit cannot overshadow the critical point that the en banc process is a key proponent for making judicial policy in circuit courts. Nor can it diminish the fact that it substantially augments the D.C. Circuit's ability to make regulatory change in administrative law, increasingly its most important judicial function in the middle tier. Still, on occasion it is a vexatious procedure that is both a boon and bane for circuit court judges.

## THE BEST TRAITS IN THE WORST LIGHT:
## THE VEXATIOUS NATURE OF EN BANC REVIEW

Ironically, the best traits of en banc review also tend to be its primary weaknesses as a method of judicial review. Four criticisms are routinely discussed. Critics argue that it promotes judicial inefficiency, undermines the finality of panel decision-making, threatens court collegiality, and compromises judicial integrity as a result of its political manipulation. En banc review is purportedly inefficient because courts expend too much time and energy convening as a whole. Thus it is pejoratively referred to as the "most time-consuming and inefficient device in the appellate judiciary's repertoire." Also, en banc decision-making allegedly hinders the finality of panel outcomes. The constant risk that a division's ruling will be upset by an en banc court hangs over the panel like the sword of Damocles. It also prevents a full ordering of legal expectations by litigants since it is never really known if the panel decision will withstand further review. Furthermore, the uncertainty of en banc review divides the circuit court since judges deciding cases on panels are resentful of having their work undone by a majority of the court. And, last, en banc review is easily capable of political exploitation by a majority of judges in active service on the circuit court. At any given moment, a disfavored panel decision may be reversed by the actions of an activist court.[21]

A more precise failing is that it is allegedly impractical. Perhaps this is why larger circuits, like the Ninth Circuit, have resorted to using limited, or "mini," en bancs as an alternative to engaging in full-blown en banc review. A mini en banc is a proceeding at which less than the full court meets to decide a case that ordinarily would be decided by the whole court. While mini en banc procedures vary among the circuits, they typically involve less judicial manpower and no oral argument. They also result in fewer opinions. In smaller circuits, like the D.C. Circuit, mini en bancs have been informally instituted through the help of case law. Under *Irons v. Diamond* (1981), for example, the court circulates an opinion to the full membership in an effort to resolve conflicts among the judges and any controlling circuit precedent. If successfully invoked, a so-called *Irons* footnote is inserted into the opinion which states, "the foregoing part of the division's decision, because it resolves an apparent conflict between two prior decisions, has been separately considered and approved by the full court, and thus constitutes the law of the circuit." Despite its timesaving potential and Congress's, by statute, recognition of the legitimacy of mini en bancs in 1978, the D.C. Circuit's mini en banc procedure has seen infrequent use.[22]

Clearly the en banc process is mostly flawed because it simply encourages abuse from counsel desiring to represent their clients vigorously, a norm that raises a variety of different ethical concerns. Even though it is supposed to be rarely invoked, circuit courts frequently are besieged with a steady influx of petitions asking for an en banc reconsideration of an adverse panel decision. Judge Irving Kaufman, a Second Circuit judge and critic of the en banc process, observed in 1985 that his court had to handle more than 750 petitions for rehearing en banc during a five-year period. Scholar Neil McFeely, in his 1987–88 comprehensive study of en banc proceedings, criticized litigants and counsel for abusing the "limited role of rehearing en banc." The difficulty, he claimed, is that "many consider [rehearings en banc] simply another level of appeal and submit suggestions for rehearing *en banc* as a matter of course," a practice that violates court-sanctioned rules of practice. In response to this problem, the local rules of the D.C. Circuit insist that suggestions for rehearings en banc be accompanied by a separate explanatory statement identifying why the case is exceptionally important; or, counsel must attach a list of applicable U.S. Supreme Court or circuit precedent purportedly conflicting with the panel's decision.[23] Clearly, permitting litigants to suggest en banc review easily burdens the circuit courts with a high volume of paperwork. To illustrate, 4,063 petitions for rehearing en banc were filed in 1995 in the circuit courts (excluding the Federal Circuit). Of that number, the Ninth (21.3 percent), Fourth (19.0 percent), Eighth (10.8 percent), Eleventh (9.8 percent), and Third (9.6 percent) Circuits had the highest percentage of rehearing petitions on the docket.[24] These numbers are substantial and, quite clearly, highlight the potential of turning the en banc procedure on its head.

While these criticisms are troubling, perhaps the most worrisome is that en banc review is too political. Judges exploit it by overturning panel outcomes that are incongruous with the prevailing ideological view of a court. The political manipulation of the en banc process, it is claimed, is the direct cause for everything that is supposedly wrong with courts: it intensifies internal conflict on a circuit court, it undermines the rule of law, and it creates uncertainty for litigants, lawyers, and judges.[25] The criticism assumes special relevance in the D.C. Circuit where, notably, en banc review has enjoyed a rich and distinctive history in the circuit.

## THE NUMBERS DON'T LIE

From 1930 to 1970, the D.C. Circuit established itself as a court that was willing, if not eager, to invoke en banc courts as a means to resolve appellate disputes. In 1930, when Congress added two more judges to the (then) extant three-judge Court of Appeals in the District of Columbia, the court shunned the practice of sitting in three-judge panels and immediately began to sit en banc. Doing so was different from the prevailing norm in other circuits at the time. So ingrained was the practice that the court did not even hear cases by division until 1938. Thereafter, even though it increased in size, the court distinguished itself by getting into the relatively routine but time-consuming habit of circulating draft opinions to determine if a case merited full-court treatment. Up until 1952, before filing any opinion D.C. Circuit panel judges sent drafts to the rest of the court for review. During circulation any judge had the right to request a hearing en banc and could vote on the matter either before or after the opinion was rendered. While all circuit courts at that time permitted judges to order an en banc hearing before decision, the D.C. Circuit convention was unique because other circuit court judges could not vote en banc if they were not on the original panel. Only four courts—the Third, Fifth, Ninth, and D.C. Circuits—had a process by which the judges could freely consult with one another regarding cases, thus increasing the chance of en banc review.[26]

The free dissemination of draft opinions contributed to the high frequency of en banc cases heard in the D.C. Circuit. From 1940 to 1964, the D.C. Circuit heard ninety-two en banc cases, exceeding the number of en banc cases disposed of in nearly all of the other circuit courts over the same time period. Although one circuit, the Third Circuit, handled more en banc cases (124), the ninety-two D.C. Circuit cases represented nearly one-fourth of all en banc cases in the circuit courts. Notably, forty-eight of the ninety-two were criminal cases, twenty-two were administrative appeals, and the balance consisted of private civil appeals (13), U.S. civil appeals (7), and original proceedings (2).[27] As a result, before 1970, the court's internal practices and its special jurisdiction developed a tradition of meeting en banc regularly, a behavioral characteristic that was unique among the federal courts.

An analysis of the workload statistics from the Administrative Office of U.S. Courts indicates that after 1970 the D.C. Circuit continued to utilize en banc review relatively often for a court that has boasted twelve or fewer authorized judgeships. Since the reported data reveal the number of appeals commenced along with the number of en banc dispositions in all circuit

TABLE 4. *En Banc Dispositions in U.S. Courts of Appeals, by Decade, 1970–1995*

| | D.C. | 1st | 2d | 3d | 4th | 5th | 6th | 7th | 8th | 9th | 10th | 11th | Total |
|---|---|---|---|---|---|---|---|---|---|---|---|---|---|
| 1970–79 | 67 | 0 | 18 | 88 | 68 | 164 | 7 | 29 | 42 | 46 | 16 | 0 | 545 |
| 1980–89 | 64 | 10 | 11 | 58 | 102 | 150 | 52 | 62 | 101 | 69 | 82 | 61 | 859 |
| 1990–95 | 21 | 18 | 5 | 34 | 67 | 63 | 38 | 82 | 56 | 52 | 51 | 98 | 548 |
| Total | 152 | 28 | 34 | 180 | 237 | 377 | 97 | 173 | 199 | 173 | 143 | 159 | 1952 |

SOURCE: *Annual Report of the Director of the Administrative Office of the U.S. Courts*, from 1970 to 1995.

courts, it is possible to assess the D.C. Circuit's en banc activity comparatively across circuits. Although the D.C. Circuit did not have the highest number of en banc dispositions in the federal circuit courts, it still had a very high percentage given the size of its membership and docket.

Table 4, for example, is a summary of the total number of en banc dispositions in the federal circuit courts from 1970 to 1995. It reveals that the Fifth (377), Fourth (237), and Eighth (199) Circuits had the most en banc adjudications. The D.C. Circuit, on the other hand, ranked seventh (152) in terms of the aggregate. The table also indicates that the total number of en banc dispositions in all courts rose sharply over time. Of the total number of en bancs from 1970 to 1989, 545 were disposed of in the 1970s and 859 were handled in the 1980s. Notably, for the first six years of the 1990s, the level of en banc activity (548) surpassed the total volume of dispositions recorded in the 1970s (545). The trend reflecting more en banc dispositions is not surprising considering that in 1970, for example, the number of total appeals filed in all circuits was 11,552, whereas for 1995 it was 50,072.[28]

The pattern in the circuit courts across time is insightful as well. In the 1970s, for example, the D.C. Circuit, with sixty-seven dispositions, ranked fourth among the courts. The Fifth (164), Third (88), and Fourth (68) Circuits were the top three. In the next decade, D.C. Circuit dispositions (64) stayed about the same as the 1970s level (67), but its overall ranking slipped to sixth, behind the Fifth (150), Fourth (102), Eighth (101), Tenth (82), and Ninth (69) Circuits, respectively. For the first half of the 1990s, however, the D.C. Circuit's en banc disposition rate fell precipitously, with the court ranking tenth (with 21 dispositions) among circuit courts. On balance, therefore, Table 4 implies that the rate of full-court review is generally increasing in all courts while, in the D.C. Circuit, it is diminishing. Nevertheless, it still confirms that comparatively speaking, the D.C. Circuit disposed of a fair number of en banc cases over time, particularly in the 1970s.

While the number of en banc dispositions, standing alone, seems impres-

TABLE 5. *Percentage of En Banc Dispositions in U.S. Courts of Appeals, by Decade, 1970–1995*

|  | D.C. | 1st | 2d | 3d | 4th | 5th | 6th | 7th | 8th | 9th | 10th | 11th | Total Average |
|---|---|---|---|---|---|---|---|---|---|---|---|---|---|
| 1970–79 | .55 | 0 | .11 | .64 | .46 | .52 | .05 | .25 | .46 | .18 | .16 | 0 | .33 |
| 1980–89 | .38 | .09 | .04 | .23 | .38 | .38 | .17 | .28 | .53 | .14 | .44 | .34 | .27 |
| 1990–95 | .21 | .22 | .02 | .17 | .28 | .17 | .14 | .44 | .31 | .11 | .34 | .20 | .20 |
| Total Average | .39 | .12 | .05 | .31 | .22 | .35 | .13 | .33 | .43 | .14 | .33 | .26 | .26 |

SOURCE: *Annual Report of the Director of the Administrative Office of the U.S. Courts*, from 1970 to 1995.

sive, in actuality they comprise only a fraction of the federal judiciary's aggregate caseload. Table 5 underscores this reality by noting that from 1970 to 1995 en banc sittings only constituted, on average, less than .50 percent of the circuit courts' docket. In fact, they represent only .26 percent. Moreover, in contrast to the raw number of en banc dispositions (considered in isolation from the total number of appeals), the rate of en banc activity actually declined over time, where the total average is .33 percent in the 1970s and .27 percent in the 1980s. Relative 1990 to 1995, the rate is only .20 percent. In light of these figures, it is plausible to believe that the aggregate number of case filings in circuit courts *proportionately* will make little difference in terms of predicting how many en banc dispositions the courts will hear in the future. Even though the raw number of appeals commenced is rising exponentially, based on the pattern of activity reflected in Table 5, it seems likely that the percentage of en banc dispositions will continue either to stay the same or decrease.

In any event, Table 5 suggests that the percentage, and not the total number, of en banc cases truly measures the extent to which circuit courts meet collectively in adjudicating appeals. Significantly, as the data highlights, the D.C. Circuit's percentage of en banc dispositions exceeds the total average percent achieved for all courts in the 1970s (.55 percent), 1980s (.38 percent), and 1990s (.21 percent), something that only the Fourth and Eighth Circuits can also boast. Of the few cases heard collectively, the Eighth Circuit (.43 percent), the D.C. Circuit (.39 percent), the Fifth Circuit (.35 percent), and the Seventh (.33 percent) and Tenth Circuits (.33 percent), respectively, rank ahead of the rest of the circuits in average en banc dispositions. Those courts, therefore, are the leaders in terms of the average percentage en banc activity from 1970 to 1995, even though the Fifth, Fourth, and Eighth Circuits actually have the highest number (see Table 5).

TABLE 6. *Annual Number of En Banc Dispositions in U.S. Courts of Appeals, 1970–1995*

| | D.C. | 1st | 2d | 3d | 4th | 5th | 6th | 7th | 8th | 9th | 10th | 11th | Total |
|---|---|---|---|---|---|---|---|---|---|---|---|---|---|
| 1970 | 4 | 0 | 0 | 5 | 15 | 20 | 1 | 2 | 2 | 5 | 3 | 0 | 57 |
| 1971 | 9 | 0 | 3 | 14 | 9 | 11 | 0 | 2 | 3 | 0 | 0 | 0 | 51 |
| 1972 | 6 | 0 | 0 | 0 | 5 | 9 | 0 | 0 | 0 | 0 | 0 | 0 | 20 |
| 1973 | 3 | 0 | 0 | 2 | 1 | 4 | 2 | 3 | 5 | 1 | 2 | 0 | 23 |
| 1974 | 11 | 0 | 2 | 12 | 6 | 29 | 0 | 2 | 3 | 15 | 2 | 0 | 81 |
| 1975 | 10 | 0 | 1 | 16 | 7 | 15 | 0 | 3 | 7 | 7 | 3 | 0 | 69 |
| 1976 | 8 | 0 | 2 | 13 | 5 | 17 | 1 | 5 | 4 | 8 | 0 | 0 | 63 |
| 1977 | 7 | 0 | 6 | 11 | 11 | 16 | 2 | 3 | 2 | 5 | 2 | 0 | 65 |
| 1978 | 5 | 0 | 2 | 5 | 2 | 30 | 1 | 5 | 9 | 4 | 1 | 0 | 64 |
| 1979 | 4 | 0 | 2 | 10 | 8 | 13 | 0 | 4 | 7 | 1 | 3 | 0 | 52 |
| 1980 | 5 | 0 | 4 | 5 | 7 | 24 | 4 | 5 | 6 | 3 | 2 | 0 | 65 |
| 1981 | 5 | 0 | 2 | 14 | 8 | 21 | 0 | 2 | 7 | 5 | 5 | 0 | 69 |
| 1982 | 5 | 0 | 1 | 5 | 8 | 12 | 4 | 7 | 7 | 9 | 2 | 14 | 74 |
| 1983 | 10 | 0 | 1 | 5 | 6 | 11 | 3 | 8 | 5 | 4 | 3 | 10 | 66 |
| 1984 | 3 | 2 | 0 | 3 | 6 | 19 | 9 | 5 | 15 | 14 | 16 | 14 | 106 |
| 1985 | 5 | 0 | 1 | 5 | 18 | 13 | 7 | 3 | 15 | 6 | 4 | 8 | 85 |
| 1986 | 2 | 1 | 1 | 5 | 6 | 18 | 5 | 7 | 9 | 5 | 12 | 19 | 90 |
| 1987 | 4 | 1 | 1 | 8 | 13 | 10 | 7 | 8 | 11 | 7 | 8 | 10 | 88 |
| 1988 | 13 | 1 | 0 | 4 | 19 | 17 | 6 | 7 | 12 | 9 | 13 | 16 | 117 |
| 1989 | 12 | 5 | 0 | 4 | 11 | 5 | 7 | 10 | 14 | 7 | 17 | 7 | 99 |
| 1990 | 1 | 4 | 0 | 2 | 13 | 10 | 4 | 7 | 7 | 6 | 19 | 12 | 85 |
| 1991 | 7 | 5 | 0 | 2 | 9 | 8 | 6 | 15 | 15 | 8 | 10 | 4 | 89 |
| 1992 | 4 | 3 | 2 | 7 | 10 | 16 | 7 | 2 | 9 | 13 | 7 | 14 | 94 |
| 1993 | 2 | 6 | 2 | 5 | 5 | 6 | 10 | 6 | 10 | 10 | 7 | 9 | 78 |
| 1994 | 1 | 0 | 0 | 9 | 10 | 5 | 5 | 48 | 6 | 7 | 4 | 11 | 106 |
| 1995 | 6 | 0 | 1 | 9 | 20 | 18 | 6 | 4 | 9 | 8 | 4 | 11 | 96 |
| Total | 152 | 28 | 34 | 180 | 237 | 377 | 97 | 173 | 199 | 173 | 143 | 159 | 1952 |

SOURCE: *Annual Report of the Director of the Administrative Office of the U.S. Courts*, from 1970 to 1995.

## THE REAGAN APPOINTMENTS AND THE
## JUDICIAL POLITICS OF EN BANC REVIEW

The foregoing tables establish that en banc review was a key element of the judicial business of the circuit court in Washington, D.C., after 1970. Even so, the data cannot accurately assess how the judicial politics of en banc review influences D.C. Circuit policy-making or collegiality. Table 6, an annual breakdown of en banc cases by circuit, tries to fill that void by identifying when en banc conflict peaked or ebbed on a court. Judicial dissension, it would seem, should intensify or diminish during those time periods when partisanship becomes more or less critical in the disposition of those special class of cases meriting full-court review. In this context, the data ought to be especially relevant in the context of the rapid membership changes occurring on the D.C. Circuit in the mid-1980's. Specifically, in 1982 and 1983 three conservative jurists, Robert Bork (1982), Antonin Scalia (1982), and Kenneth Starr (1983), were appointed. Thereafter, five more conservative judges— Laurence Silberman, James Buckley, Stephen Williams, Douglas Ginsburg, and David Sentelle—filled the bench from 1985 to 1987.[29] If political ideology became a part of the court's jurisprudence, it is plausible to think that more en banc cases should be decided in the 1980s as the court's conservative appointees began to coalesce into a majority and challenged the liberal judges for supremacy on the court.

Table 6 provides evidence that the new Reagan appointments affected the en banc process and polarized the bench along ideological grounds. While the level of collective review sharply rose during two years in the 1970s (1974–75), political conflict on the D.C. Circuit peaked early in the 1980s (1983), and then later in the same decade (1988–89). In the 1980s, thirty-five, or 54.69 percent, of the en banc cases for that decade (64) were decided. In contrast, the twenty-two en banc cases disposed of in 1974 and 1975 represent less than a third (31.3 percent) of the total number of those type of cases adjudicated in the 1970s. Since there were no significant changes in the court's membership in the mid-1970s, the data implies that the turnover in judicial personnel in the 1980s had an effect of increasing full-court review as the new judges reevaluated precedent in a time of deregulation.[30]

Notably, the percentages pertaining to the 1980s fall in the general range of time when the new conservative judges formed a majority (by 1987). Significantly, the court was not only torn over the substance of the cases compiled in Table 6; at least in some of the cases, the disharmony also centered on whether the en banc process itself is the proper means for realizing the ideological preferences of the emerging dominant bloc on the court. In referring to the 1985–86 court term, for example, Judge Patricia Wald lamented that D.C. Circuit en banc cases generally decided in the mid-1980s were particularly fractious, remarking, "Traditionally in our courts of appeals, the *en banc* process has been utilized to test the correctness of new precedents, as soon as they are issued. What is novel in our circuit right now, perhaps more than in any other circuit, is the increasing resort to en bancs to overrule venerable, heretofore respected circuit precedents. The shift is plainly a symptom of the rapidly changing makeup of the court."[31]

For Judge Wald, many of the venerable precedents at risk involved adjudication of fundamental issues comprising administrative law and regulatory social policy: the reviewability of agency action, access to the court, disclosure of government information, statutory construction, and an assortment of political concerns that inevitably divide liberal and conservative appointees on the bench. The problem was acute "in high visibility cases, involving controversial social or 'moral' issues, [where the judges'] differences in judicial philosophy, on the proper role of the courts in a democratic society, do emerge front and center." Notably, in describing the tension on the court, Wald expressed the belief that "some judges have definite 'agendas' for changing the law in certain areas, such as restricting access to the federal courts, and that they diligently pursue these agendas at every opportunity."[32] Clearly, then, Judge Wald's comments and the table's findings support the view that "the battle over en banc review that divided D.C. Circuit is one of the most telling developments of the Reagan era."[33]

Content analysis of some of the cases decided in the circuit when court's membership was in a period of flux illustrates how the en banc process became subject to D.C. Circuit judicial politics. The liberal and conservative wings reached a stalemate in 5-5 en banc ties (in party-line voting) on the issue of litigant standing in the CAFE cases (discussed in Chapter 2).[34] In another contentious en banc case, *Bartlett v. Bowen* (1987), the court was politically divided over a per curiam ruling emanating from three panel decisions, *Bartlett v. Bowen* (1987), *Martin v. D.C. Metropolitan Police Department* (1987), and *United States v. Meyer* (1987). Each of these cases—which were handed down in the summer of 1987, a time when the conservatives on the court outnumbered the liberals—accurately represents the type of result that liberals favor and conservatives routinely abhor. For instance, in *Bartlett,* the panel held that the federal courts had jurisdiction to hear a dispute involving the denial of Medicare benefits to a Christian Science practitioner's estate. In *Martin,* the court ruled that a political protester could sue federal police even though they ordinarily enjoy legal immunity from such claims. And, in *Meyer,* three D.C. Circuit judges decreed that criminal charges brought against political protesters must be dismissed due to the vindictive prosecution by prosecutor. Collectively, the cases galvanized the Democratic and Republican appointees on the court. It is unsurprising, therefore, that some scholars criticized the court for acting politically when the conservative coalition convened en banc and voted to reexamine the continued viability of the panel decisions.[35]

From one perspective it is quite unremarkable for the court to reconsider its panel decisions through en banc review. The fact that some of the en banc dispositions were ties, or evenly divided, is not even that unusual. In the 1950s, for instance, the circuit court could not reach a majority outcome in four of the seventeen en banc cases heard.[36] Still, the *Bartlett* en banc deadlock is atypical and especially susceptible to the politicalization criticism, because shortly after the trio of panel rulings were handed down, the full court—which was now in the control of the conservatives—convened en banc and granted a rehearing specifically for the purpose of revisiting the merits of the underlying liberal panel outcomes. Of course, the abrupt reversal exposed the ideological rifts between the circuit judges on substantive issues and strained collegial relationships. But, it also revealed the discordant relations existing between supposedly like-minded conservative Republican appointees about the proper employment and scope of full-court review.

Specifically, Judge Laurence Silberman, who presumably changed his mind on the issue of using an en banc court to reevaluate the panel cases, broke from the Republican ranks and cast the deciding vote to deny rehearing the cases en banc. Silberman's defection had the effect of allowing the liberal results in each panel case to remain intact. Yet, but for Judge Silberman, the rest of the D.C. Circuit divided along party lines either to concur or dissent from the denial of the rehearings: five Democratic appointees supported the denials, whereas five Republican appointees dissented. In addition to splitting evenly on the issue of whether the panel cases were exceptional enough to merit full-court consideration (recall that an en banc rehearing should be allowed only when a case presents "exceptional importance"), the ideological division in *Bartlett* discloses that the court was worried about abusing its collective discretion for political purposes. This sensitivity prompted Judge Edwards, in a concurring opinion denying review, to issue a stern admonishment about the implications of engaging in result-oriented jurisprudence: "Collegiality cannot exist if every dissenting judge feels obliged to lobby his or her colleagues to rehear the case en banc to vindicate that judge's position. Politicking will replace the thoughtful dialogue that should characterize a court where every judge respects the integrity of his or her colleagues. Furthermore, such a process would impugn the integrity of the panel judges, who are both intelligent enough to know the law and conscientious enough to abide by their oath to uphold it."[37]

## THE FINALITY OF D.C. CIRCUIT DECISION-MAKING

As the per curiam, en banc ruling in *Bartlett* implies, politically motivated en banc decision-making registers overt strife on circuit courts, undermines the court's credibility, and makes law a capricious enterprise. As one circuit court scholar, J. Woodford Howard, points out, "public clashes in dissents and en bancs understate internal disharmony. They represent the end rather than the beginning of the conflict-resolution process, the differences judges failed to compose."[38] For this reason and others, as political scientist Christopher Smith correctly maintains, en banc decisions are not only final (and also disharmonious) judicial pronouncements in public policy, but also "indicators of conflict and change within the federal judiciary."[39] The dynamics of full-court review, of course, do not only express themselves on the court or even in the final decision. Often it is a variety of social and political events that invariably draw the court into the public eye and contribute to shaping its agenda priorities. In a co-authored study of D.C. Circuit en banc adjudications, D.C. Circuit Judge Douglas Ginsburg emphasizes the same point when he reports that his court heard over ten cases en banc as a result of the Watergate affair in the mid-1970s.[40] Although the Watergate scandal is an exceptional political event, it nonetheless served as the catalyst for the court to engage in a number of instances of full-court review in which the court, in the end, acted as a final arbiter of a politically significant and contentious public affairs issue.

Yet, meeting collectively to decide cases has a number of pernicious effects, and most of them flow from the inability of the circuit court to agree on a case or the ideological direction of legal policy. When an en banc court fails to agree, the result often has a devastating impact upon the law and intracourt relationships. In some cases, conflict between judges in en banc dispositions results in irreconcilable differences that lead to more disagreements in later panel decisions and, sometimes, open defiance of en banc precedent. *Mallory v. U.S.* (1958)—a celebrated but controversial ruling dealing with the admissibility of confessions in criminal prosecutions—falls into this category since the en banc precedent created in *Mallory* was subsequently ignored by later panels who fundamentally disagreed with the original decision. Or, as indicated earlier, occasionally en banc courts end in ties, which does nothing to reconcile precedent or clarify the law.[41] Acknowledging that en banc courts are at the forefront of legal and public policy change still does not diminish the unfavorable critique that they are too politically disruptive and inefficient, a practical concern that undercuts their original purpose as defined by Justice Douglas in *Textile Mills*.

### TEXTILE MILLS RECONSIDERED

The politics of en banc review in the circuit courts raises the core issue of whether it is possible to achieve the promise of maintaining uniformity and consistency in law through collective judicial decision-making. As we have seen, the critics of the en banc procedure seem correct in asserting that sometimes the judicial politics of the court, as part of the en banc process, diminishes the finality of circuit court rulings and biases the substantive content of public policy. Abusing collective review in the middle tier also lessens the stability and consistency of the common law which, it should be recalled, was a primary justification for legitimizing en banc review in the Supreme Court's *Textile Mills* decision in 1941. Indeed, there the Court observed that en banc decision-making is supposed to be an efficient procedure of judicial administration where inter- and intra-circuit conflicts would be minimized, and not created, and finality of decision, not indecision, would ensue. According to *Textile Mills,* in theory en banc consideration thus permitted circuit courts to fulfill their institutional role as the courts of last resort in the federal judiciary in most cases; and it certainly was not supposed to compromise this role.[42]

## THE GINSBURG-FALK STUDY

One method to test the criticism that en banc review undermines the finality of decision is to determine how often D.C. Circuit en banc rulings are left intact by the United States Supreme Court upon further appellate review. In perhaps the most comprehensive account of the court's en banc decision-making ever compiled, Judge Douglas Ginsburg and his law clerk, Donald Falk, listed all of the cases that were decided en banc in the D.C. Circuit during a ten-year period spanning from 1981 to 1990. A close inspection of the cases reveals two important findings about en banc review and the finality of circuit court decisions. First, the study discloses that there were very few unanimous decisions, which in turn implies plenty of conflict and disharmony among the judges. Of sixty-one cases, only sixteen were unanimously decided, and the rest had at least one dissenting opinion. In fact, six of the forty-seven nonunanimous cases (12.8 percent) were decided by one vote, and two rulings (4.3 percent) were the product of an evenly divided court. These facts show that the majority of en banc cases reflect an inability to agree among the judges. The strife caused by full-court review probably results in more uncertainty about the rule of law and invariably less finality of decision in future appeals.[43]

Yet, a survey of the subsequent case history of each en banc case reveals that the United States Supreme Court does not actually disturb the outcome reached by the D.C. Circuit (sitting en banc) in a majority of cases. Of the sixty-one cases in the Ginsburg-Falk en banc sample, twenty-five decisions were appealed to the Supreme Court. Of those cases, three were reversed, one was vacated, and eighteen were denied certiorari. The remaining three decisions were affirmed. Hence in over eight out of ten cases, the circuit court's en banc decision remained the final decision for those litigants involved. And, it is significant to note that the litigants in the remaining thirty-six en banc cases did not appeal at all from the D.C. Circuit, constructively making the circuit the last word on legal policy in those dispositions, as well.[44]

## THE SECOND BITE OF THE APPLE: HOW THE NATION'S HIGHEST COURT SUPERVISES D.C. CIRCUIT DECISION-MAKING BY GRANTING OR DENYING CERTIORARI

The issue of finality is also significant in considering the degree to which the nation's highest court superintends lower court outcomes. Apart from internally assessing the viability of a panel decision through en banc consideration, a circuit court ruling can be modified or reversed through a second external means of appellate review if a disappointed litigant first opts to file a writ of certiorari with the U.S. Supreme Court. The writ, if granted, gives the petitioner another chance to succeed on the appeal's merits. If certiorari is denied, however, the circuit court's judgment remains intact. The latter point is especially salient because denying external review to the nation's highest federal court has the impact of affirming or rejecting what the lower court did in its decision.[45] As applied to the D.C. Circuit, the implications of limited review are also clear because explicitly or implicitly ratifying the court's work in agency cases makes the D.C. Circuit the court of last resort in its dominant area of jurisprudence after 1970: administrative law.

Fortunately, it is possible to ascertain whether the Supreme Court actively supervises D.C. Circuit decision-making by analyzing judicial workload statistics compiled by the Administrative Office of U.S. Courts. Figure 10, for example, is a portrait of the certiorari grant and denial rates of all circuit court appeals (in all circuit courts) from 1970 to 1997. As a general rule, the table shows that the Supreme Court grants certiorari infrequently. Conversely, the petition is denied quite often. Of the total number of certiorari petitions filed in the Supreme Court from the circuit courts from 1970 to 1997 (116,671), only 4,220 were granted and 81,258 were denied. For the twenty-eight year period, the Supreme Court granted certiorari slightly less than 4 percent of the time (3.6 percent) while denying it at a rate of about 70 percent (69.6 percent). Quite clearly, therefore, the nation's highest court has adopted a posture of limited review in examining the rulings coming from the intermediate tier of federal courts.

However, the data indicates that the Court has taken a more aggressive approach with the circuit court in Washington, D.C., at least insofar as the grant rate suggests. Figure 11, in particular, demonstrates that 333 of the 3,643 certiorari petitions, or 9.1 percent, coming from the D.C. Circuit were granted from 1970 to 1997. Over the same time period, 2,658, or 72.9 percent, were denied. When compared to the results of the preceding table, the data tells us that the Supreme Court chose to monitor D.C. Circuit appeals more closely; the grant rate for D.C. Circuit appeals (9.1 percent) is much higher than for all circuits combined (3.6 percent). At the same time, however, Figures 10 and 11 reveal that the denial rates for the D.C. Circuit (72.9 percent) and the rest of the circuits (69.6 percent) are virtually identical.

Moreover, as the variable pattern of the certiorari grant rate implies, Figure 11 shows that the ideological composition of each court during specific time periods affects the extent to which the High Court affirms or rejects

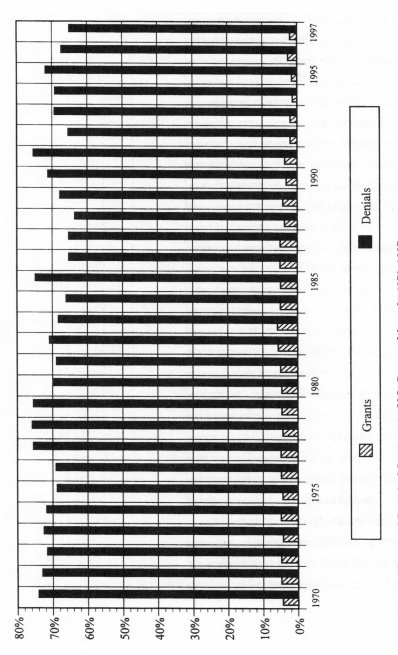

**FIGURE 10.** Rates of Grant and Denial of Certiorari in U.S. Courts of Appeals, 1970–1997

Source: *Annual Report of the Director of the Administrative Office of the United States Courts*, from 1970 to 1997 (Table B-2).

Note: All data, except the years from 1992 to 1997, are based upon a twelve-month period ending June 30; for 1992–1997, the data are based upon the annual period ending September 30. The percentages reported here only reflect the rates of certiorari grants and denials; excluded are the percentages of dismissals and pending cases (as based on the current year). Due to the exclusions, the percentages reported here do not equal 100 percent.

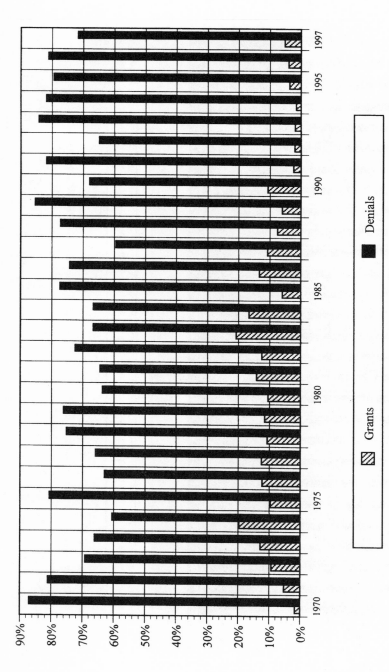

**FIGURE II.** Rates of Grant and Denial of Certiorari in D.C. Circuit Appeals, 1970–1997

Source: *Annual Report of the Director of the Administrative Office of the United States Courts*, from 1970 to 1997 (Table B-2).

Note: All data, except the years from 1992 to 1997, are based upon a twelve-month period ending June 30; for 1992–1997, the data are based upon the annual period ending September 30. The percentages reported here only reflect the rates of certiorari grants and denials; excluded are the percentages of dismissals and pending cases (as based on the current year). Due to the exclusions, the percentages reported here do not equal 100 percent.

lower courts' appeals. Prior to 1986, a more liberal D.C. Circuit clashed more with the moderate to conservative Supreme Court under the leadership of Chief Justice Warren Burger. As the D.C. Circuit's political transformation in membership took hold in the mid-1980s, the more conservative Supreme Court under Chief Justice William Rehnquist tended to condone the policy-making coming from the lower court (which was also presumably more conservative) more frequently. This type of intercourt activity is seen in Figure 11 in two ways. First, from 1970 to 1974, the data suggests an inverse relationship between the grant and denial rates over the five-year period: that is, as the grant rate increases, the denial rate decreases. Second, during the Burger Court years (1970–1985), the grant rate is generally more elevated and the denial rate is less so; whereas, with some exceptions (1986, 1987, and 1990), during the Rehnquist Court years (1986–1997) the grant rate is much lower and the denial rate is considerably higher than what transpired in the Burger Court.

A careful inspection of the specific workload statistics outlines this behavior and confirms that the Burger Court had a more discordant relationship with the D.C. Circuit. From 1970 to 1985, the United States Supreme Court granted 253 of 2,124 certiorari petitions, or 11.9 percent, coming from the lower court. Conversely, the Court denied 1,499, or 70.5 percent. The pattern is different for the Rehnquist Court. After 1985, the Supreme Court granted only 80 of 1,519 certiorari petitions, or 5.2 percent, emanating from the Washington circuit court; but, of those petitions, 1,159, or 76.3 percent, were declined review. Consequently, while the difference in denial rates across both Courts are not quite as disparate, the higher grant rate in the Burger Court years (11.9 percent as compared to 5.2 percent) illustrates that the Court opted to superintend D.C. Circuit rulings more carefully.

When the Supreme Court's certiorari treatment of D.C. Circuit regulatory appeals is considered in Figures 12 and 13, an identical pattern emerges. For example, 142 of 957 certiorari petitions involving regulation cases coming from the D.C. Circuit were granted and 637 were denied. Thus, as Figure 12 indicates, there was a relatively high grant rate of 14.8 percent and a more modest denial rate of 66.5 percent for D.C. Circuit regulatory appeals. Unlike the grant and denial rates of certiorari petitions in all (i.e., nonregulatory) D.C. Circuit cases (see Figure 11), these numbers suggest that the Supreme Court was not as willing to accept D.C. Circuit interpretations of administrative law. The higher grant and lower denial rates are especially conspicuous from 1970 to 1985, during the Burger Court tenure. This makes sense because the courts were not ideologically in sync during that time period. Also, closer supervision by the High Court was probably warranted since the lower court was very aggressive in making agencies accountable through its activist applications of the hard-look doctrine.

In order to explore this possibility further, Figure 13 pinpoints the impact of the presidential appointing process on the grant and denial rates of certiorari petitions for D.C. Circuit administrative appeals. It does so by comparing grant and denial rates across time: that is, in a period when the D.C. Circuit was more liberal in membership (before 1982) against when it was increasingly conservative (after 1982). For purposes of Figure 13, 1982 is used as a reference year because that is when President Reagan began his conservative assault (in terms of the judicial selection process) on the D.C. Circuit. It will be recalled that beginning in 1982, eight conservative judges were added to the D.C. Circuit; and, in both periods, the Supreme Court was moderate to conservative in its political composition. The comparison presupposes that the Supreme Court will challenge D.C. Circuit regulatory appeals more (through higher grant and lower denial rates) in the earlier period. An opposite pattern should develop in the latter period.

Figure 13 generally supports these expectations. It shows that there is a change in the denial and grant rates as the composition of the D.C. Circuit becomes increasingly conservative with the addition of judges appointed by Presidents Reagan and Bush. In the years prior to President Reagan's first three appointments (1970–1981), of a total of 467 regulatory certiorari petitions from the D.C. Circuit, the Supreme Court granted certiorari in ninety-one appeals, or 19.4 percent of the time; conversely, it was denied in 283 cases, or at a rate of 60.5 percent. But, after 1982, a time when a number of Republican-appointed judges began to sit on the bench, of a total of 490 regulatory certiorari petitions from the D.C. Circuit, the Supreme Court granted certiorari in 51 cases (10.4 percent) while denying it in 354, or 72.2 percent of the time.

Clearly, these findings underscore the principle that the judges sitting on the benches of each court make a considerable difference in whether D.C. Circuit administrative law policy-making was accepted by the Supreme Court. When the D.C. Circuit was more liberal and the Supreme Court was more conservative in composition (before 1982), there is a much higher grant rate and a substantially lower denial rate, suggesting more supervision by the Supreme Court. But, as the D.C. Circuit's political transformation in membership coalesced and its bench grew more conservative, it aligned itself more with the conservativism of the Supreme Court after 1982. As a result, the grant rate decreased considerably and the denial rate increased significantly.

This data is persuasive evidence that the United States Supreme Court not only has largely permitted circuit courts to be the courts of last resort for federal litigants, but also that it has let the D.C. Circuit define the scope of

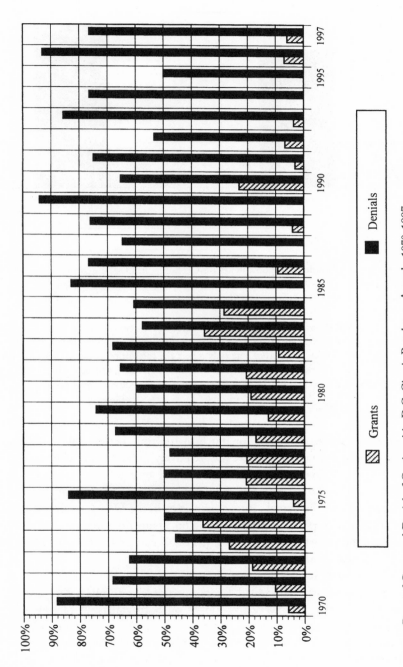

FIGURE 12. Rates of Grant and Denial of Certiorari in D.C. Circuit Regulatory Appeals, 1970–1997

Source: *Annual Report of the Director of the Administrative Office of the United States Courts*, from 1970 to 1997 (Table B-2).

Note: All data, except the years from 1992 to 1997, are based upon a twelve-month period ending June 30; for 1992–1997, the data are based upon the annual period ending September 30. The percentages reported here only reflect the rates of certiorari grants and denials; excluded are the percentages of dismissals and pending cases (as based on the current year). Due to the exclusions, the percentages reported here do not equal 100 percent.

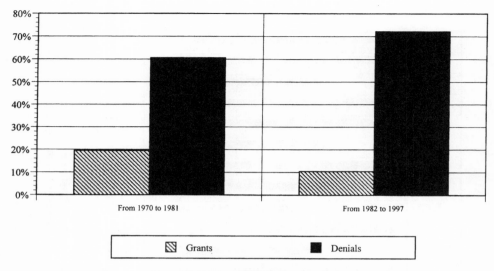

**FIGURE 13.** Impact of Judicial Appointments on Certiorari in D.C. Circuit Regulatory Appeals, 1970–1997

Source: *Annual Report of the Director of the Administrative Office of the United States Courts,* from 1970 to 1997 (Table B-2).

Note: The data, except the years 1992 and 1997, are based upon a twelve-month period ending June 30; for 1992–1997, the data are based upon the annual period ending September 30. The percentages reported here only reflect the rates of certiorari grants and denials; excluded are the percentages of dismissals and pending cases (as based on the current year). Due to the exclusions, the percentages reported here do not equal 100 percent.

legal policy in administrative law for much of the time period after 1970. While the Supreme Court's grant rate was, relatively speaking, elevated with regard to the D.C. Circuit compared to the overall average in all cases (9.1 percent compared to 3.6 percent) and regulatory appeals (14.8 percent compared to 8.5 percent), the denial rate for appeals from the D.C. Circuit in all cases and regulatory appeals (72.9 percent and 66.5 percent, respectively) still indicates that the Court opts to "affirm" (through certiorari denials) D.C. Circuit decisions a significant portion of the time.[46]

Moreover, the data reveals that there is an important distinction between how the Supreme Court treated D.C. Circuit certiorari petitions before and after the appointment of conservative judges on both courts. A plausible theory explaining the dynamic in the grant and denial rates is that an ideological rift formed in the Burger Court years between a D.C. Circuit that was relatively liberal in composition and a Supreme Court that was increasingly conservative in membership. But then, in the Rehnquist Court years and as the D.C. Circuit became more conservative in its membership, the Supreme Court became more tolerant of the policy-making emanating from that circuit court which, in turn, led to a decline in the certiorari grant rate and an increase in denials.

## CONCLUSION

Frank M. Coffin, a veteran judge on the U.S. Court of Appeals for the First Circuit, once remarked that courts sitting en banc "resemble a small legislature more than a court."[47] Judge Coffin's statement truly captures the essence of this exceptional form of appellate review in the federal courts, since the en banc process compels all the judges on circuit courts of appeals to meet at one time for the purpose of not only deciding the merits of an appeal but also making judicial policy. In addition, the procedure is controversial because of its potential for abuse, either by litigants (through their counsel) or judges. Counsel, in pursuit of a client victory, transform it into a malleable rule of process by petitioning the court for a rehearing en banc as a routine matter of course. Judges, in trying to effectuate a specific policy result, turn it into an unexceptional form of judicial review by manipulating it with their political discretion. Under either scenario, en banc review fails to conform to its original purpose, which is to promote efficient judicial administration and a uniform body of law in the federal courts. Moreover, and perhaps more telling, circuit court policy-making becomes a function of the vagaries associated with the judicial politics of the court utilizing en banc review for partisan reasons.

En banc and Supreme Court review relative to the D.C. Circuit has been an integral component of the lower court's judicial policy-making as a court of last resort, particularly in administrative law. After 1970, the D.C. Circuit utilized en banc courts frequently, and with a partisan purpose. This is best illustrated in the 1980s, when the court, in many ways, was a house divided against itself in select, politically controversial cases. As the court's political transformation in membership continued with a bevy of Reagan judicial appointments, the liberal and conservative appointees waged a battle for control of the court through the en banc process. In this way, the en banc process in the D.C. Circuit is truly indicative of political conflict and change.

Furthermore, although en banc dispositions represent only a fraction of the D.C. Circuit's docket, they still are a key part of the decisional processes of the federal courts. Like panel rulings, a majority of en banc decisions are not appealed to the Supreme Court. When appeals emanating from the circuit are subject to further appellate review, the United States Supreme

Court regularly uses its discretion to deny certiorari more and grant it less, especially if both courts are ideologically compatible in membership. As a result, the circuit court plays a critical role in defining the law and the scope of legal policy change for most litigants who sue in D.C. Circuit administrative law appeals.

With respect to regulatory appeals coming from the D.C. Circuit, the Supreme Court in all likelihood will continue its pattern of behavior and grant certiorari review less while denying it more in the indeterminate future. From this perspective, as both courts have turned to the right in recent years, the high denial and low grant rates of certiorari in the 1980s and 1990s make pundit Joseph Goulden's offhand remark that the D.C. Circuit is a "mini" Supreme Court in administrative law seem more accurate as time elapses.[48]

# The D. C. Circuit Court and Its Future

Since they are courts of last resort for most federal litigants, few would deny that the U.S. Courts of Appeals are mechanisms for creating national legal-policy change in America. To be sure, the D.C. Circuit has achieved prominence as an influential policy-maker in the family of federal courts. Although it was once known as a liberal activist court that expanded criminal defendants' rights under Chief Justice David Bazelon in the 1960s, afterward the court underwent a fundamental political transformation that greatly affected its authority to hear certain types of cases and its jurisprudence. As a result, since the 1970s prominent scholars and judges who have intimate knowledge of the court characterize it as a "dominant judicial force" in adjudicating a large volume of complex and important regulatory appeals. For these reasons as well as others, the D.C. Circuit has been alternatively referred to as generally the nation's second most powerful court or, more narrowly, a "mini" Supreme Court of administrative law.[1]

Despite its legal and political significance, the D.C. Circuit still faces the type of institutional constraints plaguing all federal courts. Since 1960 the federal judiciary has been besieged by an avalanche of appeals, something that threatens to impede the courts' commitment to deliver adequate legal services to litigants over the next century. As Table 7 shows, the difficulty is especially acute in the courts of appeals, where caseloads are demonstrably higher than in the district courts. While the sheer number of appeals filed has grown exponentially since 1960 (from 3,899 to 52,319), more troublesome is the rapid increase in the number of pending cases that are clogging the circuit courts' dockets (from 2,220 to 39,899). With only 167 authorized court of appeals judgeships to handle the massive caseload, it is little wonder that Chief Justice Rehnquist of the United States Supreme Court laments that Congress is too slow in not filling the large number of judicial vacancies that exist on the federal bench.[2] For the chief justice, the achievement of federal appellate justice suffers because vacancies "contribute to a backlog of cases, undue delays in civil cases, and stopgap measures to shift judicial personnel where they are most needed." For others, Congress's reluctance to create

TABLE 7. *Appeals Filed, Terminated, and Pending in U.S. Courts of Appeals,*
*1960–1997*

|  | Authorized Judges | Cases Filed | Cases Terminated | Cases Pending |
|---|---|---|---|---|
| 1960 | 68 | 3,899 | 3,713 | 2,220 |
| 1965 | 78 | 6,766 | 5,771 | 4,775 |
| 1970 | 97 | 11,662 | 10,699 | 8,812 |
| 1975 | 97 | 16,658 | 16,000 | 12,128 |
| 1980 | 132 | 23,200 | 20,887 | 20,252 |
| 1985 | 156 | 33,360 | 31,387 | 24,758 |
| 1990 | 156 | 40,898 | 38,520 | 32,396 |
| 1997 | 167 | 52,319 | 51,194 | 39,899 |

SOURCE: *Annual Report of the Director of Administrative Offices of the U.S. Courts,* from
1960 to 1997 (Table B).
NOTE: "Cases Pending" refers to cases pending at end of current fiscal year. The data for
the U.S. Court of Appeals for the Federal Circuit are excluded.

more authorized judgeships simply increases the median disposition time for
each case.[3]

Even though Congress occasionally addresses the issue of court reform
with moderate success, its recent efforts have been minimal and arguably
inconsequential. While circuit courts have created many intramural (i.e., from
within the court) reforms to alleviate the caseload problem, the failure to
achieve meaningful extramural (i.e., from outside the court) reform raises the
issue of whether future circuit courts will be able to dispense the kind of justice
that has been traditionally part of the appellate courts' legacy. This topic has
been described by scholars and judges as the quest to achieve a "visibly rational
appellate process." Visible rationality means that litigants in the federal court
of appeals should have the right to seek relief in a judicial process delineated
by fairness, timeliness, due deliberation, and equal treatment.[4] A variety of
studies of the intermediate tier have debated the question of whether these
traditional ideals are compromised by unmanageable caseloads and limited
judicial resources. More specifically, the research often centers around the
extent to which the caseload crisis causes more delegation of judicial responsibilities to staff, fewer oral arguments, more unpublished opinions, less collegial deliberation about cases, and unclear statements of legal precedent.[5]

A burgeoning caseload and the problems of judicial inefficiency facing the
middle tier prompt an inquiry of whether the D.C. Circuit, a court with a
unique role in the federal court system, can maintain its basic *evolving* purpose as a judicial institution that has a substantial impact on regulatory

policy. In response to this concern, some legal scholars assert that the circuit courts should be restructured to accommodate subject matter court reform which, in turn, helps to mollify partially the difficulties posed by the dramatic upswing in cases. They also say that subject matter courts, which are given exclusive power to hear only certain types of cases, better promote uniformity of law because courts would dispose of only those kinds of appeals that most likely are going to appear on the docket. While the proposals creating national subject matter courts vary, in the case of the D.C. Circuit this generally means that the court adjudicates specific types of administrative law appeals which are generated from agencies like the National Labor Relations Board or the Federal Communications Commission.[6]

Despite the recommendations of the Judicial Conference of the United States which suggest otherwise, envisioning the D.C. Circuit as a national subject matter (as opposed, arguably, to a "specialized") court has some initial appeal since it is functioning as a de facto administrative law court of appeals.[7] Although some hint that the court's dominance in the field may be waning, it still makes sense to explore the issue further with some fresh data and perhaps a different perspective.[8] At a minimum, the findings presented in this book raise a number of questions about whether court reform in the D.C. Circuit is achievable or wise, especially in light of the caseload crisis. Therefore, after surveying the nature of the D.C. Circuit's business and its modern judicial role, the general purposes of appellate courts are outlined in order to address, in broad terms, the feasibility of adopting subject matter reform in the D.C. Circuit in the future.

## THE D.C. CIRCUIT AS A DE FACTO NATIONAL ADMINISTRATIVE LAW COURT

The D.C. Circuit's evolution after 1970 has made it into a de facto administrative law court in terms of its agenda, membership, and the national influence of its regulatory jurisprudence. Ironically, its development as a quasi-specialized venue indirectly results from congressional court reform legislation (the D.C. Crime bill) that was partially designed to increase judicial efficiency and the ability of police to fight street crime in the district. Yet one overlooked feature of the 1970 legislation is an ulterior political purpose: to curb the court's liberal activism in criminal law because conservative critics thought that the circuit was too soft on crime. After the 1968 presidential campaign, where the return to "law and order" was a key Republican strategy and an important feature of electoral success, President Richard Nixon joined with Congress to curtail the liberal policy initiatives of the Bazelon Court by using the bill to take away the circuit's local authority to hear the district's criminal appeals.

The political excision of the court's power to hear local criminal appeals had the unintended effect of initiating the process of substantially restructuring the circuit's docket and jurisprudence. For this reason, the 1970 D.C. Crime bill is the most important enactment influencing the court's present function because it permitted the court to redefine itself as a leader in administrative law. As Congress churned out laws in the 1970s, an era of burgeoning social regulation, the void left in the D.C. Circuit's criminal docket was quickly filled with administrative law cases because Congress increasingly granted the court exclusive jurisdiction to hear a variety of appeals from key executive agencies. The 1970 legislation had a pronounced impact on the D.C. Circuit, because criminal case filings precipitously declined and there was a dramatic surge of regulatory appeals after 1973.

Tables 8 and 9 and Figure 14 suggest that the D.C. Circuit Crime bill had a lasting effect on the court; they reveal three general trends in the data. Table 8 identifies the first pattern by demonstrating that since 1970 nearly 41 percent of the D.C. Circuit's docket has consisted of administrative appeals, a level that far exceeds any other circuit court. Second, as Table 9 indicates, the D.C. Circuit ranks first among the circuits in terms of both the total number and the total percent of administrative appeal filings in all circuits from 1970 to 1997. The third trend, outlined in Figure 14, concerns the rapid increase in agency appeals in the D.C. Circuit since the mid-1970s. Specifically, after 1975 the percentage of regulatory appeals in the circuit remains, for most years, above 40 percent. In fact, the 40 percent level was reached or exceeded in seventeen years of the twenty-three-year period from 1975 to 1997 (or 73.9 percent of the time). Moreover, from 1975 agency appeals consumed 50 percent or more of the court's docket twice (in 1981 and 1988).

Collectively, the tables and figure emphasize that since 1970 the D.C. Circuit has handled more regulatory cases than any other regionally based circuit court.[9] Notably, too, the actual number of agency cases heard by the court may be understated since the Administrative Office of U.S. Courts reports the data reflected in the tables and figure by treating U.S. civil appeals independently from agency cases. Legal scholar Harold Bruff, for example, points out that a significant portion of civil cases that have the United States as a party most likely concern administrative law issues that in fact are a part of the D.C. Circuit's docket.[10] Moreover, while Table 9 suggests that the Ninth Circuit is nearly an equal to the D.C. Circuit in regards to the number and percentage of administrative cases heard in all circuits, it should be acknowledged that the D.C. Circuit is a much smaller court than the Ninth. The number of authorized judges to hear cases makes a difference in evaluat-

**TABLE 8.** *Percentage of Case Filings in U.S. Courts of Appeals, by Subject Matter, 1970–1997*

|      | Private Civil | Criminal | U.S. Civil | Administrative | Other |
|------|---------------|----------|------------|----------------|-------|
| D.C. | 15.44 | 12.99 | 28.07 | 40.66 | 2.84 |
| 1st  | 47.28 | 22.74 | 19.56 | 6.67  | 3.76 |
| 2d   | 49.88 | 21.48 | 15.35 | 8.40  | 4.90 |
| 3d   | 53.01 | 17.23 | 17.12 | 7.67  | 4.96 |
| 4th  | 52.55 | 18.68 | 18.18 | 6.49  | 4.09 |
| 5th  | 54.11 | 21.03 | 14.02 | 6.69  | 4.15 |
| 6th  | 52.78 | 17.99 | 18.40 | 7.84  | 2.99 |
| 7th  | 51.53 | 18.78 | 18.05 | 7.64  | 4.00 |
| 8th  | 51.02 | 19.02 | 20.86 | 5.09  | 4.01 |
| 9th  | 41.59 | 22.84 | 17.81 | 11.44 | 6.33 |
| 10th | 48.03 | 18.93 | 21.57 | 5.46  | 6.01 |
| 11th | 47.61 | 29.33 | 15.69 | 3.43  | 4.51 |

SOURCE: *Annual Report of the Administrative Office of the U.S. Courts,* from 1970 to 1997 (Appendix 1, Table B-1).
NOTE: The data represent the percentage of filed appeals in each circuit court's docket. Except for fiscal years 1992–97, where data is based upon fiscal year ending September 30, the data is based upon a twelve-month period ending June 30. In Table 8, the category "Other" includes appeals reported under bankruptcy and original proceedings appeals. The reported categories under the heading "Cases Commenced" in the statistical tables change in fiscal years 1979–83. As a result, "Prisoner Petitions" (appearing once, in FY 1981), "U.S. Prisoner Petitions" (appearing first in FY 1982 and afterward), and "Private Prisoner Petitions" (appearing first in FY 1982 and afterward) are, according to the Statistics Division of the Administrative Office of the U.S. Courts, civil appeals. In order to maintain consistency between categories across time, "U.S. Civil" in Table 8 includes appeals reported under the "U.S. Civil" (appearing for the last time in FY 1980), "Other U.S. Civil" (appearing first in FY 1981 and afterward), and "U.S. Prisoner Petitions." The "Private Civil" category in Table 8 thus includes appeals reported under "Private Civil" (appearing for the last time in FY 1980), "Other Private Civil" (appearing first in FY 1981 and afterward) and "Private Prisoner Petitions." Since, for fiscal year 1981, no distinction is made in the reports whether appeals under the "Prisoner Petitions" category are U.S. or private in nature, those appeals are arbitrarily placed in the "U.S. Civil" category in Table 8.

ing the extent to which the court's judicial resources are devoted to adjudicating complex regulatory appeals. For instance, with only twelve authorized judgeships, the ratio of the average number of agency appeals to judges is 51:1 in the D.C. Circuit; whereas, with twenty-eight judgeships, the ratio is 20:1 in the Ninth. (The ratio is computed by dividing the number of authorized judgeships into the total number of administrative appeal filings in the U.S. Courts of Appeals.) In raw terms, this means that the D.C. Circuit's

TABLE 9. *Percentage of Administrative Appeal Filings in U.S. Courts of Appeals, 1970–1997*

| | 1970–79 | 1980–89 | 1990–97 | Total Number (All Circuits) | Total Percent (All Circuits) |
|------|---------|---------|---------|-----------------------------|------------------------------|
| D.C. | 19.68 | 24.23 | 20.60 | 17,087 | 21.79 |
| 9th | 18.40 | 18.78 | 24.07 | 16,041 | 20.46 |
| 5th | 13.37 | 9.50 | 9.21 | 8,179 | 10.43 |
| 2d | 10.99 | 7.03 | 8.01 | 6,598 | 8.41 |
| 6th | 8.54 | 8.92 | 7.07 | 6,424 | 8.19 |
| 3d | 7.48 | 7.00 | 4.94 | 5,044 | 6.43 |
| 4th | 4.93 | 5.92 | 7.69 | 4,902 | 6.25 |
| 7th | 6.63 | 6.00 | 4.86 | 4,536 | 5.78 |
| 8th | 3.92 | 3.52 | 2.93 | 2,688 | 3.42 |
| 10th | 3.32 | 3.73 | 3.04 | 2,658 | 3.39 |
| 11th | 0.00 | 3.35 | 5.51 | 2,495 | 3.18 |
| 1st | 2.75 | 1.99 | 2.08 | 1,743 | 2.22 |

SOURCE: *Annual Report of the Administrative Office of the U.S. Courts,* from 1970 to 1997.
NOTE: The data represent the percentage of filed administrative appeals in each circuit court relative to the total number of administrative appeals filed in all circuits.

agency docket is more than twice as large as that of the Ninth Circuit. With fewer judges on the D.C. Circuit bench to decide more cases, it is more relevant, and accurate, to rank the courts by the percentage of regulatory appeals they hear in the context of their respective judicial resources. In regard to the circuit courts' judicial workload, all the tables infer that the D.C. Circuit is the foremost regionally based jurisdiction that handles administrative law cases in America.

Apart from its docket, there are other reasons why the D.C. Circuit has emerged as a de facto administrative law court with considerable power in the past quarter century. Since the District of Columbia is not a state, presidents enjoy the freedom to appoint judges from a national pool of candidates, because a state senator cannot exert political influence to sabotage a judicial selection with a blue slip, or veto. With no home-state senators to be concerned about, presidents appoint judges that tend to be more meritorious and maybe even less politically driven. In sum, the appointment process for selecting D.C. Circuit judges, which is handled differently by presidents because of the court's location, has an obvious repercussion on the court's decision-making and the ease with which it handles thorny issues of administrative law.[11]

Moreover, the professional expertise of prospective D.C. Circuit judges is apparent, with several former and present jurists possessing a wide range of

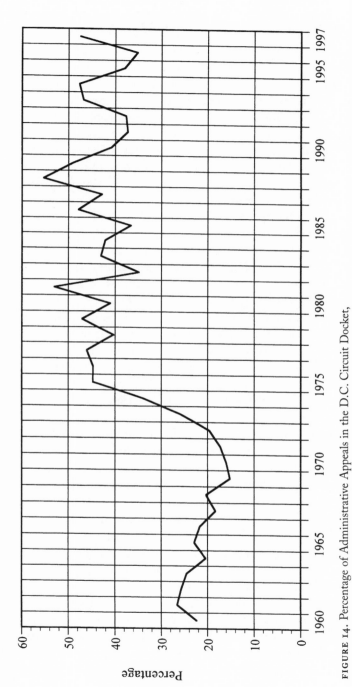

FIGURE 14. Percentage of Administrative Appeals in the D.C. Circuit Docket, 1960–1997

Source: *Annual Report of the Director of the Administrative Office of the United States Courts*, from 1960 to 1997 (Table B-2).

Note: All data, except the years 1992 to 1997, are based upon a twelve-month period ending June 30; for 1992–1997, the data are based upon the annual period ending September 30. Percentages are derived by dividing the number of administrative appeals commenced in the D.C. Circuit annually by the number of total appeals commenced for that year.

knowledge about subjects that invariably touch upon the modern bureaucracy. The D.C. Circuit bench is stocked with talented judges who are intellectual, pedantic, and well equipped to handle the inherent complexity of administrative law appeals. A student of the D.C. Circuit has noted that a sizable number of D.C. Circuit judges "have written, during their tenure as judges, legal articles and academic books that would put most academics to shame." Furthermore, several former and present judges have significant political experience in the federal government and, presumably, regulation. Former D.C. Circuit judge Abner Mikva served in Congress and Robert Bork served as U.S. solicitor general. Among his many accomplishments, Bork wrote *The Antitrust Paradox: A Policy at War with Itself* (1978). Former D.C. Circuit judge and present associate justice of the U.S. Supreme Court, Antonin Scalia acted as general counsel in the Office of Telecommunications. Prior to assuming his spot on the circuit, Judge Douglas Ginsburg worked as a deputy assistant to the attorney for regulatory affairs, Antitrust Division Department, and as an assistant attorney general, Antitrust Division, Department of Justice. Chief Judge Harry Edwards, among other things, is an expert in the field of labor relations; he is the author of fifty articles dealing with labor law, equal employment opportunity, labor arbitration, higher education law, alternative dispute resolution, federalism, and the judicial process. Before his appointment, Judge Laurence Silberman gained experience in the Appellate Division, National Labor Relations Board and for the Department of Labor. While there are many other examples from which to draw, suffice it to say that the legal talent of the D.C. Circuit inherently aids in making the court's membership achieve a high degree of administrative law expertise.[12]

The court's location, when combined with the unique nature of the judicial selection process, creates a dynamic intellectual environment that facilitates excellence in the district's administrative law community. Agencies frequently appearing before the court are at the forefront of this group. Since Congress made the court the exclusive venue to challenge certain agency appeals, the D.C. Circuit has evolved into a natural situs for deciding agency cases. Inherently, therefore, it has become an attractive forum for hearing regulation cases that affect key areas of national policy; it often hears appeals from powerful agencies such as the Federal Energy Regulatory Commission, the Federal Communications Commission, the Environmental Protection Agency, and the Federal Labor Relations Authority.[13] Since the U.S. Supreme Court does not often disturb circuit court rulings, the D.C. Circuit insures, particularly through the hard-look doctrine, that these repeat-player agencies are accountable for their policy decisions. In the process, the D.C. Circuit is a court of last resort in defining the scope of national policy in key areas of energy, telecommunications, and environmental and labor regulation.

Moreover, the degree of judicial control that the court exercises over agencies necessarily determines the way in which lawyers in the district practice administrative law before the circuit. As administrative law scholar Paul Verkuil observes, the relationship between bench and bar is one of the most unusual characteristics of the D.C. Circuit because "[the] bar in the District of Columbia . . . is committed to the administrative law field in a way few other bars are in their respective circuits. It is as close as we come, really, to having something like the English system, where a select group of lawyers appear frequently before the court, deal with recurring problems, get to know each other, and gain real confidence in and respect for each other. As a result . . . counsel take outrageous stands reluctantly, because they know they have to return. . . . This sustained interaction is a very important reason why [the D.C. Circuit] is distinctive, why its opinions are unusually rich and influential."[14] In addition to fostering an intellectual climate that is defined by high competence among the bench and bar, perhaps the dynamic between agencies, lawyers, and D.C. Circuit judges explains why D.C. Circuit judges are often perceived as being exceptional candidates for subsequent appointment to the U.S. Supreme Court. In past years, Warren Burger, Fred Vinson, and Wiley Rutledge were on the circuit court bench before serving on the Supreme Court. In the post-1970 period, former judge Robert Bork and sitting judge Douglas Ginsburg were nominated as associate justices (but were not confirmed by the U.S. Senate). Other appointees have enjoyed more success, with a total of six D.C. Circuit judges going to the Court. As of 1998, this represents one-third of the Supreme Court's present membership (Antonin Scalia, Clarence Thomas, and Ruth Bader Ginsburg). The selection process, it seems, is not only confined to circuit court judges. In one year, for example, eighteen of thirty-three law clerks (54.5 percent) for the U.S. Supreme Court had prior D.C. Circuit clerkships.[15]

For all these reasons, modern D.C. Circuit rulings carry particular weight which, of course, enhances its notoriety as a de facto administrative law court. The circuit's regulatory reputation emerged from the aggressive style of judicial review it began to use routinely in checking the policy initiatives of bureaucracies after 1970. With the hard-look doctrine and through a number of other salient rulings concerning the doctrine of standing, agency inaction, environmental regulation, and judicial deference to agencies (through statutory construction), the D.C. Circuit became famous for deciding the type of cases that find their way into the pages of administrative law textbooks and become hornbook law. Best describing the inherent difficulty of establishing that the D.C. Circuit is a special court, Judge Patricia Wald said, "But how do we prove distinctiveness in roles of circuit courts? I started to count up the cases in the administrative law case books that involve the D.C. Circuit: after a while that got to be a pointless activity, since there were so many. So, I hope that you will take it on faith that something like half the opinions in most of the major casebooks and treatises derive from this court. Its influence is profound for that reason alone."[16] It is not too much of a leap of faith to assert that the D.C. Circuit exerts wide authority over regulation in the modern administrative law state. It presents another question, though, as to whether its reputation makes it a reasonable candidate for court reform.

## THE APPELLATE FUNCTION AND THE PROSPECT OF JUDICIAL REFORM IN THE D.C. CIRCUIT

A basic issue in considering the viability of judicial reform is whether changing the D.C. Circuit would undermine some or all of the reasons why circuit courts were created in the first place. From a historical perspective, the enactments of the 1891 Evarts Act and the 1911 Judicial Code demonstrate that the function of appeals courts is to superintend trial level (district) courts and regulate the flow of appeals to the nation's highest court, the U.S. Supreme Court. A primary original purpose, therefore, is error correction (of trial courts), not law declaration. Even though law declaration, or the act of establishing a uniform body of federal jurisprudence, is by original design a function of the U.S. Supreme Court, this task has become an essential element of the modern middle tier function as well, which only increases the judicial authority of circuit courts in the federal system of courts.[17]

Nonetheless, a second, and perhaps even more basic aim of circuit courts is to preserve the right to appeal for litigants *through* error correction. Guaranteeing litigants the opportunity for appealing adverse judgments is an intrinsic goal, if not a core value, of circuit courts. Broadly conceived, this means that each party filing an appeal has a fair opportunity to have their legal dispute heard on a timely basis. Procedurally, it signifies that appellate courts assemble a trial record upon filing and take all the requisite steps to insure that litigants have their cases completely adjudicated without undue delay. Thus, *traditional* appellate justice—or the type of judicial review that fairly airs legal disputes in an expeditious fashion—exemplifies that courts afford the chance to be heard (through briefs and oral argument); that courts take the time to deliberate an appeal's merits in a collegial manner (through conference and circulation of draft opinions prior to judgment); and, ultimately, that courts legitimize final judgments by explaining applicable legal rationale in written, published opinions. All this presupposes, of course, that judges have the requisite time and judicial resources to accomplish these tasks so that they can actively participate in every phase of an appeal. Still, an appellate court delivering conventional justice goes a long way in promoting judicial integrity because the public believes that legal decisions are equitably made under a stable rule of law.[18]

Until the caseload crisis, circuit courts had been able to remain true to their traditional moorings and dispense justice fairly. But, as Table 7 and other studies on circuit court reform indicate, the growth of the circuit court docket after 1960 has outpaced the circuit courts' institutional ability to handle cases efficiently. A cursory examination of how well circuit courts dispose of cases points up the problem. While the rate of case terminations, for example, has remained fairly proportionate to the number of cases filed, the addition of almost one hundred judges since 1960 has not reduced filings or decreased the number of pending cases in the circuit courts.[19] Nor have they stemmed the rising number of filings per authorized judgeship. In 1960, there were 57.3 filings per judge. By 1997, the rate increased five-fold, to 313.3.[20] It is little wonder, then, that some court watchers argue that a partial solution to the caseload crisis can be found in increasing the capacity of circuit courts to hear cases, either by adding more judges or creating more courts.[21]

For some critics, though, the pressure to dispose of cases quickly means that the vital assumption of achieving equal and expedient appellate justice has all but vanished. Legal scholar Thomas Baker thus quips, "In far too many appeals being decided by the Courts of Appeals today, what remains of the federal appellate tradition and ideal resembles Alice's Cheshire Cat; only the smile is left and it is growing fainter and fainter."[22] Worse still, with the exception of the legislative decisions to divide the Fifth Circuit (1980) and create a Federal Circuit (1982), Congress has not implemented any major extramural reforms to rectify the problem.[23] Consequently, to solve the caseload crisis, circuit courts have been forced to create intramural reforms, which, to some, have already fully run their course.[24]

Even so, the method by which circuit courts have confronted the issue are instructive in terms of comprehending the nature of the burden imposed on courts in dealing with an expanded docket. One popular intramural measure is to employ administrative staff to move appeals through the courts and out of the judicial system. Circuit courts have thus relied upon more law clerks and central staff attorneys to help judges screen and decide cases. Also, courts have created internal operating procedures (behind-the-scenes decisional rules and processes) to push appeals out the courthouse door. Other strategies for reducing the backlog of cases include eliminating oral argument and conferences, issuing summary orders, rendering unpublished opinions, and using "differentiated internal decisional tracks" to fulfill the circuit court's obsession to end cases in a hurry.[25]

While these measures may assist in docket management, the fact that courts are incessantly pressed for time has a number of consequences that adversely affect the delivery of legal services and strengthen the argument that traditional appellate justice is waning. First, with so many cases on the docket, all appeals cannot be treated equally. Second, the caseload crisis undermines collegiality since there is less time for deliberation in chambers. And, third, it increases internal conflict on the bench, thereby making it difficult for the court to reach agreement in cases and promoting an incoherent body of decisional law from the circuit. It is not surprising that some in Congress argue that the federal judiciary is sorely in need of additional funding and staffing in order to meet the demands of a burgeoning caseload.[26]

Another subtle effect that is not discussed much in the literature relates to the type of advocacy practiced by counsel. Trial attorneys operating in a pressure-cooker judicial environment must learn a brand of advocacy that emphasizes brevity in all aspects of appellate litigation. Even the ability to persuade the judge personally on the finer points of a brief is lost since circuit courts do not have the time or inclination to hear oral argument in many cases. The strategy of litigating cases is altered too, since attorneys must frame their arguments for the perspective of the harried judge who has little time or interest to listen to counsel. A necessary by-product of this nontraditional style of appellate representation is the reality that the appellate bar is becoming more specialized in its approach to litigation.[27]

Since the caseload crisis has changed the way courts and counsel litigate, it is worth considering whether it significantly obstructs the goal of receiving appeals court justice. While court delay and bureaucratic justice are not welcomed under *ideal* circumstances, it is clear that those model conditions simply do not exist in modern litigation. Perhaps the best argument in favor of reform, then, is one that takes into account the original purposes of circuit courts with an understanding that the judicial process has evolved into something that is quite different than before. This realization makes solutions to the caseload crisis more palatable since they operate from the practical assumption that the large number of appeals in the circuit courts' dockets is not going to abate soon. As one commentator put it, "Underlying all proposed solutions are two basic strategies: either reduce the flow of cases, or find a way to accommodate the rising tide."[28] In that it is improbable that Americans will litigate less, or that courts will be able to decrease case filings with more intramural measures, the best strategy is accommodation through extramural reform. Perhaps the only feasible answer is to devise, and ultimately enact through congressional legislation, a reform proposal that manages the caseload well in light of the original *and* new purposes (or characteristics) of circuit courts, even if some aspects of the traditional form of appellate justice invariably dissipate.

## THE D.C. CIRCUIT AS A LABORATORY FOR EXPLORING THE NECESSITY FOR JUDICIAL REFORM

Judge S. Jay Plager of the U.S. Court of Appeals for the Federal Circuit once inferred that some of the negative "widely held assumptions" about subject matter courts in the federal judiciary need to be reexamined and perhaps discarded.[29] While Judge Plager's remarks were directed at some of the misconceptions surrounding the U.S. Court of Appeals for the Federal Circuit, they also may apply to the modern D.C. Circuit. Indeed, a few scholars who are informed about the appellate judicial process steadfastly maintain the court is a working model for subject matter reform.[30]

In other words, many of the assumptions supporting the view that the D.C. Circuit should not be converted into a subject matter court are, for some, untenable. At least superficially, their arguments have appeal because enacting subject matter reform does not seem to contravene the contemporary goals or purposes of circuit courts. Arguably, reform does nothing to diminish the likelihood that appellate justice will be delivered in a timely manner and on a fair basis in the future. More significantly, effectuating the change may be consistent with a legal system that is increasingly characterized by statutory construction cases and a professional bar inexorably moving toward specialization. Indeed, the conventional wisdom about circuit courts—that they should remain exclusively generalist in their judicial orientation and must adhere to a regional format—may not be really that persuasive, since legal scholars and judges have noticed that certain circuit courts, like the Second, Third, Fifth, and Ninth Circuits, are already organized along a division of labor that is increasingly subject matter oriented. Several years ago legal scholar Daniel Meador observed, in fact, that

> there is already a de facto division of judicial labor along subject matter lines. The judges on one regional court of appeals have dockets that vary in significant ways from those of judges on other regional courts of appeals. The differences are often extreme; in some categories of cases there are no appeals at all in some circuits, while their number is substantial in others. In fiscal year (FY) 1987, for example, the Second Circuit had forty-one appeals in securities cases brought by the government, while the First, Sixth, Seventh, and Eleventh Circuits had none. The Ninth Circuit had twenty-seven appeals in real property actions against the governments; the First Circuit had none. In marine injury cases, the Fifth Circuit had 180 appeals;

the Sixth, Tenth, and D.C. Circuits had none. In Social Security cases, the Sixth Circuit had 252 appeals, while the D.C. Circuit had only twenty-two. In environmental suits against the government, the Ninth Circuit had thirty-one appeals, while the First, Fourth, and Seventh had only one each. In prisoners' civil rights suits (excluding habeas corpus), the Fifth Circuit had 509 appeals; the D.C. Circuit had twenty three. The Ninth Circuit had 109 appeals under the National Labor Management Relations Act; the D.C. Circuit had one. This substantial variation in the nationwide distribution of appellate business shows that even without a formal allocation of appellate jurisdiction by subject matter we have a de facto division of labor on that basis.[31]

Professor Meador's comments are more prescient in light of the descriptive data presented in Table 10, a synopsis of the frequency of agency litigation in the circuits in the 1990s. The results tabulate the extent to which a particular agency litigates in a specific court of appeals. It reveals that the D.C. Circuit adjudicated the bulk of appeals emanating from six agencies (Federal Energy Regulatory Commission, Federal Communications Commission, Environmental Protection Agency, Federal Labor Relations Authority, Interstate Commerce Commission, and Department of Transportation) that are instrumental in regulating the nation's energy, telecommunications, environmental, labor, commerce, and transportation policy from 1990 to 1997. The table indicates, too, that the Ninth Circuit handles much of the country's immigration (48.01 percent, from the Immigration and Naturalization Service), tax (31.39 percent, from the Internal Revenue Service) and aviation (33.28 percent, from the Federal Aviation Administration) regulatory appellate litigation. Moreover, it shows that the Fourth Circuit (with 40.40 percent of Benefits Review Board cases), the Sixth Circuit (with 17.73 percent of National Labor Relations Board and 19.55 percent of Department of Labor cases), and the Eleventh Circuit (with 39.60 percent of Office of Workers' Compensation Programs cases) each carry their fair share of regulatory matters, albeit in a disparate fashion. Therefore, the data infers that Meador is correct in asserting that some circuit courts are organized on a de facto basis, at least in terms of the percentage of agency regulation; and, not surprisingly, that the D.C. Circuit is a dominant forum for hearing cases from important agencies that define public policy. These findings tend to underscore the growing reality that specialization is rapidly becoming a conspicuous part of the landscape of American legal culture.[32]

Also, it should be borne in mind that giving the D.C. Circuit exclusive subject matter jurisdiction in regulatory appeals does not necessarily mean

TABLE 10. *Percentage of Agencies Litigating in U.S. Courts of Appeals, 1990–1997*

| Agency | D.C. | 1st | 2d | 3d | 4th | 5th | 6th | 7th | 8th | 9th | 10th | 11th |
|--------|------|-----|-----|-----|------|------|------|------|------|------|------|------|
| INS | 1.95 | 2.70 | 8.58 | 2.25 | 3.93 | 15.57 | 1.89 | 5.24 | 1.38 | **48.01** | 3.67 | 6.28 |
| NLRB | 7.33 | 3.76 | 15.42 | 10.12 | 8.96 | 4.35 | **17.73** | 9.66 | 5.86 | 11.84 | 2.21 | 2.75 |
| IRS | 2.28 | 1.50 | 13.84 | 6.18 | 6.10 | 9.28 | 6.43 | 5.32 | 4.08 | **31.39** | 6.02 | 7.02 |
| BRB | 2.03 | .73 | 1.65 | 12.30 | **40.40** | 13.19 | 16.78 | 4.39 | 1.08 | 5.57 | .42 | 1.26 |
| FERC | **83.93** | .80 | 4.01 | .20 | .41 | 3.34 | .23 | .49 | .17 | 2.18 | .86 | 3.39 |
| FCC | **65.54** | .04 | 1.0 | .19 | .18 | 1.74 | 2.99 | 1.66 | 3.36 | 2.61 | 1.07 | .90 |
| EPA | **67.18** | 1.81 | 1.32 | 4.08 | 3.10 | 2.76 | 4.91 | 2.78 | .99 | 7.24 | 2.59 | 1.25 |
| FLRA | **48.56** | 1.69 | 1.51 | 3.27 | 10.48 | 3.06 | 1.26 | .70 | 5.30 | 19.46 | 2.30 | 5.51 |
| ICC | **45.15** | .40 | 6.42 | 4.95 | .81 | 7.70 | 9.72 | 6.83 | 6.08 | 7.70 | .82 | 2.38 |
| TRAN | **43.71** | 2.62 | .91 | 2.78 | 2.24 | 2.89 | 2.24 | 1.26 | 5.57 | 19.64 | 5.71 | 7.33 |
| FAA | 25.41 | 2.77 | 3.59 | 1.18 | 2.74 | 5.41 | 5.46 | 1.60 | 4.86 | **33.28** | 5.64 | 6.96 |
| LABR | 5.38 | 7.99 | 11.23 | 8.84 | 3.49 | 8.41 | **19.55** | 2.88 | 2.85 | 11.40 | 5.54 | 12.45 |
| OWCP | .35 | 0 | .37 | 0 | 4.30 | 1.08 | 1.67 | 6.51 | 4.03 | 26.13 | 15.92 | **39.60** |

SOURCE: Unpublished Table B-3B, *Annual Report of the Director of Administrative Office of the U.S. Courts,* from 1990 to 1997.

NOTE: INS = Immigration & Naturalization Service; NLRB = National Labor Relations Board; IRS = Internal Revenue Service; BRB = Benefits Review Board; FERC = Federal Energy Regulatory Commission; FCC = Federal Communications Commission; EPA = Environmental Protection Agency; FLRA = Federal Labor Relations Authority; ICC = Interstate Commerce Commission; TRAN = Department of Transportation; FAA = Federal Aviation Administration; LABR = Department of Labor; OWCP = Office of Workers' Compensation Programs. The table reports only those agencies that have litigated at least fifteen appeals relative to all circuits in at least one of the years from 1990 to 1997. Excluding original proceedings and bankruptcies, 98.61 percent of agencies are reported. Agencies that are not listed in the table thus have a litigation rate of less than 1 percent and are excluded from the analysis; as a result, the reported percentages do not total 100 percent. For all years except 1990, the fiscal year ending September 30 is used; for 1990, fiscal year June 30 is used.

that the court will be impeded in obtaining the traditional objective of correcting lower court errors and, simultaneously, declare principles of administrative law a nontraditional concern. Since the U.S. Supreme Court exercises little supervision over circuit courts, the rulings from a subject matter court are final judgments for most agency appeal litigants. This is consistent with the judicial role of today's circuit courts: they are final reviewing courts for many parties who seek the right of appeal in the intermediate tier of courts. Likewise, when appropriate, the D.C. Circuit could still act as a buffer to the U.S. Supreme Court, and the Supreme Court still remains the final arbiter of administrative law in the nation, an important rationale behind its original judicial function. Nor will subject matter reform undercut from the prospect that the D.C. Circuit will still be able to guarantee the right to appeal adverse judgments, a core purpose of a federal circuit court.

Finally, as proponents of specialization emphasize, it is plausible to believe that subject matter reform has the institutional advantage of maintaining judicial economy and perhaps mitigating the effect of the caseload crisis. In other words, "Cases of nationwide significance should be subject to review by a single, national forum . . . the benefits from nationwide administrative review would not lie principally in reducing the caseload of the regional circuits, although the collective effect of such a jurisdictional shift would not be insignificant. Instead, the principal benefit would lie in preserving nation-wide uniformity."[33] By creating uniformity in the law, hearing cases on a subject matter basis tends to expedite rulings from expert judges. This is especially significant in administrative law, where numerous trial and agency records are typically part of the trial transcript under appellate review. With increased judicial efficiency, predictability in the law and a better ordering of legal expectations result as well.[34] As it will be discussed shortly, this type of efficiency may be achievable in light of a judicial workload statistics report that states that the D.C. Circuit ranked first or second among the federal courts in terminating administrative agency appeals on the merits in the 1990s. This kind of proof aids proponents of subject matter reform in arguing that the D.C. Circuit may operate well as a subject matter court with limited jurisdiction. It also buttresses the basic claim of those who think that reform is a pragmatic solution, and one that is highly consistent with the modern circuit court function in a judicial world beset by massive caseloads and limited judicial resources.

## THE FEDERAL COURTS STUDY COMMITTEE AND THE LONG-RANGE PLAN FOR FEDERAL COURTS

At a minimum, the foregoing establishes that it is not that difficult to con-ceptualize the D.C. Circuit as a national administrative law court that can be structured in terms of specific subject matter. However, before Congress acts, more research is needed, especially in light of at least two prior Judicial Conference recommendations against reforming the judiciary along subject matter lines or making the D.C. Circuit into a specialized court. By statute, Congress created a fifteen-member committee to study the courts of the United States in the context of analyzing alternate dispute resolution, federal court structure and administration, intra- and intercircuit conflicts in the U.S. Courts of Appeals, and the scope of federal jurisdiction. The committee's charge was also to make recommendations as to how the law might be revised and, more broadly, to develop a long-range plan for the judicial system. While both studies explore, but ultimately reject, the idea of creating a specialized national court of administrative law in the courts of appeals, an examination of the first study's rationale infers that more work needs to be done in order to make a convincing argument that the D.C. Circuit should not be reformed into a national administrative law court.

The first study, an April 1990 *Report of the Federal Courts Study Committee* (FCSC), opposed the new court because "a court with a monopoly over review of agency cases would necessarily be too large to be effectively administered."[35] It suggests that the complexity of administrative law makes it impractical for the court to handle the number of cases that it would be expected to hear. In fact, the report stresses that the influx of agency cases—some from direct review, but most derived from district court appeals and informal adjudications—requires the creation of a "large, multi-divisional court." For the FCSC, "the gains of such centralization" are "not worth [the] costs." In addition, the report asserts that the D.C. Circuit should not become a national court; nor should it be vested with national, in banc authority to review administrative decisions from the remaining circuits. According to the FCSC, in order to meet the administrative burden of deciding more agency cases the D.C. Circuit would have to be "greatly enlarged" and, if it was, there would be "only incremental gains in uniformity."

The formulation of a long-range plan for the federal courts is the basis for the second report, issued in December of 1995. Like its predecessor, it rebuffs the idea that any new specialized or subject matter courts should be put into the regional design of the courts of appeals. Recommendation no. 16 instead reaffirms that the appellate function in the middle tier should remain generalist in scope and regionally based. Moreover, it suggests that only one preexisting court, the U.S. Court of Appeals for the Federal Circuit, ought to be a national, subject matter court. Additional specialized courts beyond the Federal Circuit, the plan states, are not favored since "in most instances the well-known dangers of judicial specialization outweigh any such benefits." What may be more feasible, it states, is to give the Federal Circuit more authority to hear "those limited categories of cases in which centralized review is helpful."[36]

These positions echo many of the familiar bugaboos associated with specialized courts. Opponents of specialized courts typically assert, for example, that they destroy the value of having a generalist judiciary decide appeals; that they are less prestigious and attract a lower caliber of judicial nominees for court service; and that they produce bias, which makes them vulnerable to political temptations and capture by special interests.[37] But, with few exceptions, neither study fully explains the rationale for making their conclusions, an omission that makes any neutral evaluation of their merits extremely difficult. Still, one of the two reports provides some clues as to why the Judicial Conference has been resistant to change. While analogous reports are not available from the Long Range Planning Committee, the FCSC's publication of its working papers and subcommittee reports (working papers, dated July 1, 1990) makes it possible to discern why the FCSC dismissed specialization as a reform possibility. While the papers do not necessarily reflect the FCSC's final conclusions, they are significant because they are an informal legislative history of the FCSC's deliberations. As such, they give a solid point of departure for analyzing whether its recommendations are sound.

In its working papers, the FCSC's Subcommittee on the Federal Courts and Their Relation to the States examined the judicial experience of the D.C. Circuit before concluding that it could not meet the promise of functioning well as a specialized court.[38] Despite observing that the D.C. Circuit "already specializes in administrative law to a large extent" and that it is "a natural candidate for conversion into a specialized tribunal," the subcommittee concluded that any plan to make the D.C. Circuit into a national administrative law court is unmanageable, impractical, and counterproductive. In addition to listing many of the familiar arguments against specialization, the subcommittee gave three broad but interrelated reasons why it could not endorse creating a court of administrative appeals in the circuit courts. While the first one is more generic, the last two are directed specifically at the D.C. Circuit experience.

According to the subcommittee, the "greatest obstacle" to implementing reform is creating a court that would be big enough to adjudicate complex and time-consuming agency appeals. Using workload statistics from fiscal year 1988 in the Administrative Office data as a baseline for analysis, the subcommittee noted that the court must be able to handle at least 3,043 total direct appeals if all agency appeals in the circuits were funneled to the D.C. Circuit. Even though doing so makes the new court's docket roughly equivalent to the average size of a typical circuit court's docket, the subcommittee hypothesized that the specialized court would have to accommodate not only "hard" administrative law cases but also informal adjudications originating from the district courts (and thus are not direct because they do not come from agencies). In sum, by deciding very few easy cases, which typically "pad" the docket of regional courts of appeals, the subcommittee reasoned that this "inflate[s]" the new court's docket beyond the point of workability," especially when combined with the prospect of deciding direct appeals *and* informal adjudications.

This subcommittee finding, however, is suspect in two ways. Before a credible recommendation can be formulated, more information is needed about the number (and type) of agency appeals that the D.C. Circuit would hypothetically decide as a national court. By using only one fiscal year (1988) to draw its conclusion that the court's docket would be unmanageable, the subcommittee fixates on an unrepresentative reference point because it is the *only* year when the D.C. Circuit's percentage of agency appeals was that high after 1960. In fact, as Figure 14 illustrates, the 50 percent mark is breached only one other time, in 1981 (53.05 percent). Using the highest percentage at an isolated point in time is biased and misleading. It is more relevant, and fair, to judge the court's potential workload by inspecting its agency docket over several years. For example, had the subcommittee inspected the five-year period preceding the date when the *Final Report* was issued (1985–89), it would have discovered that the average D.C. Circuit agency appeals docket is 46.21 percent, not 53.05 percent. The most current data is even more informative, since the court's agency docket from 1990 to 1997 averages only 41.57 percent.[39]

Another difficulty with the subcommittee's finding is that it is derived from ambiguous data about the extent to which the direct appeals docket fails to include informal adjudications. While informal adjudications should be part of the analysis, the subcommittee erred by generalizing about how many informal actions comprise the agency docket. Stating in the working papers that "there are no statistics indicating the exact number of such cases" and relying, instead, upon "knowledgeable estimates suggest[ing] that they far outnumber direct appeals from the agency," the subcommittee has not given conclusive proof that the D.C. Circuit cannot handle the number of appeals if it is made into a specialized court. The obscurity of these remarks do not enlighten; rather, they merely whet the appetite for engaging in further review about what type of appeals comprise the regulatory docket. Nor do they provide a cogent justification for jettisoning the idea of constructing a national adminstrative law court in the federal courts.[40]

The subcommittee next evaluated the "D.C. Circuit example" to buttress its second reason why it believed that it is impractical to make the D.C. Circuit into a national regulatory court. In asserting that "the D.C. Circuit's twelve judges handle about 35 percent of the nation's administrative appeals" and that "these cases [make up] 50 percent of the court's docket," the subcommittee reasoned that the "anecdotal evidence suggests that these cases actually occupy a much larger percentage of the court's time." Even if agency cases are substituted for the court's nonadministrative appeals, the subcommittee still believed that the court would have to become as large as the Ninth Circuit to handle its new workload. Furthermore, when informal cases are considered part of the D.C. Circuit's regulatory workload, the subcommittee felt that this will "yield an impossibly large docket"; but, if they are excluded, then this will "impair the court's ability to produce a uniform and consistent body of administrative law."[41]

The subcommittee's claim that the D.C. Circuit cannot efficiently process complex and numerous agency appeals is again dubious because it wrongly uses the data from the Administrative Office to sustain its position. For example, in making the point that the D.C. Circuit cannot handle its own regulatory cases efficiently even before reform, the subcommittee indicated that the court decides fewer cases annually per judge (136) than the rest of the circuits (240, the national average). Not only is there some doubt about how the subcommittee arrived at these figures, but this inference is questionable for other reasons.[42]

While it is true that the D.C. Circuit adjudicated 35 percent of the nation's administrative appeals in one year (FY 1988), it is fallacious to imply that it remained at that level for any length of time before or afterward. As Table 9 reveals, from 1970 to 1997 the D.C. Circuit heard 21.80 percent of the nation's regulatory cases. In addition, the annual "appeals per judge" percentage is not a reliable measurement of how well a U.S. Court of Appeals handles its caseload. Stating that the D.C. Circuit decided fewer cases (allegedly 136 per year, per judge) as compared to the national average (240 per year, per judge) fails to take into account that circuit courts decide cases (typically) in panels of three. What is more pertinent is the "actions per panel," a caseload statistic that shows that the D.C. Circuit is quite adept at handling complex administrative cases. For example, from 1990 to 1997 the D.C. Circuit ranked first or second among the federal courts in terminating administrative agency appeals on the merits, even though the court at times was operating with less than a full complement of authorized judgeships. In fact, the court ranked consistently last (or near last) in terminating *all other types of cases* on its docket over the same time period. Rather than proving that the D.C. Circuit cannot superintend agency cases, the actions per panel, merit termination statistic only strengthens the argument that the D.C. Circuit uses its administrative law expertise well and that the remaining nonadministrative cases should be removed from its docket due to judicial inefficiency. In short, it is proof that the D.C. Circuit operates best as a specialized court.[43]

The subcommittee makes one final point in rejecting the D.C. Circuit as a specialized administrative law forum. Primarily due to the number of agency cases the D.C. Circuit would possibly hear, the subcommittee doubted that uniformity of the law—the principal justification for establishing a specialized court—would occur. In claiming that the court "has struggled throughout the 1970s and 1980s to discharge its administrative review functions," the subcommittee observed that the D.C. Circuit has "experimented with different approaches" in interpreting the vague provisions of the Administrative Procedure Act, but has remained unsuccessful. For the subcommittee, the D.C. Circuit's "semi-specialization" compounds, rather than ameliorates, the problem of "doctrinal distortion" by the U.S. Supreme Court in administrative law, principally due to the "uneasy relationship" (as evidenced by a high grant and high reversal rates of D.C. Circuit appeals) it has with the D.C. Circuit in select cases.[44]

Any discussion of D.C. Circuit administrative law jurisprudence, however, should take into account the creation and evolution of the hard-look doctrine in the D.C. Circuit, a major legal contribution of the lower federal court, something the subcommittee conspicuously underemphasizes. Furthermore, the subcommittee cites three landmark cases to suggest that the intercourt relationship impairs the stability of administrative law.[45] Yet, identifying only three cases is not a very representative sample of the "uneasy relationship" with the High Court. Without more empirical proof, it is also overstatement to assert—as the subcommittee does—that the Supreme Court takes and reverses more cases from the D.C. Circuit. Not only is this finding incorrectly referenced in the subcommittee report, it is also weakened by analogous findings presented elsewhere.[46]

For instance, inspecting the grant and denial rates of appeals coming from the D.C. Circuit provides an indication of the extent to which the Supreme Court ratifies or rejects the circuit's regulatory decision-making. As Chapter 4 showed, from 1970 to 1997, the Supreme Court granted certiorari less than 10 percent of all D.C. Circuit appeals while denying it more than 70 percent of the time. More importantly, even though grant rate for D.C. Circuit regulatory appeals is slightly more elevated over the same time period (14.8 percent), the denial rate also remained high at 66.5 percent. This evidence shows that the Supreme Court is prone to accepting what the lower court does through denial "affirmances." Also, a case could be made that the Supreme Court has been increasingly *receptive* to D.C. Circuit policy-making in regulation in the 1980s and afterward, since each court's membership became more conservative through the presidential appointing process. Indeed, in the 1990s both courts are still moderate to conservative in their political composition. As a result, it might be more accurate to imply that the political relationship between the courts is responsible for *increasing* the level of doctrinal coherence in regulation instead of distorting it.[47]

While it may be easy to dismiss any criticism of the FCSC's work product, the data generated in this book simply invite more scrutiny of the committee's rationale. With more study, it would be possible to assess the issue of subject matter reform on its merits for the purpose of determining if the status quo ought to be maintained. Conducting more research could also explore some of the concerns that were not fully addressed by the 1990 Federal Courts Subcommittee, and perhaps in either the April 1990 *FCSC Report* or the December 1995 *Federal Courts Long Range Plan*. If additional research is undertaken, for example, it would be useful to know:

- how many informal appeals are heard annually in the D.C. Circuit and the rest of the circuit courts over time;

- whether informal appeals come exclusively from the U.S. district courts or elsewhere;

- how many U.S. Civil appeals in the D.C. Circuit and the rest of the circuit courts contain administrative law issues;

- how consolidated appeals are treated as a caseload statistic and whether these "overstate" the number of agency appeals heard by the D.C. Circuit and the rest of the circuit courts;

- to what extent the hard-look doctrine contributes or diminishes doctrinal coherence in administrative law; and,

- the reversal rate of D.C. Circuit administrative appeals in comparison to the rest of the circuits over time.

These issues are only the beginning of the inquiry, and many more questions could be raised in trying to determine if altering the structure of the D.C. Circuit is a feasible or unmanageable reform endeavor. More answers to these and similar questions are necessary to see if there is a cogent and convincing rationale against specialized courts in general, or, for that matter, why the D.C. Circuit specifically could not be one. On the surface, though, there seems to be enough evidence to make a plausible argument that Congress or the judiciary ought to investigate further into whether the D.C. Circuit should be formally recognized as a national court of administrative law in the intermediate tier of courts.

## CONCLUSION

From the foregoing discussion, it is clear that the issue of judicial reform in the D.C. Circuit should be reconsidered by the political branches and courts as the federal judiciary moves into the next century. Even though the Judicial Conference of the United States has recommended against enacting change, there are a number of reasons why Congress, the executive committees representing the courts, and scholars ought to reexamine the issue of subject matter reform before closing the proverbial book on the possibility of effectuating it in a practical and politically workable fashion.[48]

First, the court is already a pilot project for seriously considering whether making any changes to the appellate function or structure is wise. Even though the 1990 Federal Courts Study Committee formally recommended against the creation of an administrative law court, it was receptive toward instituting a new Article III appellate division of the U.S. Tax Court (with exclusive but limited jurisdiction over certain appeals). Moreover, the reasons (which are stated in the formal report in only a general way) why the D.C. Circuit *specifically* should not be a national administrative law court are not that convincing in light of what is disclosed in the working papers of the subcommittee that dismissed the prospect. If anything, the subcommittee's work, which presumably became a part of what the full committee decided to do in the formal report, provides more questions than answers in trying to ascertain if "the D.C. Circuit experience" as a semispecialized bench conclusively mitigates against the creation of a national court. Because of the subcommittee's weak arguments, and particularly since the Federal Courts Study Committee is not completely against the notion of creating some form of subject matter court, and especially because this book's findings offer a new perspective on the D.C. Circuit, the time is ripe to take another look at the issue.

A second justification for reexamining it is to discover (particularly as applied to the D.C. Circuit) if the usual forceful arguments that are made against specialization, like the fear of capture and the destruction of a judiciary that is committed to remaining regional and generalist in scope, are still persuasive in the face of the contemporary problems confronting appeals courts. As law professor Thomas E. Baker points out, even if a court is captured, the likelihood is that the decision-making of the court would not change that much, particularly in the prevailing political climate; and, the adverse consequences flowing from capture or specialization (such as lost percolation of issues) are indeterminate at best. Furthermore, as this book and many others maintain, the D.C. Circuit is already operating more like a national, and not a regional, court. With this in mind, on the surface it seems incongruous to insist that a court remain generalist and regionally based when it is already acting like a national, semispecialized court, especially when the practice of law is increasingly becoming more specialized as well. In light of these facts, simply harboring disdain for specialized courts because specialization is a threat to generalist tradition is not a compelling reason to reject it out of hand in the D.C. Circuit. On the other hand, it is relatively safe to claim that implementing national subject matter or specialized courts has tangible benefits, such as centralizing review of complex administrative law cases and promoting uniformity. At a minimum, the potentiality for reaping the rewards of these advantages should be explored more carefully in light of the evidence (and questions) raised in this book.

It is plausible to think, too, that instilling subject matter reform in the

D.C. Circuit does not necessarily entail the kind of radical restructuring of the appellate system that some fear. Since the court is presently functioning as a de facto regulatory forum, it makes little sense to overhaul the entire system to accommodate one court. But, as the 1989 American Bar Association Standing Committee on Federal Judicial Improvements indicated, an "all-or-nothing solution" is not warranted; that is, it is feasible to give the court more exclusive jurisdiction over certain agency cases as well as increasing the number of judgeships serving on the circuit. These modest changes, which would give the court exclusive and concurrent power over agency appeals, would not require that the court lose its regional (and, in some ways, its generalist) character. In the process, they may allow the D.C. Circuit to handle efficiently the type of subject matter that is already frequently appearing on its docket (as suggested by Table 10). The changes are likely to permit the court to develop new areas of regulatory expertise as Congress, through new legislation, creates additional administrative programs. Although taking this type of preliminary step would probably not do much to alleviate the caseload crisis, it still may aid in making regulatory law more stable and uniform throughout the nation, an explicit goal of circuit courts. That, in and of itself, is something that is worth pursuing, with more study. Yet, more research on this vital question is needed before any recommendation on how to proceed can be seriously entertained.

Of course, making the argument that it is necessary to revisit the question of D.C. Circuit court reform is one thing, and convincing those in power to implement it is quite another. As legal scholar Thomas Baker reminds us, all of the arguments for and against enacting subject matter reform are superfluous in consideration of the bottom-line question of "what good will it do?" That is a very good question, and one that is impossible to answer at the present time. But that is the point. Certainly it is impossible to know what the future holds for the D.C. Circuit and the rest of the federal judiciary if Congress, the courts, and scholars interested in the judicial process are not asking the right questions. Hopefully, the data in this book provides a vehicle for making the correct inquiries about the feasibility of reform in the circuit court in Washington, D.C., and perhaps elsewhere. As legal scholar Baker explains:

> More needs to be understood about the appellate subject matter jurisdiction already in place in the federal system . . . Just as the Ninth Circuit performs as a kind of laboratory for administering the large circuit, the Federal Circuit and the District of Columbia Circuit are both laboratories for subject matter specialization. While the former is more often mentioned in discussions of appellate specialization, the jurisdiction of each is characterized to some degree by special subject matter appeals that are

included along with a more traditional and general mixture of other appeals. More data needs to be collected and evaluated from these two existing courts of appeals. This should be accomplished independent of other proposed experiments with appellate subject matter specialization. It may well be that the perceived drawbacks can be ameliorated and the benefits enhanced by some synergetic combination of subject matter designation with general appellate jurisdiction. There may be a possible solution to some of the problems of the courts of appeals right under our noses.[49]

Only time will tell if the D.C. Circuit, as a special court with a unique legal and political function in the American administrative state, will continue to meet the challenges and burdens imposed by the caseload crisis in the new millennium. Without further study, however, we might never discover if the solution to some of the problems of circuit courts is really as plainly obvious as Professor Baker maintains.

# Notes

PREFACE

1. J. Woodford Howard, Jr., *Courts of Appeals in the Federal Judicial System: A Study of the Second, Fifth, and District of Columbia Circuits* (Princeton, N.J.: Princeton University Press, 1981).

2. Francis J. Flaherty, "Inside the 'Invisible' Courts: As Their Importance Grows, U.S. Circuits Remain 'Unnoticed,'" *National Law Journal*, May 2, 1983 p. 1.

3. Most, but not all, scholarly studies are outdated or have explored D.C. Circuit judicial behavior relative to only a limited range of issues or other courts. See, e.g., Howard, *Courts of Appeals in the Federal Judicial System;* Sue Davis and Donald R. Songer, "The Changing Role of the United States Courts of Appeals: The Flow of Litigation Revisited," *Justice System Journal* 13 (1988–89): 323–40; Charles M. Lamb, "A Microlevel Analysis of Appeals Court Conflict: Warren Burger and His Colleagues on the D.C. Circuit," in *Judicial Conflict and Consensus: Behavioral Studies of American Appellate Courts,* ed. Sheldon Goldman and Charles M. Lamb (Lexington: University Press of Kentucky, 1986): 179–96; R. Shep Melnick, *Regulation and the Courts: The Case of the Clean Air Act* (Washington, D.C.: Brookings Institution, 1983); Sheldon Goldman, "Conflict and Consensus in the United States Courts of Appeals," *Wisconsin Law Review* (1968): 461–82; Louis S. Loeb, "Judicial Blocs and Judicial Values in Civil Liberties Cases Decided by the Supreme Court and the United States Court of Appeals for the District of Columbia Circuit," *American University Law Review* 14 (1964): 146–77.

4. Quoted by Patricia Wald in Patricia M. Wald et al., "The Contribution of the D.C. Circuit to Administrative Law," *Administrative Law Review* 40 (1988): 509.

5. See the online materials relating to the final report of the Commission on Structural Alternatives for the Federal Courts of Appeals, available at http://app.comm.uscourts.gov/ [December 18, 1998]. See also Judicial Conference of the United States, Committee on Long Range Planning, Long Range Plan for the Federal Courts (Washington, D.C.: Judicial Conference of the United States, 1995).

6. See, e.g., Christopher P. Banks, "Judicial Politics in the 'Mini–Supreme Court': Legal-Policy Change in the U.S. Court of Appeals for the District of Columbia Circuit, 1960–1993" (Ph.D. diss., University of Virginia, 1995); Christopher P. Banks, "The Politics of En Banc Review in the 'Mini–Supreme Court,'" *Journal of Law and Politics* 13 (1997): 377–414; Christopher P. Banks, "Ideology and Judicial Deference in the D.C. Circuit," *Southeastern Political Review* 26 (1998): 861–88.

# CHAPTER 1. AN ANOMALOUS COURT OF "GREAT AUTHORITY"

1. J. Woodford Howard, Jr., *Courts of Appeals in the Federal Judicial System: A Study of the Second, Fifth, and District of Columbia Circuits* (Princeton, N.J.: Princeton University Press, 1981), xvii n.3; Felix Frankfurter and James M. Landis, *The Business of the Supreme Court: A Study in the Federal Judicial System* (New York: Macmillan Co., 1928), 258. Other relevant studies of circuit courts include Thomas E. Baker, *Rationing Justice on Appeal: The Problems of the U.S. Courts of Appeals* (St. Paul, Minn.: West Publishing Co., 1994); Daniel J. Meador and Jordana Simone Bernstein, *Appellate Courts in the United States* (St. Paul, Minn.: West Publishing Co., 1994); Sheldon Goldman and Charles M. Lamb, eds., *Judicial Conflict and Consensus: Behavioral Studies of American Appellate Courts* (Lexington: University of Kentucky Press, 1986); Philip L. DuBois, ed., *The Analysis of Judicial Reform* (Lexington, Mass.: Lexington Books, 1982); Deborah J. Barrow and Thomas G. Walker, *A Court Divided: The Fifth Circuit Court of Appeals and the Politics of Judicial Reform* (New Haven, Conn.: Yale University Press, 1988).

2. Joseph C. Goulden, *The Benchwarmers: The Private World of the Powerful Federal Judges* (New York: Weybright and Talley, 1974); 227. See also Jeffrey B. Morris, "The Second Most Important Court: The United States Court of Appeals for the District of Columbia Circuit" (Ph.D. diss., University of Columbia, 1972).

3. See Patricia M. Wald et al., "The Contribution of the D.C. Circuit to Administrative Law," *Administrative Law Review* 40 (1988): 509; Meador and Bernstein, *Appellate Courts in the United States,* 21–22. See also Judicial Conference of the United States, Committee on Long Range Planning, *Long Range Plan for the Federal Courts* (Washington, D.C.: Judicial Conference of the United States, 1995), 43–44.

4. As quoted by Paul Verkuil in Wald et al., "The Contribution of the D.C. Circuit," 532.

5. Judge Mikva's remark was made during a televised interview with Fred Graham on October 22, 1993. Part of the interview is reprinted in "Mikva: 'No Political Views, Just Opinions,'" *Legal Times,* October 25, 1993, p. 14.

6. Karen O'Connor and Larry J. Sabato, *American Government: Continuity and Change,* 2d ed. (Boston: Allyn and Bacon, 1997), 335.

7. As quoted by Paul Verkuil in Wald et al., "The Contribution of the D.C. Circuit," 532.

8. Jonathan B. Groner, "Just What Is It about the D.C. Circuit?" *Legal Times,* June 21, 1993, p. 1; Abner J. Mikva, "Sturm Und Drang at the D.C. Circuit," *George Washington Law Review* 57 (1989): 1063–64.

9. Garry Sturgess, "The Court Also Aches: D.C. Circuit Rocked Again by Nomination Politics," *Legal Times,* October 14, 1991, p. 1.

10. Groner, "Just What Is It?," 1.

11. As of 1998, Wiley Rutledge, Fred Vinson, Warren Burger, Antonin Scalia, Clarence Thomas, and Ruth Bader Ginsburg have served or are presently serving on the Court. See Groner, "Just What Is It?" 1; Morris, "The Second Most Important Court," 190–91, Chart IV-3, 972; Patricia M. Wald, "Life on the District of Columbia Circuit: Literally and Figuratively Halfway between the Capitol and the White House," *Minnesota Law Review* 72 (1987): 1–22. Notably, Abner Mikva resigned from the D.C. Circuit bench to become President Bill Clinton's counsel and Kenneth Starr left the court

to become special prosecutor investigating the Whitewater scandal involving President Clinton. See Groner, "Just What Is It?" 1; Marcia Coyle, "The Liberal D.C. Circuit Judge Is Called an Affable and Able Political Operator," *National Law Journal*, August 22, 1994, sec. A, p. 1; Eva Rodriguez, "Political Veteran Joins a Troubled White House: New Counsel Abner Mikva Bills Himself as Pragmatist," *The Recorder*, August 30, 1994, p. 5; Harvey Berkman, "Charges of Partisanship Fly over Appointment of Starr," *National Law Journal*, September 2, 1994, sec. A, p. 13.

12. Mikva, "Sturm Und Drang at the D.C. Circuit," 1063; Neil A. Lewis, "Presiding as Ideas Clash in Capital Appeals Court," *New York Times*, February 1, 1991, sec. B, p. 4. As to how the judicial politics of the D.C. Circuit affects the court's regulatory decision-making, see Richard J. Pierce, Jr., "Two Problems in Administrative Law: Political Polarity on the District of Columbia Circuit and Judicial Deterrence of Agency Rulemaking," *Duke Law Journal* (1988): 300–28.

13. United States Court of Appeals for the District of Columbia Circuit, *History of the United States Court of Appeals for the District of Columbia Circuit in the Country's Bicentennial Year* (Washington, D.C.: U.S. Court of Appeals for the District of Columbia Circuit, 1977), 7–8, citing *Bush v. District of Columbia*, 1 App. D.C. 1 (1893).

14. Mikva, "Sturm Und Drang at the D.C. Circuit," 1063–64.

15. James F. Simon, *In His Own Image: The Supreme Court in Richard Nixon's America* (New York: David McKay Co., 1972), 79–80; Wald, "Life on the District of Columbia Circuit," 7–8; Pierce, "Two Problems in Administrative Law," 300–7.

16. In 1991, for example, several D.C. Circuit judges caused a stir when they refused to record the race of the persons they interviewed for law clerk positions, a practice followed by most federal judges in accordance with an affirmative action policy set by the Judicial Conference of the United States. Garry Sturgess, "Five Judges Won't Report on Clerks' Race, Gender: Affirmative Action Rebellion in D.C. Circuit," *Legal Times*, August 5, 1991, p. 1.

17. A statistical survey of published opinions decided in 1987 indicates that the court often split along ideological lines in 17 percent of the cases. Kenneth Karpay, "Bork or No Bork, GOP Bloc a Force on the D.C. Circuit," *Legal Times*, January 18, 1988, p. 10. In 1993 Judge Mikva also said that while the court unanimously agrees in 80 percent of cases that do not involve "sharp issues," "polarity" and "chemistry" on the court emerge in "another 10, 15, 20 percent which are the diverse issues within our society where the Supreme Court has not yet spoken clearly or where there are just honest disagreements about how [the D.C. Circuit] should approach the problem." See "Mikva: 'No Political Views, Just Opinions,'" 14.

18. Lewis, "Presiding as Ideas Clash in Capital Appeals Court," 4. Although the *New York Times* first printed the story, the incident was broadcast earlier over National Public Radio. The *Legal Times* speculated that the case provoking the argument was *Hammon v. Barry*, 813 F. 2d 412 (D.C. Cir. 1987), a case that struck down the hiring provisions of the D.C. Fire Department affirmative action plan as a violation of Title VII of the Civil Rights Act of 1964. Ann Pelham, "Silberman, Dogged by Story, Provides Details of Outburst," *Legal Times*, March 11, 1991, p. 7. In the end, in an opinion determining if a petition for rehearing the *Hammon* panel decision should be granted, the circuit declined to grant the rehearing and upheld the attack on the affirmative action plan. See *Hammon v. Barry*, 826 F. 2d 73 (D.C. Cir. 1987).

19. David M. O'Brien is quoted in Groner, "Just What Is It?" 1. See also Thomas M. Susman's comments in Wald et al., "The Contribution of the D.C. Circuit," 507.

20. Theodore Voorhees, "The District of Columbia Courts: A Judicial Anomaly," *Catholic University Law Review* 29 (1980): 917–37.

21. United States Court of Appeals for the District of Columbia Circuit, *History of the United States Court of Appeals*, 2. See also Edwin C. Surrency, *History of the Federal Courts* (New York: Oceana Publications, 1987), 333–35; Voorhees, "The District of Columbia Courts," 919–21; Morris, "The Second Most Important Court," 89–90.

22. Surrency, *History of the Federal Courts*, 335–36; Voorhees, "The District of Columbia Courts," 921–24; Morris, "The Second Most Important Court," 91.

23. Surrency, *History of the Federal Courts*, 336–37. See also United States Court of Appeals for the District of Columbia Circuit, *History of the United States Court of Appeals*, 3.

24. Surrency, *History of the Federal Courts*, 337.

25. This only implies that the Supreme Court has the final say in matters of policy or law, but not necessarily in terms of the number of case dispositions. Robert A. Carp and Ronald Stidham, *The Federal Courts*, 2d ed. (Washington, D.C.: CQ Press, 1991), 16. See also Voorhees, "The District of Columbia Courts," 925. For a discussion of the legislation responsible for creating the modern middle tier of courts, see generally Thomas E. Baker, *A Primer on the Jurisdiction of the U.S. Courts of Appeals* (Washington, D.C.: Federal Judicial Center, 1989); Russell R. Wheeler and Cynthia Harrison, *Creating the Federal Judicial System*, 2d ed. (Washington, D.C.: Federal Judicial Center, 1994).

26. Goulden, *The Benchwarmers*, 230–31.

27. Morris's remark is found in Garry Sturgess, "Fighting for Second," *Legal Times*, July 8, 1991, p. 7.

28. The pertinent cases include *Fall v. United States*, 49 F. 2d 506 (D.C. Cir. 1931), *Means v. United States*, 65 F. 2d 206 (D.C. Cir. 1933), *Whitaker v. United States*, 72 F. 2d 739 (D.C. Cir. 1934), *Viereck v. United States*, 130 F. 2d 945 (D.C. Cir. 1942), and *Viereck v. United States*, 139 F. 2d 847 (D.C. Cir. 1944). See *History of the United States Court of Appeals*, 20–29.

29. Morris, "The Second Most Important Court," 162. Judge Bazelon, appointed in 1949 by President Truman, served as chief judge for sixteen years (1962–78) and thereafter took senior status in 1979. He died in 1993. For an insightful summary of the man and jurist, see Patricia M. Wald, "David Bazelon: Warrior of the Bench," *Legal Times*, March 1, 1993, p. 25. See also Goulden, *The Benchwarmers*, 231.

30. Goulden, *The Benchwarmers*, 227–28. For analysis of some of the internal disagreements on the D.C. Circuit bench over politically contentious criminal law issues, see Charles M. Lamb, "A Microlevel Analysis of Appeals Court Conflict: Warren Burger and His Colleagues on the D.C. Circuit," in Goldman and Lamb, eds., *Judicial Conflict and Consensus*, 179–96; Charles M. Lamb, "Warren Burger and the Insanity Defense: Judicial Philosophy and Voting Behavior on a U.S. Court of Appeals," *The American University Law Review* 24 (1974): 91–128.

31. Howard, *Courts of Appeals in the Federal Judicial System*, 3–56.

32. Fifty-eight and three tenths percent represents the total number of criminal cases disposed of after a hearing in all the circuits (7,567) divided by the total number of criminal cases commenced in all the circuits (12,972) from 1960 to 1969. The remaining

41.7 percent are criminal appeals not disposed of after a hearing (i.e., pending cases and those cases not terminated on the merits) in relation to the total number of criminal cases commenced in all the circuits.

33. William J. Brennan, Jr., Introduction to "Chief Judge Bazelon's Contributions to the Law," *Georgetown Law Journal* 63 (1974–75): 3. See also Morris, "The Second Most Important Court," 281; Note, "The United States Court of Appeals for the District of Columbia Circuit: 1965–66 Term," *Georgetown Law Journal* 55 (1966–67): 1–68.

34. Abner J. Mikva, "The Real Judge Bazelon," *Georgetown Law Journal* 82 (1993): 2; Morris, "The Second Most Important Court," 298–99, 462–65. For a sample of Judge Bazelon's writings, see David L. Bazelon, "Implementing the Right to Treatment," *University of Chicago Law Review* 36 (1969): 742–54; David L. Bazelon, "The Morality of the Criminal Law," *Southern California Law Review* 49 (1976): 385–405; David L. Bazelon, "The Dilemma of Criminal Responsibility," *Kentucky Law Journal* 72 (1983–84): 263–77.

35. *Durham v. United States*, 214 F. 2d 862 (D.C. Cir. 1954). A sample of the academic treatment of the issues raised by *Durham* include Abe Krash, "The Durham Rule and Judicial Administration of the Insanity Defense in the District of Columbia," *Yale Law Journal* 70 (1960–61): 905–52; Charles W. Halleck, "The Insanity Defense in the District of Columbia: A Legal Lorelei," *Georgetown Law Journal* 49 (1960): 294–320.

36. *M'Naghten's Case*, 8 Eng. Rep. 718 (H.L. 1843).

37. *Durham v. United States*, 214 F. 2d 862 (D.C. Cir. 1954), 873. See also Bazelon, "The Morality of the Criminal Law," 390.

38. *McDonald v. United States*, 312 F. 2d 847 (D.C. Cir. 1962). See also *Stewart v. United States*, 214 F. 2d 879 (D.C. Cir. 1954), raising the issue of who should decide the insanity question. For a thorough recitation of the treatment of the *Durham* case in the D.C. Circuit and elsewhere, see Morris, "The Second Most Important Court," 388–444.

39. *United States v. Brawner*, 471 F. 2d 969 (D.C. Cir. 1972) (en banc). See also Heathcote W. Wales, "The Rise, the Fall, and the Resurrection of the Medical Model," *Georgetown Law Journal* 63 (1974–75): 89–95.

40. Morris, "The Second Most Important Court," 389.

41. *Easter v. District of Columbia*, 361 F. 2d 50 (D.C. Cir. 1966).

42. *Powell v. Texas*, 392 U.S. 514 (1968). See also Patricia M. Wald, "Alcohol, Drugs, and Criminal Responsibility," *Georgetown Law Journal* 63 (1974–75): 71; Morris, "The Second Most Important Court," 340–42.

43. See *Rouse v. Cameron*, 373 F. 2d 451 (D.C. Cir. 1966); *Lake v. Cameron*, 364 F. 2d 657 (D.C. Cir. 1966).

44. See Morris, "The Second Most Important Court," 450–60. See generally Bazelon, "Implementing the Right to Treatment," 742–54.

45. Morris, "The Second Most Important Court," 299–312.

46. *Luck v. United States*, 348 F. 2d 763 (D.C. Cir. 1965). See also Note, "The United States Court of Appeals for the District of Columbia Circuit: 1964–65 Term," *Georgetown Law Journal* 54 (1965): 263; Morris, "The Second Most Important Court," 325–26.

47. *Blue v. United States*, 342 F. 2d 894 (D.C. Cir. 1964). See also Note, "United States Court of Appeals for the District of Columbia Circuit: 1964–65 Term," 193–96.

48. The "liberal" or "due process" wing of the D.C. Circuit, which coalesced in 1962 and 1963, included Judges David Bazelon, J. Skelly Wright, Charles Fahy, Spottswood

Robinson, Henry W. Edgerton, Harold Leventhal, George T. Washington, and Carl McGowan. The "conservative" or "crime control" wing consisted of Judges Warren Burger, John Danaher, Wilbur Miller, and Walter M. Bastian. Morris, "The Second Most Important Court," 228–348.

49. Goulden, *The Benchwarmers,* 225.

50. Howard, *Courts of Appeals in the Federal Judicial System,* 8. See also, Morris, "The Second Most Important Court," 87.

51. Morris, "The Second Most Important Court," 259–60.

52. *Fisher v. United States,* 328 U.S. 463 (1946), 476–77. See also *Griffin v. United States,* 336 U.S. 704 (1949).

53. Note, "The Judge-Made Supervisory Power of the Federal Courts," *Georgetown Law Journal* 53 (1964–65): 1077.

54. See generally Leonard W. Levy, *Against the Law: The Nixon Court and Criminal Justice* (New York: Harper & Row, 1974), 1–60; Jeffrey A. Segal and Harold J. Spaeth, "Rehnquist Court Dispositions of Lower Court Decisions: Affirmation and Not Reversal," *Judicature* 74 (1990): 84–88; Harold J. Spaeth, "Supreme Court Disposition of Federal Circuit Court Decisions," *Judicature* 68 (1985): 245–50.


## CHAPTER 2. MOLLYCODDLING JUDGES AND THE POLITICS OF D.C. CIRCUIT COURT REFORM

Epigraph sources can be found in David L. Bazelon, Foreword to "The Morality of the Criminal Law: Rights of the Accused," *Journal of Criminal Law & Criminology* 72 (1981): 1151; and Nicholas deB. Katzenbach's remarks in a letter to David L. Bazelon dated June 24, 1965, reprinted in Yale Kasimar, "Has the Court Left the Attorney General Behind? The Bazelon-Katzenbach Letters on Poverty, Equality and the Administration of Criminal Justice," *Kentucky Law Journal* 54 (1955): 490–91.

1. Joseph C. Goulden, *The Benchwarmers: The Private World of the Powerful Federal Judges* (New York: Weybright and Talley, 1974), 225.

2. See, e.g., *Durham v. United States,* 214 F. 2d 862 (D.C. Cir. 1954); Bazelon's letter to the editor of the *New York Times,* reprinted in *New York Times,* December 12, 1965, p. 34 (criticizing American Law Institute's proposed code on pre-arraignment procedures that, in Bazelon's view, deprived indigent criminal suspects of their constitutional rights). His extrajudicial writings illustrate a liberal approach to deciding criminal appeals: e.g., David L. Bazelon, "The Morality of Criminal Law," *Southern California Law Review* 49 (1975): 385–405; David L. Bazelon, "New Gods for Old: 'Efficient' Courts in a Democratic Society," *New York University Law Review* 46 (1971): 653–74; David L. Bazelon, "The Defective Assistance of Counsel," *University of Cincinnati Law Review* 42 (1973): 1–46; David L. Bazelon, "Civil Liberties: Protecting Old Values in the New Century," *New York University Law Review* 51 (1976): 505–15; David L. Bazelon, "The Dilemma of Criminal Responsibility," *Kentucky Law Journal* 72 (1983–84): 263–77.

3. See Bazelon's letter to Nicholas deB. Katzenbach, dated June 16, 1965, and deB. Katzenbach's response, dated June 24, 1965, reprinted in Appendices A and B in Kasimar, "Has the Court Left the Attorney General Behind?," pp. 486–94.

4. See, e.g., "Courts Too Soft on Criminals: A Warning by Attorney General," *U.S. News & World Report*, 59 (August 16, 1965): 66.

5. The empirical data discussed in the next few paragraphs is analyzed from *The Annual Report of the Director of the Administrative Office of the United States Courts* (Washington, D.C.: U.S. Government Printing Office, 1960–69), Table B-1.

6. See "Statement of the Managers of the Part of the Senate Submitted Regarding the Conference Action upon S. 2601, the President's Crime Legislation for the District of Columbia," in *Congressional Record*, 91st Cong., 2d Sess., 1970, 116, pt. 18: 24340–51; President's Commission on Law Enforcement and the Administration of Justice, *The Challenge of Crime in a Free Society: A Report* (Washington, D.C.: U.S. Government Printing Office, 1967); United Press International, "Legal Experts Find Armed Robberies Rampant in Capital," *New York Times*, December 5, 1969, p. 65. Ben A. Franklin, "City of Fear and Crime: Nixon Faces Capital Test," *New York Times*, January 22, 1969, p. 49.

7. See Leonard W. Levy, *Against the Law: The Nixon Court and Criminal Justice* (New York: Harper & Row, 1974), 2–3; Fred P. Graham, "Warren Says All Share Crime Onus," *New York Times*, August 2, 1968, p. 1. See also, "An Assist For Police: Congress Tackles Crime," *U.S. News & World Report* 61 (October 31, 1966): 46 (stating that the *Durham* insanity rule is proof that courts are protecting criminals at the expense of law enforcement); "Breakdown of Courts in America," *U.S. News & World Report* 66 (March 10, 1969): 58 (arguing that the backload of criminal cases in courts is caused by Supreme Court decisions expanding the rights of criminal defendants).

8. "Transcripts of Acceptance Speeches By Nixon & Agnew to GOP Convention," *New York Times*, August 9, 1968, p. 20.

9. Public Law 91-358, 91st Cong., 2d sess. (July 29, 1970); Wesley S. Williams, Jr., "District of Columbia Court Reorganization, 1970," *Georgetown Law Journal* 59 (1971): 477–560.

10. Joseph D. Tydings, Foreword to Williams, "District of Columbia Court Reorganization, 1970," 477–80. See also Christopher Lyndon, "Congress Gets Nixon Bill for Preventative Detention," *New York Times*, July 12, 1969, p. 1; Paul Delaney, "Concern Voiced over Crime Bill," *New York Times*, May 24, 1970, p. 66.

11. Lyndon, "Congress Gets Nixon Bill," 1. See generally Jeffrey B. Morris, "The Second Most Important Court: The United States Court of Appeals for the District of Columbia Circuit" (Ph.D. diss., University of Columbia, 1972), 478 (intimating that the court reform bill was "neutral" in scope). The commentary describing the political nature of the D.C. Circuit includes Abner J. Mikva, "Sturm Und Drang at the D.C. Circuit," *George Washington Law Review* 57 (1989): 1063; Patricia M. Wald, "Life on the District of Columbia Circuit: Literally and Figuratively Halfway Between the Capitol and the White House," *Minnesota Law Review* 72 (1987): 1.

12. See Levy, *Against the Law*, 2–3; Goulden, *The Benchwarmers*, 233; Morris, "The Second Most Important Court," 478.

13. Much of the ensuing discussion relating to the D.C. Crime bill's legislation history is derived from "Statement of the Managers of Part of the Senate Submitted Regarding the Conference Action upon S. 2601"; U.S. Senate, *Reorganizing the Courts of the District of Columbia, and for Other Purposes: Report [To Accompany S. 2601]*, 91st Cong., 1st sess., 1969. S. Rept. 91-405 (Washington, D.C.: U.S. Government Printing

Office); U.S. House of Representatives, *District of Columbia Court Reform and Criminal Procedure Act of 1970: Report of the Committee on the District of Columbia on H.R. 16196,* 91st Cong., 2d sess., 1970. H. Rept. 91-907 (Washington, D.C.: U.S. Government Printing Office); U.S. Senate, *Hearings before the Committee on the District of Columbia,* 91st Cong., 1st and 2d sess., 1969, pts. 1–12 in *Crime in the National Capital* (Washington, D.C.: U.S. Government Printing Office). Part of the House and Senate debate is found in *Congressional Record,* 91st Cong., 2d sess., 1970, 116, pt. 18: 24454–77; 24704–17; 24836–99; 25037–56; 25141–42, 25183–90, 25197–12; 25376–87, 25419–33, 25441–52; 25525–29, 25532–33, 25554–91.

14. *Congressional Record,* 91st Cong., 2d sess., 1970, 116, pt. 18: 25566. The remarks of Representatives Broyhill and Abernethy are found in *Congressional Record,* 91st Cong., 2d sess., 1970, 116, pt. 18: 8091–92, 8095.

15. United States Court of Appeals for the District of Columbia Circuit, *History of the United States Court of Appeals for the District of Columbia Circuit in the Country's Bicentennial Year* (Washington, D.C.: U.S. Court of Appeals for the District of Columbia Circuit, 1977), 77–79; Morris, "The Second Most Important Court," 262–70.

16. Tydings, Foreword, 478–79.

17. "Statement of the Managers of Part of the Senate Submitted Regarding the Conference Action upon S. 2601," 24347. Criticisms of the *Luck* doctrine, created by *Luck v. United States,* 348 F. 2d 763 (D.C. Cir. 1965), are found in U.S. House of Representatives, H. Rept. 91–907, 62–63.

18. See *United States v. Leathers,* 412 F. 2d 169 (D.C. Cir. 1969) and *United States v. Alston,* 420 F. 2d 176 (D.C. Cir. 1969). See U.S. House of Representatives, *Report of the Committee on the District of Columbia on H.R. 16196,* 91st Cong., 2d sess., 1970, H. Rept. 91-907, 87–94; Morris, "The Second Most Important Court," 310–11.

19. Prior law was established by *Davis v. United States,* 160 U.S. 469 (1895), when the U.S. Supreme Court held that the burden of proving sanity beyond a reasonable doubt rested upon the government. This rule was followed by the federal courts. See *U.S. v. Greene,* 834 F. 2d 1067 (D.C. Cir. 1987), 1069.

20. See *Bolton v. Harris,* 395 F. 2d 642 (D.C. Cir. 1968). See also U.S. House of Representatives, *Report on H.R. 16196,* H. Rept. 91-907, 73–75; "Statement of the Managers of Part of the Senate Submitted Regarding the Conference Action upon S. 2601," 24348.

21. "Statement of Donald E. Santarelli" reprinted in U.S. Senate, *Crime in the National Capital,* 1395–96. See *Kent v. United States,* 401 F. 2d 408 (D.C. Cir. 1968); *Haziel v. United States,* 404 F. 2d 1275 (D.C. Cir. 1968). See generally, Morris, "The Second Most Important Court," 318–19.

22. "Statement of the Managers of Part of the Senate Submitted Regarding the Conference Action upon S. 2601," 24346.

23. Ibid., 24346–50.

24. Robert L. Rabin, "Federal Regulation in Historical Perspective," *Stanford Law Review* 38 (1986): 1278–95; William Lilley III and James C. Miller, "The New 'Social Regulation,'" *Public Interest* 47 (1977): 52, Table 2.

25. Alfred C. Aman, Jr., *Administrative Law in a Global Era* (Ithaca, N.Y.: Cornell University Press, 1992), 27–29; Peter H. Schuck, review of *The Politics of Regulation,* edited by James Q. Wilson, *Yale Law Journal* 90 (1981): 702–25. See also R. Shep

Melnick, *Regulation and the Courts: The Case of the Clean Air Act* (Washington, D.C.: Brookings Institution, 1983), 5–9.

26. Rabin, "Federal Regulation in Historical Perspective," 1291; Kenneth Culp Davis and Richard J. Pierce, Jr., *Administrative Law Treatise,* vol. 3, 3d ed. (Boston: Little, Brown & Company, 1993), 22.

27. The empirical data from Figure 3 and ensuing discussion on the judicial workload statistics in the next few paragraphs is analyzed from *The Annual Report of the Director of the Administrative Office of the United States Courts* (Washington, D.C.: U.S. Government Printing Office, 1970–79), Table B-1.

28. As stated by Patricia Wald, in Patricia M. Wald et al., "The Contribution of the D.C. Circuit to Administrative Law," *Administrative Law Review* 40 (1988): 508–18. At one time the court had exclusive jurisdiction over parts of thirteen federal statutes and had concurrent power with other circuits regarding sixty-one federal statutes. Francis J. Flaherty, "Inside the 'Invisible' Courts: As Their Importance Grows, U.S. Circuits Remain 'Unnoticed,'" *Legal Times,* May 2, 1983, p. 1. See also David M. O'Brien, *What Process Is Due? Courts and Science-Policy Disputes* (New York: Russell Sage Foundation, 1987), 155.

29. Judge Wald's comment appears in Wald et al., "The Contribution of the D.C. Circuit," 509. But see Paul Verkuil's remark that "while the D.C. Circuit has in a sense had greatness thrust upon it in administrative law, it has also done a lot to earn its reputation." Ibid., 531.

30. Rabin, "Federal Regulation in Historical Perspective," 1311.

31. *Office of Communication of the United Church of Christ v. Federal Communication Commission,* 359 F. 2d 994 (D.C. Cir. 1966); *Office of Communication of the United Church of Christ v. Federal Communication Commission,* 425 F. 2d 543 (D.C. Cir. 1969). The *Church* opinions, along with the Second Circuit's decision in *Scenic Hudson Preservation Conference v. Federal Power Commission,* 354 F. 2d 608 (2d Cir. 1966) (reversing FPC's grant of a license to build a hydroelectric plant without adequate consideration of the environmental impact), were indicative of the new trend. Rabin, "Federal Regulation in Historical Perspective," 1296–301.

32. Wald et al., "The Contribution of the D.C. Circuit," 516.

33. Ibid., 511, 532–33.

34. Harold Leventhal, "Principled Fairness and Regulatory Urgency," *Case Western Reserve Law Review* 25 (1974): 66–81. See also, Harold Leventhal, "Environmental Decisionmaking and the Role of Courts," *University of Pennsylvania Law Review* 122 (1974): 511–12. For a discussion on the origin and significance of hard-look review, see Alfred C. Aman, Jr., "Administrative Law in a Global Era: Progress, Deregulatory Change, and the Rise of the Administrative Presidency," *Cornell Law Review* 73 (1988): 1143–44; William H. Rogers, Jr., "A Hard Look at *Vermont Yankee*: Environmental Law under Close Scrutiny," *Georgetown Law Journal* 67 (1979): 699–727.

35. *Greater Boston Television Corporation v. Federal Communication Commission,* 444 F. 2d 841 (D.C. Cir. 1970), 851–52.

36. *Environmental Defense Fund, Inc. v. Ruckelshaus,* 439 F. 2d 584 (D.C. Cir. 1971), 597–98 (where Judge Bazelon, in remanding a case back to the Department of Agriculture because the secretary failed to suspend federal registration for the pesticide DDT, took advantage of the court-agency collaboration on the basis that "judicial review alone

can correct only the most egregious abuses"). See Henry J. Friendly, "Some Kind of Hearing," *University of Pennsylvania Law Review* 123 (1975): 1311 n.221.

37. Glen O. Robinson, Ernest Gellhorn, and Harold H. Bruff, *The Administrative Process,* 4th ed. (St. Paul, Minn.: West Publishing Co., 1993), 432; David M. O'Brien, "The Courts and Science-Policy Disputes: A Review and Commentary on the Role of the Judiciary in Regulatory Politics," *Journal of Energy Law and Policy* 4 (1983): 108; Patricia M. Wald, "Negotiation of Environmental Disputes: A New Role for the Courts?" *Columbia Journal of Environmental Law* 10 (1985): 2; Samuel Estreicher, "Pragmatic Justice: The Contributions of Judge Harold Leventhal to Administrative Law," *Columbia Law Review* 80 (1980): 904–5.

38. O'Brien, "The Courts and Science-Policy Disputes," 108.

39. *Calvert Cliffs Coordinating Committee, Inc. v. United States Atomic Energy Commission,* 449 F. 2d 1109 (D.C. Cir. 1971), 1111. Notably, the primary device to compel agencies to consider environmental considerations was the preparation and filing of an environmental impact statement, an action-forcing element akin to cost-benefit analysis. Martin Shapiro, *Who Guards the Guardians? Judicial Control of Administration* (Athens: University of Georgia Press, 1988), 98–101.

40. *People Against Nuclear Energy v. United States Nuclear Regulatory Commission,* 678 F. 2d 222 (D.C. Cir. 1982). See also O'Brien, *What Process Is Due?* 177; Aman, "Administrative Law in a Global Era," 1142.

41. Leventhal, "Environmental Decisionmaking and the Role of Courts," 510.

42. Samuel Estreicher served as a law clerk for Judge Leventhal. The concept of "danger signals" is indirectly articulated by Judge Leventhal in a per curiam opinion in *Joseph v. Federal Communications Commission,* 404 F.C. 207 (D.C. Cir. 1968), 212. Much of the discussion in the next few paragraphs relies upon the insight revealed in Estreicher, "Pragmatic Justice," and the judicial opinions from the D.C. Circuit and the U.S. Supreme Court in *Volkswagenwerk Aktiengesellschaft v. Federal Maritime Commission,* 390 U.S. 261 (1968), 272; *Portland Cement Association v. Ruckelshaus,* 486 F. 2d 375 (D.C. Cir. 1973), 390–401; and, *Monsanto Company v. Kennedy,* 613 F. 2d 947 (D.C. Cir. 1979).

43. *Ethyl Corporation v. Environmental Protection Agency,* 541 F.2d 1 (D.C. Cir. 1976) (en banc), 66.

44. O'Brien, *What Process Is Due?* 107, 154–58. Judge Bazelon's judicial philosophy is explained in David L. Bazelon, "Coping with Technology through the Legal Process," *Cornell Law Review* 62 (1977): 817–32; David L. Bazelon, "Science and Uncertainty: A Jurist's View," *Harvard Environmental Law Review* 5 (1981): 209–15; *International Harvester Company v. Ruckelshaus,* 478 F. 2d 615 (D.C. Cir. 1973), 650–53 (Judge Bazelon, concurring). For a sample of the Bazelon-Leventhal debate, see *International Harvester Company v. Ruckelshaus,* 478 F. 2d 615 (D.C. Cir. 1973).

45. Aman, "Administrative Law in a Global Era," 1145. Cases invoking procedural hard look include *Mobil Oil Corporation v. Federal Power Commission,* 483 F. 2d 1238 (D.C. Cir. 1973); *Walter Holm & Company v. Hardin,* 449 F. 2d 1009 (D.C. Cir. 1971); *American Airlines, Inc. v. Civil Aeronautics Board,* 359 F. 2d 624 (1966) (en banc). See also Merrick B. Garland, "Deregulation and Judicial Review," *Harvard Law Review* 98 (1985): 526–27; Shapiro, *Who Guards the Guardians?* 49–54.

46. Only the D.C. Circuit, the Fifth Circuit, and the Ninth Circuit individually had more than five hundred agency affirmances and more than one thousand total

number of merit terminations from 1970 to 1979. The Second Circuit had over five hundred agency affirmances (601), but less than one thousand total merit terminations (823). All other circuit courts had fewer. The average percentages for each circuit for the 1970–79 period are as follows: D.C., 57.06 percent; First, 66.55 percent; Second, 73.03 percent; Third, 53.98 percent; Fourth, 61.72 percent; Fifth, 77.86 percent; Sixth, 75.44 percent; Seventh, 64.33 percent; Eighth, 71.20 percent; Ninth, 70.93 percent; and Tenth, 67.0 percent. The average rate of affirmance for all circuits is 69.09 percent, inclusive of the D.C. Circuit. *Annual Reports* from 1970 to 1979, Table B-1.

47. *United States v. Allegheny-Ludlum Steel Corporation,* 406 U.S. 742 (1972) and *United States v. Florida East Coast Railroad Co.,* 410 U.S. 224 (1973). But see *Citizens to Preserve Overton Park, Inc. v. Volpe,* 401 U.S. 402 (1971). See generally Robinson, Gellhorn, and Bruff, *The Administrative Process,* 507.

48. *Vermont Yankee Nuclear Power Corp. v. Natural Resources Defense Council, Inc.,* 435 U.S. 519 (1978). Two D.C. Circuit opinions are actually at issue in *Vermont Yankee.* The first, *National Resources Defense Council, Inc. v. United States Nuclear Regulatory Commission,* 547 F. 2d 633 (D.C. Cir. 1976), concerns whether the Atomic Energy Commission (to which the NRC assumed its jurisdiction after the AEC was abolished in 1974) correctly assessed the environmental effects of nuclear waste disposal in licensing and rule-making proceedings relating to the Vermont Yankee Nuclear Power Station in Vernon, Vermont. The second, *Aeschliman v. United States Nuclear Regulatory Commission,* 547 F. 2d 622 (D.C. Cir. 1976), involves the agency's decision to grant construction permits for two nuclear reactors in Midland, Michigan, without considering alternatives to nuclear energy (i.e., other energy conservation methods).

49. *Natural Resources Defense Council, Inc. v. United States Nuclear Regulatory Commission,* 643–55. Bazelon suggests, for example, that the agency use informal conferences, discovery, interrogatories, technical advisory committees, surveys, and limited cross-examination as extra procedural devices to air the issues and create a dialogue. Ibid., 653. Bazelon also filed a separate statement (reiterating his views), which responded to Judge Edward Tamm's special concurrence (in the result). Judge Tamm voted for a remand because the agency failed to develop an adequate record explaining its decision. But Tamm also argued that "more procedure would not . . . guarantee a better record," and criticized Bazelon for "over-formalizing" the agency decision-making process. Ibid., 658–61 (Judge Tamm, concurring).

50. *Vermont Yankee Nuclear Power Corporation v. Natural Resources Defense Council, Inc.,* 525–57.

51. See *People Against Nuclear Energy v. United States Nuclear Regulatory Commission.*


## CHAPTER 3. JUDICIAL POLITICS IN THE D.C. CIRCUIT COURT

Epigraph source can be found in *Chevron U.S.A. Inc. v. Natural Resources Defense Council, Inc.,* 467 U.S. 837 (1984).

1. Harry T. Edwards, "Public Misperceptions Concerning the 'Politics' of Judging: Dispelling Some Myths about the D.C. Circuit," *University of Colorado Law Review* 56 (1985): 621, 636. Judge Edwards seems to have distanced himself from his earlier

comments. See Harry T. Edwards, "The Judicial Function and the Elusive Goal of Principled Decisionmaking," *Wisconsin Law Review* (1991): 836–65.

2. *Bartlett v. Bowen,* 824 F. 2d 1240 (D.C. Cir. 1987), 1243–44 (en banc) (Judge Edwards, concurring). Judge Mikva's remarks can be found in Abner J. Mikva, "Sturm Und Drang at the D.C. Circuit," *George Washington Law Review* 57 (1989): 1068.

3. Jeffrey A. Segal and Harold J. Spaeth, *The Supreme Court and the Attitudinal Model* (New York: Cambridge University Press, 1993), 17–19.

4. The language referring to the court as a "de facto" court is used by Judge Patricia Wald and legal scholar Paul Verkuil in Patricia M. Wald et al., "The Contribution of the D.C. Circuit to Administrative Law," *Administrative Law Review* 40 (1988): 509, 534. The phrase "historical accident" is employed by Wald on page 509.

5. Patricia M. Wald, in Wald et al., "The Contribution of the D.C. Circuit," 522–30. See also Jon Gottschall, "Reagan's Appointments to the U.S. Courts of Appeals: The Continuation of a Judicial Revolution," *Judicature* 70 (1986): 48–54.

6. Deregulation is analyzed in Robert L. Rabin, "Federal Regulation in Historical Perspective," *Stanford Law Review* 38 (1986): 1315–27; Abner J. Mikva, "Deregulating through the Back Door: The Hard Way to Fight a Revolution," *University of Chicago Law Review* 57 (1990): 522–33; Cass Sunstein, "Deregulation and the Courts," *Journal of Policy Analysis and Management* 5 (1986): 518–19; Alfred C. Aman, Jr., *Administrative Law in a Global Era* (Ithaca, N.Y.: Cornell University Press, 1993), 43–77.

7. Wald et al., "The Contribution of the D.C. Circuit," 522–23. See also *1993 Judicial Staff Directory* (Mt. Vernon, Va.: Congressional Staff Directory, 1993); *1992 Want's Federal-State Court Directory* (Washington, D.C.: Want Publication Co., 1992).

8. Harold J. Spaeth and Stuart H. Teger, "Activism and Restraint: A Cloak for the Justices' Policy Preferences," in *U.S. Supreme Court Behavior Studies,* ed., Harold J. Spaeth and Saul Brenner (New York: Garland Publishing, 1990), 240. See also Wald et al., "The Contribution of the D.C. Circuit," 524–27; Glen O. Robinson, Ernest Gellhorn, and Harold H. Bruff, *The Administrative Process,* 4th ed. (St. Paul, Minn.: West Publishing Co., 1993), 280.

9. The litigation efforts of the National Association for the Advancement of Colored People, for example, were instrumental in securing equal educational opportunity for African Americans, as evidenced by the ruling handed down by the United States Supreme Court in *Brown v. Board of Education,* 347 U.S. 483 (1954). David M. O'Brien, *Constitutional Law and Politics: Civil Rights and Civil Liberties,* vol. 2, 2d ed. (New York: W. W. Norton & Co., 1994), 1317–38.

10. David M. O'Brien, *Storm Center: The Supreme Court in American Politics,* 3d ed. (New York: W. W. Norton & Co., 1993), 210–26; Walter Gellhorn and Ronald M. Levin, *Administrative Law in a Nutshell,* 3d ed. (St. Paul, Minn.: West Publishing Co., 1990), 378–87.

11. Charles Alan Wright, Arthur R. Miller, and Edward H. Cooper, *Federal Practice and Procedure: Jurisdiction,* 2d ed., sec. 3531 (St. Paul, Minn.: West Publishing Co., 1984), 348; H. W. Perry, Jr., "Agenda Setting and Case Selection," in *The American Courts: A Critical Assessment,* ed. John B. Gates and Charles A. Johnson (Washington, D.C.: CQ Press, 1990), 241.

12. Daniel J. Balz et al., "Special Report: America Faces Turning Point in its Long Love Affair with the Automobile," *National Journal* 8, no. 1 (1976): 6; Elder Witt, "Final

Energy Policy Bill Faces Uncertain Fate," *Congressional Weekly Report* 37, no. 50 (1975): 2689, 2766–67.

13. Public Law 94-163, 94th Congress, 1st sess. (December 22, 1975) 89 Stat. 871. Title III amended the Motor Vehicle Information and Cost Savings Act, which in fact became a new Title V to that act. Elder Witt, "Congress Sends Ford Energy Policy Bill," *Congressional Weekly Report* 33, no. 51 (1975): 2691.

14. Witt, "Congress Sends Ford Energy Policy Bill," 2692; Warren Brown, "EPA Grants Ford, GM Break in Fuel Penalty," *Washington Post,* January 18, 1985, sec. E, p. 1; Timothy B. Clark, "The Two Billion Dollar Question: Will Economy Fines Hit Auto Companies?" *National Journal,* November 19, 1983; Warren Brown, "NHTSA Seeks Freeze in Fuel-Mileage Standards," *Washington Post,* June 27, 1986, sec. C, p. 1.

15. See e.g., *Center for Auto Safety v. Claybrook,* 627 F. 2d 346 (D.C. Cir. 1980); *Center for Auto Safety v. National Highway Traffic Safety Administration,* 710 F. 2d 842 (D.C. Cir. 1983); *Center for Auto Safety v. National Highway Traffic Safety Administration,* 793 F. 2d 1322 (D.C. Cir. 1986) (*CAS I*); *In Re Center for Auto Safety,* 793 F. 2d 1346 (D.C. Cir. 1986), *Center for Auto Safety v. Thomas,* 806 F. 2d 1071 (D.C. Cir. 1986) (*CAS II*), *Public Citizen v. National Highway Traffic Safety Administration,* 848 F. 2d 256 (D.C. Cir. 1988); *Competitive Enterprise Institute v. National Traffic Highway Safety Administration,* 901 F. 2d 107 (D.C. Cir. 1990); *General Motors Corporation v. National Highway Traffic Safety Administration,* 898 F. 2d 165 (D.C. Cir. 1990); *City of Los Angeles v. National Highway Traffic Safety Administration,* 912 F. 2d 478 (D.C. Cir. 1990); *Mercedes–Benz of N.A., Inc. v. National Highway Traffic Safety Administration,* 291 F. 2d 29 (D.C. Cir. 1991); and, *Competitive Enterprise Institute v. National Highway Traffic Safety Administration,* 956 F. 2d 321 (D.C. Cir. 1992). Of the cases, only three, *Center for Auto Safety v. Claybrook, General Motors Corporation v. National Highway Traffic Safety Administration,* and *Mercedes–Benz of N.A., Inc. v. National Highway Traffic Safety Administration,* did not raise justiciability issues. The eleven cases are published opinions generated through a search by Lexis, an online legal information service.

16. *CAS I; CAS II.* See also Kenneth Culp Davis and Richard J. Pierce, Jr., *Administrative Law Treatise,* vol. 3, 3d ed., sec. 16.1–16.4 (Boston: Little, Brown & Company, 1993), 1–28; Glenn D. Grant, "Standing on Shaky Ground," *George Washington Law Review* 57 (1989): 1408–37; Cass R. Sunstein, "Standing and the Privatization of Public Law," *Columbia Law Review* 88 (1988): 1432–81.

17. *CAS I,* 1323–41.

18. Ibid., 1341–45.

19. *CAS II,* 1075.

20. Ibid., 1080.

21. *Center for Auto Safety v. Thomas,* 810 F. 2d 302 (D.C. Cir. 1987) (en banc, vacating panel opinion); *Center for Auto Safety v. Thomas,* 847 F. 2d 843 (D.C. Cir. 1988) (en banc, 5-5 tie). In the 5-5 en banc tie ruling, the opinion representing the Democratic appointees (granting standing) is found at *Center for Auto Safety v. Thomas,* 847 F. 2d 843 (D.C. Cir. 1988) (en banc), 844–63; and, the opinion on behalf of the Republican appointees (denying standing) is at *Center for Auto Safety v. Thomas,* 847 F. 2d 843 (D.C. Cir. 1988) (en banc): 863–76.

22. Glenn D. Grant, "Standing on Shaky Ground," *George Washington Law Review* 57 (1989): 1416.

23. *Center for Auto Safety v. Thomas,* 856 F. 2d 1557 (D.C. Cir. 1988) (en banc).

24. Grant, "Standing on Shaky Ground," 1414.

25. By the fall of 1988, the D.C. Circuit consisted of eight Republican appointees and six Democratic appointees. *1993 Judicial Staff Directory* (Mt. Vernon, Va.: Congressional Staff Directory, 1993); *1992 Want's Federal-State Court Directory* (Washington, D.C.: Want Publication Co., 1992). See also Lee Hockstader, "Automakers Win Case on Fuel Economy," *Washington Post,* September 17, 1988, sec. D, p. 14.

26. See, e.g., Mikva, "Sturm Und Drang at the D.C. Circuit," 1063–68; Antonin Scalia, "The Doctrine of Standing As an Essential Element of the Separation of Powers," *Suffolk University Law Review* 17 (1983): 881–99.

27. John C. Yang, "Standing . . . In the Doorway of Justice," *George Washington Law Review* 59 (1991): 1357–58.

28. The vagaries of D.C. Circuit standing jurisprudence in the 1980s raises an empirical question about the precise impact that ideology or other nonlegal factors have on the outcome of court access decisions. One study confirms that there is a subtle and complex relationship between law and politics in D.C. Circuit access policy-making involving agency appeals. See Chapter 2 of Christopher P. Banks, "Judicial Politics in the 'Mini–Supreme Court': Legal-Policy Change in the U.S. Court of Appeals for the District of Columbia Circuit, 1960–1993" (Ph.D. diss., University of Virginia, 1995).

29. See Glen O. Robinson, *American Bureaucracy: Public Choice and Public Law* (Ann Arbor: University of Michigan Press, 1991): 177–78; George B. Shepherd, "Fierce Compromise: The Administrative Procedure Act Emerges from New Deal Politics," *Northwestern University Law Review* 90 (1996): 1557–683; See also Martin Shapiro, *Who Guards the Guardians? Judicial Control of Administration* (Athens: University of Georgia Press, 1988), 33–41.

30. Martin Shapiro, "APA: Past, Present, and Future," *Virginia Law Review* 72 (1986): 450–51; Alfred C. Aman, Jr., "Administrative Law in a Global Era: Progress, Deregulatory Change, and the Rise of the Administrative Presidency," *Cornell Law Review* 73 (1988): 1109–31; Shapiro, *Who Guards the Guardians?* 36–38; Paul R. Verkuil, "The Emerging Concept of Administrative Procedure," *Columbia Law Review* 78 (1978): 261–76; Rabin, "Federal Regulation in Historical Perspective," 1253–62.

31. Peter H. Aranson, Ernest Gellhorn, and Glen O. Robinson, "A Theory of Legislative Delegation," *Cornell Law Review* 68 (1983): 1–67. The Court eviscerated the New Deal by its rulings in *Panama Refining Company v. Ryan,* 293 U.S. 388 (1935) (invalidating the Petroleum Code of the National Industrial Recovery Act [NIRA]); *Schechter Poultry Corporation v. United States,* 295 U.S. 495 (1935) (invalidating the Live Poultry Code under the NIRA); *United States v. Butler,* 297 U.S. 1 (1936) (invalidating the Agricultural Adjustment Act); and *Carter v. Carter Coal Company,* 298 U.S. 238 (1936) (invalidating Bituminous Coal Conservation Act). See Rabin, "Federal Regulation in Historical Perspective," 1253–59.

32. See *West Coast Hotel Co. v. Parrish,* 300 U.S. 379 (1937); *National Labor Relations Board v. Jones & Laughlin Steel Corporation,* 301 U.S. 1 (1937); *Helvering v. Davis,* 301 U.S. 619 (1937); and *Steward Machine Company v. Davis,* 301 U.S. 548 (1937). The "switch-in time-to-save-nine" decision is associated generally with the *West Coast* ruling. Henry J. Abraham, *Justices and Presidents: A Political History of Appointments to the*

*Supreme Court* 2d ed. (New York: Oxford University Press, 1985), 209–10. See also Rabin, "Federal Regulation in Historical Perspective," 1259–60.

33. Abraham, *Justices and Presidents,* 209–10.

34. Ronald A. Cass, "Models of Administrative Action," *Virginia Law Review* 72 (1986): 364. Other scholars make similar points. See, e.g., Rabin, "Federal Regulation in Historical Perspective," 1262–63.

35. The ABA's efforts to reform administrative procedure, although fairly ineffectual, began in earnest as early as 1933. Walter Gellhorn, "The Administrative Procedure Act: The Beginnings," *Virginia Law Review* 72 (1986): 219. Reform became attractive since administrative law was loosely characterized as being anything done by government officials, without regard to law properly understood; it thus was analogized to being "Marxist" or more socialist in nature. See Gellhorn, "The Administrative Procedure Act," 221–22; Verkuil, "The Emerging Concept of Administrative Procedure," 261–76.

36. "Report of the Special Committee on Administrative Law," *American Bar Association Journal* 63 (1938): 331. See also Gellhorn, "The Administrative Procedure Act," 221–23; Shepherd, "Fierce Compromise," 1590–93. Much of the antiagency rhetoric appears in articles written by lawyers. See e.g., Arthur A. Ballantine, "Administrative Agencies and the Law," *American Bar Association Journal* 24 (1938): 109–12; Arthur T. Vanderbilt, "The Place of the Administrative Tribunal in Our Legal System," *American Bar Association Journal* 24 (1938): 261–73; Blyth E. Stason, "Methods of Judicial Relief from Administrative Action," *American Bar Association Journal* 24 (1938): 274–78.

37. *Final Report of the Attorney General's Committee on Administrative Procedure, Administrative Procedure in Government Agencies,* 77th Cong., 1st Sess., 1941, S. Doc. 8 (Washington, D.C.: U.S. Government Printing Office), 1. Paul Verkuil opines that the *Final Report* is the most influential document in administrative law. See Verkuil, "The Emerging Concept of Administrative Procedure," 271–78. See also Gellhorn, "The Administrative Procedure Act," 224–32; Rabin, "Federal Regulation in Historical Perspective," 1264–65.

38. Shapiro, *Who Guards the Guardians?* 57.

39. Shapiro, "APA," 452–54. See Shapiro, *Who Guards the Guardians?,* 36–58; Rabin, "Federal Regulation in Historical Perspective," 1265–68.

40. Shapiro, *Who Guards the Guardians?* 39–44, 56; Shapiro, "APA," 453–54.

41. David M. O'Brien, *What Process Is Due? Courts and Science-Policy Disputes* (New York: Russell Sage Foundation, 1987), 113–15; Rabin, "Federal Regulation in Historical Perspective," 1266; Aman, "Administrative Law in a Global Era," 1116–21. For an assessment of the significance of the APA and related issues on administrative law, see "The Administrative Procedure Act: A Fortieth Anniversary Symposium," *Virginia Law Review* 72 (1986): 215–492.

42. O'Brien, *What Process Is Due?* 114–15; Wald et al., "The Contribution of the D.C. Circuit," 514.

43. Aman, *Administrative Law in a Global Era,* 44.

44. *National Lime Association v. Environmental Protection Agency,* 627 F. 2d 416 (D.C. Cir. 1980), 452–53. See also Merrick B. Garland, "Deregulation and Judicial Review," *Harvard Law Review* 98 (1985): 505–91.

45. The discussion in the next few paragraphs is derived from *State Farm Mutual Automobile Insurance Company v. Department of Transportation,* 680 F. 2d 206 (D.C. Cir. 1982) and Abner J. Mikva, "The Changing Role of Judicial Review," *Administrative*

*Law Review* 38 (1986): 115–40. See also *Chrysler Corporation v. Department of Transportation*, 472 F. 2d 659 (6th Cir. 1972); *Pacific Legal Foundation v. Department of Transportation*, 593 F. 2d 1338 (D.C. Cir. 1979).

46. *Motor Vehicle Manufacturers Association of the United States, Inc. v. State Farm Mutual Automobile Insurance Company*, 463 U.S. 29 (1983), 50. Scholarly assessment of the air bags controversy and hard-look review is found in Robinson, Gellhorn, and Bruff, *The Administrative Process*, 527; Shapiro, *Who Guards the Guardians?* 165. Notably, Judge Wald, in Wald et al., "The Contribution of the D.C. Circuit," 519–22, suggests the decision is more akin to a substantive hard-look review decision, whereas Garland calls it a "ringing endorsement of the quasi-procedural hard look." Garland, "Deregulation and Judicial Review," 543. Others observe that the Court's reasoning is similar to a D.C. Circuit analysis. Alfred C. Aman, Jr. and William T. Mayton, *Administrative Law*, Hornbook Series (St. Paul, Minn.: West Publishing Co., 1993): 509–12.

47. *International Ladies' Garment Workers' Union v. Donovan*, 722 F. 2d 795 (D.C. Cir. 1983), 818–26, 828.

48. Wald et al., "The Contribution of the D.C. Circuit," 522.

49. The discussion in the next few paragraphs is based upon the D.C. Circuit's opinion in *Natural Resources Defense Council, Inc. v. Gorsuch*, 685 F. 2d 718 (D.C. Cir. 1982). See also *Chevron U.S.A. Inc. v. Natural Resources Defense Council, Inc.*

50. Thomas W. Merrill, "Judicial Deference to Executive Precedent," *Yale Law Journal* 101 (1992): 971.

51. *Chevron U.S.A. Inc. v. Natural Resources Defense Council, Inc.*, 865.

52. Judge Kenneth Starr called the decision the "*Chevron* two-step" in a panel discussion at a meeting of the Section of Administrative Law in 1986, reprinted in Kenneth W. Starr et al., "Judicial Review of Administrative Action in a Conservative Era," *Administrative Law Review* 39 (1987): 360. For a sense of the scholarly assessment about *Chevron's* impact, see Peter H. Schuck and E. Donald Elliott, "To the *Chevron* Station: An Empirical Study of Federal Administrative Law," *Duke Law Journal* (1990): 1035–36; Davis and Pierce, *Administrative Law Treatise*, vol. 1, sec. 3.4, 117–19; Merrill, "Judicial Deference to Executive Precedent," 980–93.

53. Merrill, "Judicial Deference to Executive Precedent," 969–1033; Kenneth W. Starr, "Observations about the Use of Legislative History," *Duke Law Journal* (1987): 371–79; Abner J. Mikva, "A Reply to Judge Starr's Observations," *Duke Law Journal* (1987): 380–86. For a sample of some extrajudicial writings of D.C. Circuit judges or Supreme Court justices on the subject of judicial deference and statutory interpretation, see Antonin Scalia, "Judicial Deference to Administrative Interpretations of Law," *Duke Law Journal* (1989): 511–21; Abner J. Mikva, "Statutory Interpretation: Getting the Law to Be Less Common," *Ohio State Law Journal* 50 (1990): 980–82; Laurence H. Silberman, "*Chevron*: The Intersection of Law and Policy," *George Washington Law Review* 58 (1990): 821–28; Stephen Breyer, "Judicial Review of Questions of Law and Policy," *Administrative Law Review* 38 (1986): 363–98.

54. The discussion in the next few paragraphs is derived from Merrill, "Judicial Deference to Executive Precedent"; Kenneth W. Starr, "Judicial Review in the Post-*Chevron* Era," *Yale Journal on Regulation* 3 (1986): 283–312; and, Scalia, "Judicial Deference to Administrative Interpretations of Law." The divergent views of former judges Kenneth Starr and Abner Mikva concerning the manner in which a court should con-

strue statutes can be found in Starr, "Observations about the Use of Legislative History," and Mikva, "A Reply to Judge Starr's Observations."

55. Scalia, "Judicial Deference to Administrative Interpretations of Law," 515.

56. See, e.g., *Natural Resources Defense Council, Inc. v. Reilly*, 976 F. 2d 36 (D.C. Cir. 1992); *Wolverine Power Company v. Federal Energy Regulatory Commission*, 963 F. 2d 446 (D.C. Cir. 1992); and *Illinois Bell Telephone Company v. Federal Communications Commission*, 966 F. 2d 1478 (D.C. Cir. 1992). Each case illustrates that the court shows little deference under *Chevron*'s step one when using a "plain language" approach to statutory construction. Compare with *Committee to Save WEAM v. Federal Communications Commission*, 808 F. 2d 113 (D.C. Cir. 1986); *Puerto Rico Electric Power Authority v. Federal Energy Regulatory Commission*, 848 F. 2d 243 (D.C. Cir. 1988); *ANR Pipeline Company v. Federal Energy Regulatory Commission*, 870 F. 2d 717 (D.C. Cir. 1989); *National Wildlife Federation, Inc. v. United States Environmental Protection Agency*, 925 F. 2d 470 (D.C. Cir. 1991); *American Paper Institute, Inc. v. United States Environmental Protection Agency*, 996 F. 2d 346 (D.C. Cir. 1993). Each of the latter set of cases applies *Chevron*'s step two to defer to the agency.

57. Some scholars suggest *Chevron* has a deference effect. E.g., Davis and Pierce, *Administrative Law Treatise*, vol. 3, sec. 3.4, 117–19; Schuck and Elliott, "To the *Chevron* Station," 984–1077. Others are more skeptical. E.g., Linda R. Cohen and Matthew L. Spitzer, "Solving the *Chevron* Puzzle," *Law and Contemporary Problems* 57 (1994): 65–110; Merrill, "Judicial Deference to Executive Precedent," 980–93; and, William S. Jordan III, "Deference Revisited: Politics As a Determinant of Deference Doctrine and the End of the Apparent *Chevron* Consensus," *Nebraska Law Review* 68 (1989): 454–515. Still others, like John F. Belcaster, "The D.C. Circuit's Use of the *Chevron* Test: Constructing a Positive Theory of Judicial Obedience and Disobedience," *Administrative Law Review* 44 (1992): 745–65, are more ambivalent.

58. Gottschall, "Reagan's Appointments to the U.S. Courts of Appeals."

59. The workload statistics from the Administrative Office of U.S. Courts do not report how many merit terminations of agency appeals are statutory versus those that are nonstatutory. For that reason and others, using their data makes it difficult to establish whether *Chevron* has a causal effect of commanding more or less judicial deference.

60. One study, in fact, confirms that judicial deference in the D.C. Circuit is explained, in part, by an interaction between political variables. Still, the findings also reveal that nonideological factors—like U.S. Supreme Court precedent—affect court outcomes as well. In other words, as with D.C. Circuit access policy-making, legal and political variables affect judicial deference to agencies in the D.C. Circuit. See Christopher P. Banks, "Ideology and Judicial Deference in the D.C. Circuit," *Southeastern Political Review* 26 (1998): 861–88.

61. Segal and Spaeth, *The Supreme Court and the Attitudinal Model*, 17.

## CHAPTER 4. THE JUDICIAL POLITICS OF EN BANC REVIEW AND THE FINALITY OF D.C. CIRCUIT COURT DECISIONS

Epigraph sources can be found in Patricia M. Wald, "Changing Course: The Use of Precedent in the District of Columbia Circuit," *Cleveland State Law Review* 34 (1987):

477; and from a remark of Arthur E. Bonfield in Patricia M. Wald et al., "The Contribution of the D.C. Circuit to Administrative Law," *Administrative Law Review* 40 (1988): 507.

1. Abner J. Mikva, "Sturm Und Drang at the D.C. Circuit," *Georgetown Law Review* 57 (1989): 1064. See also Paul Verkuil's comment in Patricia Wald et al., "The Contribution of the D.C. Circuit," 534.

2. Notably, if a particularly important issue needs to be addressed immediately, en banc review also can be utilized before any panel has decided a case. Daniel J. Meador and Jordana Simone Bernstein, *Appellate Courts in the United States* (St. Paul, Minn.: West Publishing Co., 1994), 38.

3. G. Alan Tarr, *Judicial Process and Judicial Policymaking,* 2d ed. (St. Paul, Minn.: West Publishing Co., 1998), 41, Figure 2-3 (noting that the U.S. Supreme Court granted certiorari in less than 1 percent of court of appeals cases terminated on the merits in 1989). See also David M. O'Brien, "The Dynamics of the Judicial Process," *Judges on Judging: Views from the Bench,* ed. David M. O'Brien (Chatham, N.J.: Chatham House Publishers, Inc., 1997), 33.

4. Donald R. Songer, Jeffrey A. Segal, and Charles M. Cameron, "The Hierarchy of Justice: Testing a Principal-Agent Model of Supreme Court–Circuit Court Interactions," *American Journal of Political Science* 38 (1994): 690.

5. As quoted by Patricia Wald, in Patricia M. Wald et al., "The Contribution of the D.C. Circuit," 512–13. Judge Wald states that the D.C. Circuit's "unique task [is] to frame the difficult issues, to ventilate the big and small ideas, to bring to bear our special, immensely diverse knowledge and viewpoints, and above all, to strive always for fairness to litigants and faithfulness to the legislature and the law. *That* is our job; our distinctive contribution to administrative law." Ibid., 530.

6. Songer, Segal, and Cameron, "The Hierarchy of Justice," 692–93.

7. See Alex Kozinski, "What I Ate for Breakfast and Other Mysteries of Judicial Decision Making," *Judges on Judging,* 72–73.

8. Daniel Egger, "Court of Appeals Review of Agency Action: The Problem of *En Banc* Ties," *Yale Law Journal,* 100 (1990): 477; Paul M. Bator et al., eds., *Hart and Wechsler's The Federal Courts and the Federal System* (Westbury, N.Y.: Foundation Press, 1988), 39.

9. Felix Frankfurter and James M. Landis, *The Business of the Supreme Court: A Study in the Federal Judicial System* (New York: MacMillan, 1928), 59–78; Bator et al., *Hart and Wechsler's The Federal Courts,* 37; A. Lamar Alexander, Jr., "En Banc Hearings in the Federal Courts of Appeals: Accommodating Institutional Responsibilities," part 1, *New York University Law Review* 40 (1965): 569.

10. Neil D. McFeely, "*En Banc* Proceedings in the United States Courts of Appeals," *Idaho Law Review* 24 (1987–88): 255–56; Bator et al., *Hart and Wechsler's The Federal Courts,* 31–39; Alexander, "*En Banc* Hearings in the Federal Courts of Appeals," part 1, 569–70.

11. Bator et al., *Hart and Wechsler's The Federal Courts,* 38–39; Alexander, "*En Banc* Hearings in the Federal Courts of Appeals," part 1, 570; Egger, "Court of Appeals Review of Agency Action, 477.

12. *Lang's Estate v. Commissioner of Internal Revenue,* 97 F. 2d 867 (9th Cir. 1938), 869–70.

13. *Commissioner of Internal Revenue v. Textile Mills Securities Corporation,* 117 F. 2d 62 (3d Cir. 1940), *aff'd* 314 U.S. 326 (1941), 69–71.

14. *Textile Mills Securities Corporation v. Commissioner of Internal Revenue,* 314 U.S. 326 (1941), 334–35.

15. Note, "Playing with Numbers: Determining the Majority of Judges Required to Grant *En Banc* Sittings in the United States Courts of Appeals," *Virginia Law Review* 70 (1984): 1507–8. The modern version of the 1948 legislation appears in 28 United States Code, Sect. 46 (1998).

16. *Western Pacific Railroad Corporation v. Western Pacific Railroad Company,* 345 U.S. 247 (1953), 249–59, 267–68.

17. Egger, "Court of Appeals Review of Agency Action," 478; Alexander, "*En Banc* Hearings in the Federal Courts of Appeals," part 2, 729; Judah I. Labovitz, "*En Banc* Procedure in the Federal Courts of Appeals," *University of Pennsylvania Law Review* 111 (1962): 220–21; Peter Michael Madden, "In Banc Procedures in the United States Courts of Appeals," *Fordham Law Review* 43 (1974): 403.

18. Rule of Appellate Procedure, Rule 35(a). See also Madden, "In Banc Procedures in the United States Courts of Appeals," 403, 405 n.40; Egger, "Court of Appeals Review of Agency Action," 478.

19. *United States v. American-Foreign Steamship Corporation* , 363 U.S. 685 (1960), 688–91.

20. *United States v. American-Foreign Steamship Corporation,* 689–90; Douglas H. Ginsburg and Donald Falk, "The Court *En Banc*: 1981–1990," *George Washington Law Review* 59 (1991): 1022–23; Note, "*En Banc* Review in Federal Circuit Courts: A Reassessment," *Michigan Law Review* 72 (1974): 1639; Irving R. Kaufman, "Do the Costs of the *En Banc* Proceeding Outweigh Its Advantages?" *Judicature* 69 (1985): 7.

21. Kaufman, "Do the Costs of the *En Banc* Proceeding Outweigh Its Advantages?," 7–8; Michael E. Solimine, "Ideology and *En Banc* Review," *North Carolina Law Review* 67 (1988): 30–31; Note, "The Politics of *En Banc* Review," *Harvard Law Review* 102 (1989): 866.

22. A limited en banc is authorized by a 1978 statute (Section 6 of the Omnibus Judgeship Act) and lets courts with more than fifteen judges convene en banc before a limited panel that does not include all of the judges on the court. Thomas E. Baker, *Rationing Justice on Appeal: The Problems of the U.S. Courts of Appeals* (St. Paul, Minn.: West Publishing Co., 1994), 155–58. The "mini in banc" process in the D.C. Circuit is described in Steven Bennett and Christine Pembroke, "'Mini' In Banc Proceedings: A Survey of Circuit Practices," *Cleveland State Law Review* 34 (1986): 531–65. See generally, *Irons v. Diamond,* 670 F. 2d 265 (D.C. Cir. 1981).

23. Rule 35(c), D.C. Circuit Rules 1994. See Kaufman, "Do the Costs of the *En Banc* Proceeding Outweigh Its Advantages?," 7; McFeely, "*En Banc* Proceedings in the United States Courts of Appeals," 273–74.

24. Administrative Office of the U.S. Courts, Statistics Division, *Petitions for Rehearings Filed (en banc)—10/1/94 through 9/30/95* (unpublished table, on file with the author).

25. Note, "The Politics of En Banc Review," 879–81.

26. Harold M. Stephens, "Shop Talk Concerning the Business of the Court," *Journal of the Bar Association, District of Columbia* 20 (1953): 105–9; Comment, "The *En Banc*

Procedures of the United States Courts of Appeals," *University of Chicago Law Review* 21 (1954): 450 n.21, 451–52. See also Douglas H. Ginsburg and Donald Falk, "The Court *En Banc*: 1981–1990," 59 (1991): 1010; Note, "The Power of a Circuit Court of Appeals to Sit *En Banc*," *Harvard Law Review* 55 (1942): 666 n.16; Alexander, "*En Banc* Hearings in the Federal Courts of Appeals," part 2, 571 n.60.

27. From 1960 to 1964, only one circuit, the Third Circuit, handled more en banc cases (124). Alexander, "*En Banc* Hearings in the Federal Courts of Appeals," part 2, 746 (Appendix 5).

28. *Annual Report of the Director of the Administrative Office of the United States Courts* (Washington, D.C.: U.S. Government Printing Office, 1970–95), tables B and B-1.

29. *1997 Judicial Staff Directory* (Mt. Vernon, Va.: Congressional Staff Directory, Ltd. 1997): 642–45.

30. D.C. Circuit Judge Douglas Ginsburg observes that a multitude of D.C. Circuit en banc cases surfaced in the mid-1970s as a result of the Watergate crisis. Ginsburg and Falk, "The Court *En Banc*: 1981–1990," 1025–26, and 1026 n.91.

31. Patricia M. Wald, "Changing Course," 486.

32. Ibid., 479, 482 n.19, 486 n.29. See also Patricia M. Wald, "The D.C. Circuit: Here and Now," *George Washington Law Review* 55 (1987): 719.

33. Kenneth Karpay, "*En Banc* Furor, Liberal Fury," *The American Lawyer* (Supplement: *Reagan Justice; D.C. Circuit*) June 1988, p. 10.

34. See also *Hotel and Restaurant Employees Union, Local 25 v. Smith*, 846 F. 2d 1499 (D.C. Cir. 1988) (en banc, 4-4 tie in deciding litigant standing and ripeness, where Democratic appointees favored access and Republican appointees objected); *Ginsburg, Feldman & Bress v. Federal Energy Administration*, 591 F. 2d 752 (D.C. Cir. 1978) (en banc, 4-4 tie on disclosure under Freedom of Information Act); *Center for Auto Safety v. Thomas*, 847 F. 2d 843 (D.C. Cir. 1988) (en banc, discussed in Chapter 2).

35. Note, "The Politics of *En Banc* Review." *See Bartlett v. Bowen*, 816 F. 2d 695 (D.C. Cir. 1987); *Martin v. D.C. Metropolitan Police Department*, 812 F. 2d 1425 (D.C. Cir. 1987); *United States v. Meyer*, 810 F. 2d 1242 (D.C. Cir. 1987).

36. Alexander, "*En Banc* Hearings in the Federal Courts of Appeals," part 1, 584 n.125. This problem was exacerbated because the court sat en banc with an even number of judges. Ibid.

37. *Bartlett v Bowen*, 824 F. 2d 1240 (D.C. Cir. 1987): 1243–44. Judges Harry T. Edwards, Patricia Wald, Spottswood W. Robinson, Abner Mikva, and Ruth Bader Ginsburg, all Democratic appointees, voted to deny, whereas Judges Robert Bork, Kenneth Starr, James Buckley, Douglas H. Ginsburg, and Stephen Williams, all Republican appointees, dissented.

38. J. Woodford Howard, Jr., *Courts of Appeals in the Federal Judicial System: A Study of the Second, Fifth, and District of Columbia Circuits* (Princeton, N.J.: Princeton University Press, 1981), 193.

39. Christopher E. Smith, "Polarization and Change in the Federal Courts: *En Banc* Decisions in the Courts of Appeals," *Judicature* 74 (1990): 134.

40. Ginsburg and Falk, "The Court *En Banc*: 1981–1990," 1025–26, 1026 n.91.

41. Alexander, "En Banc Hearings in the Federal Courts of Appeals," part 1, 583 n.122. See also *Mallory v. United States*, 259 F. 2d 801 (D.C. Cir. 1958).

42. *Textile Mills Securities Corporation v. Commissioner of Internal Revenue*, 334–35.

43. The authors actually list sixty-three en banc cases. Two cases (number 14, a table case, and number 32, an unpublished case) are excluded from the present analysis because of the manner in which they were disposed. See Ginsburg and Falk, "The Court *En Banc*: 1981–1990."

44. Subsequent treatment of appeals was analyzed through Westlaw (Insta-Cite) and Lexis (Auto-Cite) service. A list of the pertinent cases and their subsequent treatment by the U.S. Supreme Court is provided in Christopher P. Banks, "The Politics of *En Banc* Review in the 'Mini–Supreme Court,'" *Journal of Law and Politics*, 13 (1997): 406 nn. 145–48.

45. See Peter L. Strauss, "One Hundred Fifty Cases Per Year: Some Implications of the Supreme Court's Limited Resources for Judicial Review of Agency Action," *Columbia Law Review*, 87 (1987): 1105–16.

46. *Annual Report of the Director,* Tables B-1 and B-2.

47. Frank M. Coffin, *On Appeal: Courts, Lawyering, and Judging* (New York: W.W. Norton & Co., 1994), 5.

48. Joseph C. Goulden, *The Benchwarmers: The Private World of the Powerful Federal Judges* (New York: Weybright and Talley, 1974), 227.


## CHAPTER 5. THE D.C. CIRCUIT COURT AND ITS FUTURE

1. The D.C. Circuit's superiority in administrative law is suggested by D.C. Circuit Judge Patricia Wald in Patricia M. Wald et al., "The Contribution of the D.C. Circuit to Administrative Law," *Administrative Law Review*, 40 (1988): 509. See also Richard J. Pierce, Jr., "Two Problems in Administrative Law: Political Polarity on the District of Columbia Circuit and Judicial Deterrence of Agency Rulemaking," *Duke Law Journal*, (1988): 304. Other scholars generally agree with these assessments. See Jeffrey B. Morris, "The Second Most Important Court: The United States Court of Appeals for the District of Columbia Circuit" (Ph.D. diss., University of Columbia, 1972); Christopher P. Banks, "Judicial Politics in the 'Mini–Supreme Court': Legal-Policy Change in the U.S. Court of Appeals for the District of Columbia Circuit, 1960–1993" (Ph.D. diss., University of Virginia, 1995); Joseph C. Goulden, *The Benchwarmers: The Private World of the Powerful Federal Judges* (New York: Weybright and Talley, 1974), 227.

2. As of August 1, 1998, a total of fifty-four judicial vacancies existed on the U.S. Courts of Appeals (16), U.S. District Court (37), and U.S. Court of International Trade (1). Judicial Vacancies (as of 12/01/98) available at http://www.uscourts.gov/cgi-bin/vacancy-index.pl [December 18, 1998]. An online copy of a study by the Administrative Office of the U.S. Courts shows that filings from 1993 to 1997 of new cases in appellate courts have reached record highs. Administrative Office of the U.S. Courts, *Federal Judicial Caseload: A Five-Year Retrospective,* available at http://www.uscourts.gov/[December 18, 1998].

3. William H. Rehnquist (1998). *The 1997 Year-End Report on the Federal Judiciary,* available at http://www.uscourts.gov/uscourts.gov/cj97.htm [February 11, 1998]. The chief justice also blames Congress for "federalizing" new crimes and civil causes of action, which compromises the traditional idea that the federal courts ought to have limited jurisdiction. Ibid., p. 3 of 8 web pages. See also "Remarks of Chief Justice

William H. Rehnquist," American Law Institute Annual Meeting, Mayflower Hotel, May 11, 1998, available at http://www.uscourts.gov/ALI.htm [July 22, 1998]. Second Circuit Judge Roger Miner concurs by saying that delays in the courts are inevitable when Congress federalizes more laws but fails to add more judgeships. Roger J. Miner, "Federal Court Reform Should Start at the Top," *Judicature* 77 (1993): 104–8.

4. Thomas E. Baker, *Rationing Justice on Appeal: The Problems of the U.S. Courts of Appeals* (St. Paul, Minn.: West Publishing Co., 1994), 22. "Visible rationality" suggests that litigants can petition courts and orally argue cases before an impartial judiciary which, among other things, decides appeals in a timely fashion after due consideration. Federal Judicial Center, *Structural and Other Alternatives for the Federal Courts of Appeals: A Report to the United States Congress and the Judicial Conference of the United States* (Washington, D.C.: Federal Judicial Center, 1993), 10.

5. Federal Judicial Center, *Structural and Other Alternatives for the Federal Courts of Appeals,* 9–10. These issues have surfaced again in the politically volatile context of whether the Ninth Circuit ought to be split. See the online materials relating to the final report of the Commission on Structural Alternatives for the Federal Courts of Appeals, available at http://app.comm.uscourts.gov/ [December 18, 1998]. See also Judicial Conference of the United States and the Committee on Long Range Planning, *Long Range Plan for the Federal Courts* (Washington, D.C.: Judicial Conference of the United States, 1995).

6. Daniel J. Meador and Jordana Simone Bernstein, *Appellate Courts in the United States* (St. Paul, Minn.: West Publishing Co., 1994), 23–24; Daniel J. Meador, "An Appellate Court Dilemma and a Solution through Subject Matter Organization," *University of Michigan Journal of Law Reform* 16 (1983): 471–85; Daniel J. Meador, "A Challenge to Judicial Architecture: Modifying the Regional Design of the U.S. Courts of Appeals," *University of Chicago Law Review* 56 (1989): 626. For a sample of the different types of subject matter reform plans that appear in the literature, see Baker, *Rationing Justice on Appeal,* 261–69; Federal Judicial Center, *Structural and Other Alternatives for the Federal Courts of Appeals,* 84–91.

7. The position of the Judicial Conference is stated in The Federal Courts Study Committee, *Report of the Federal Courts Study Committee* (Washington, D.C.: Judicial Conference of the United States, 1990); Judicial Conference of the United States and the Committee on Long Range Planning, *Long Range Plan for the Federal Courts.* See also Federal Courts Study Committee, *Working Papers and Subcommittee Reports, July 1, 1990,* vols. 1 and 2 (Washington, D.C.: Judicial Conference of the United States, 1990). Yet, as Judge S. Jay Plager observes, "Probably, the clearest lesson to be drawn both from the literature and from experience is that the term 'specialized' should be dropped from the discussion, since there is no agreement on what it means or on what it connotes." S. Jay Plager, "The United States Courts of Appeals, the Federal Circuit, and the Non-Regional Subject Matter Concept: Reflections on the Search for a Model," *American University Law Review* 39 (1990): 860. Daniel Meador, an advocate of subject matter courts, goes further and sees a distinction between subject matter and specialized courts. Whereas the former has exclusive power over a mixture of case categories presenting different legal issues, the latter are courts that hear appeals in a single, myopic category of case. For Meador, then, subject matter courts avoid becoming specialized since they review a greater diversity of cases. Meador and Bernstein, *Appellate Courts in the United*

*States*, 21–24, 129. However, the literature tends to blur the distinction, if any, between the two courts. See, e.g., Federal Judicial Center, *Structural and Other Alternatives for the Federal Courts of Appeals*, 84–91 (referring to national subject matter courts as "subject-matter specialization"). For purposes of the present discussion, no distinction is made and the terms are used interchangeably.

8. Bruce D. Brown, "Agency Appeals in Washington in Decline; D.C. Circuit's Workload Faces Fresh Scrutiny," *Legal Times*, November 25, 1996, p. 1. See also, Thomas E. Baker, "Imagining the Alternative Futures of the U.S. Courts of Appeals," *Georgia Law Review* 28 (1994): 957.

9. Some scholars, however, observe that the U.S. Court of Appeals for the Federal Circuit, a national, nonregional court of appeals that was created in 1982, handles as many (or more) agency appeals. Plager, "The United States Courts of Appeals, the Federal Circuit, and the Non-Regional Subject Matter Concept," 861; Peter H. Schuck and E. Donald Elliott, "To the *Chevron* Station: An Empirical Study of Federal Administrative Law," *Duke Law Journal* (1990): 1018–19.

10. Harold H. Bruff, "Coordinating Judicial Review in Administrative Law," *University of California Los Angeles Law Review* 39 (1992), partially reprinted in Glen O. Robinson, Ernest Gellhorn, and Harold H. Bruff, *The Administrative Process*, 4th ed. (St. Paul, Minn.: West Publishing Co., 1993), 166.

11. Carl Tobias, "The D.C. Circuit As a National Court," *University of Miami Law Review* 48 (1993): 159–91; Henry J. Abraham, *The Judicial Process: An Introductory Analysis of the Courts of the United States, England, and France*, 7th ed. (New York: Oxford University Press, 1998), 22–24.

12. That D.C. judges are prolific was noticed by Paul Verkuil in Wald et al., "The Contribution of the D.C. Circuit," 532. Verkuil also observed that Judges David Bazelon (35 articles) and Skelley Wright (36 articles) were especially prolific in their off-the-bench writings. Ibid., p. 533. For a biographical description of some of the D.C. Circuit judges, see Ann L. Brownson, ed., *1996 Judicial Staff Directory* (Mount Vernon, Va.: Staff Directories, 1996); W. Stuart Dornette and Robert R. Cross, eds., *Federal Judiciary Almanac 1986* (New York: John Wiley & Sons, 1984).

13. The District of Columbia Court Reform and Criminal Procedure Act of 1970 greatly increased the D.C. Circuit's jurisdiction over agency appeals. *History of the United States Court of Appeals for the District of Columbia Circuit in the County's Bicentennial Year* (Washington, D.C.: U.S. Court of Appeals for the District of Columbia Circuit, 1977): 79–80.

14. Comments by Paul Verkuil in Wald et al., "The Contribution of the D.C. Circuit," 533.

15. Jonathan Groner, "Just What Is It about the D.C. Circuit?" *Legal Times*, June 21, 1993, p. 1. See Paul Verkuil's commentary in Wald et al., "The Contribution of the D.C. Circuit," 533; Morris, "The Second Most Important Court," 190–91.

16. As quoted by Patricia Wald in Wald et al., "The Contribution of the D.C. Circuit," 532. See also Robert L. Rabin, "Federal Regulation in Historical Perspective," *Stanford Law Review* 38 (1986): 1296–301; Ernest Gellhorn and Ronald M. Levin, *Administrative Law and Process: In a Nutshell* (St. Paul, Minn.: West Publishing Co., 1990) (especially Chapter 3).

17. Federal Judicial Center, *Structural and Other Alternatives for the Federal Courts of Appeals*, 7–9. See also Meador and Bernstein, *Appellate Courts in the United States*, 70–91.

18. Judicial Conference of the United States and the Committee on Long Range Planning, *Long Range Plan for the Federal Courts*, 7–9, 41. The rule of law, equal justice, judicial independence, national courts of limited jurisdiction, excellence, and accountability of the federal judiciary are identified as core values in an analogous fashion by the Judicial Conference. See also Baker, *Rationing Justice on Appeal*, 14–51.

19. In 1960, total case terminations (not case terminations on the merits) equaled 62.58 percent of the total number of cases commenced in the current fiscal year and cases pending from the prior fiscal year. In 1997, they equaled 56.20 percent. Compare *Annual Report of the Director of the Administrative Office of the United States Courts* (Washington, D.C.: U.S. Government Printing Office, 1960, 1997), Table B-1.

20. The rate of filings per authorized judgeship for each year listed in Table 7 are for 1960, 57.3; for 1965, 86.7; for 1970, 120.2; for 1975, 171.7; for 1980, 175.8; for 1985, 213.8; for 1990, 262.2; and for 1997, 313.3. *Annual Report of the Director of the Administrative Office of the United States Courts* (FY 1960–1997). These figures, of course, only provide a rough sense of how many appeals a judge may have to handle. For an analysis of the rate of filings per active judge from 1973 to 1992, see Federal Judicial Center, *Structural and Other Alternatives for the Federal Courts of Appeals*, 17–22.

21. This issue is debated extensively throughout the public hearings and testimony found online in the proceedings of the Commission on Structural Alternatives for the Federal Courts of Appeals. See the commission's web page at http://app.comm/uscourts.gov/ [December 18, 1998].

22. Baker, *Rationing Justice on Appeal*, 181. See also Judicial Conference of the United States and the Committee on Long Range Planning, *Long Range Plan for the Federal Courts*, 14–15.

23. This is not to say that Congress or the Judicial Conference of the United States has not studied the possibility of enacting court reform in a variety of contexts. In November 1997, for example, by statute Congress created the Commission on Structural Alternatives for the Federal Courts of Appeals. The commission, which is chaired by retired U.S. Supreme Court Justice Byron White, is charged with exploring the structure and alignment of the federal appellate courts, with special reference to the Ninth Circuit. For a summary of the commission's final report, see Commission on Structural Alternatives for the Federal Courts of Appeals, *Final Report* (Washington, D.C.: Commission on Structural Alternatives for the Federal Courts of Appeals, 1998). Apart from structural reform, Congress has considered passing legislation (H.R. 1252, or the Judicial Reform Act of 1998) that would curb the so-called judicial activism of courts. "House Passes 'Judicial Activism Bill,'" *The Third Branch* (May 1998), available at http://www.uscourts.gov/ttb/may98ttb/mayttb98.html [July 29, 1998].

24. See generally Baker, *Rationing Justice on Appeal*; Martha J. Dragich, "Once a Century: Time for a Structural Overhaul of the Federal Courts," *Wisconsin Law Review* (1996): 11–73.

25. Meador and Bernstein, *Appellate Courts in the United States*, 78–91.

26. The House Judiciary Subcommittee on Courts and Intellectual Property, for example, is active in studying the caseload crisis and its effect on the federal judiciary. "Oversight Hearings Shows Increasing Workload is Straining Resources of Federal

Judiciary," *News Release: Administrative Office of the United States Courts (June 11, 1998)*, available at http://www.uscourts.gov/Press_Releases/pr061198.html [July 22, 1998].

27. Dragich, "Once a Century," 28–39; Meador and Bernstein, *Appellate Courts in the United States,* 114–21; Baker, *Rationing Justice on Appeal,* 262.

28. Dragich, "Once a Century," 15–16.

29. See Plager, "The United States Courts of Appeals, the Federal Circuit, and the Non-Regional Subject Matter Concept," 853–57.

30. See Meador, "A Challenge to Judicial Architecture," 626.

31. Ibid., 614.

32. Dragich, "Once a Century," 44, nn. 185–86 (noting that the creation of special-ized federal courts dispels the hypothesis that all courts should remain generalist; and that the Second, Third, Fifth, and Ninth Circuits are reputed to "experts" in certain areas of the law). See also Meador, "A Challenge to Judicial Architecture," 614; Lawrence Baum, "Specializing the Federal Courts: Neutral Reforms or Efforts to Shape Judicial Policy?" *Judicature* 74 (1991): 218; Baker, *Rationing Justice on Appeal,* 262. For a discus-sion on the extent to which courts are inherently generalist in their legal orientation, see Donald L. Horowitz, *The Courts and Social Policy* (Washington, D.C.: Brookings Insti-tution, 1976).

33. American Bar Association Standing Committee on Federal Judicial Improve-ments, "The United States Courts of Appeals: Reexamining Structure and Process after a Century of Growth: Report of the American Bar Association Standing Committee on Federal Judicial Improvements (March 1989)," reprinted in 125 Federal Rules Decision 523 (1989): 538–39.

34. Jeffrey W. Stempel, "Two Cheers for Specialization," *Brooklyn Law Review* 61 (1995): 88–89.

35. The quotations in the text discussion are derived from The Federal Courts Study Committee, *Report of the Federal Courts Study Committee,* 72–73.

36. Judicial Conference of the United States and the Committee on Long Range Planning, *Long Range Plan for the Federal Courts,* 43. Recommendation no. 20 also stated, "No new specialized Article III court should be created for review of agency action or Article I court decisions." Ibid., 46.

37. Meador, "A Challenge to Judicial Architecture," 634–36 (identifying the "buga-boos"); Harold H. Bruff, "Specialized Courts in Administrative Law," *Administrative Law Review* 43 (1991): 330–32; The Federal Courts Study Committee, *Report of the Federal Courts Study Committee,* 11–12.

38. The discussion in the next few paragraphs is derived from volume 1 of the Federal Courts Study Committee, *Working Papers and Subcommittee Reports,* 248–60. Circuit Judge Richard A. Posner served as the subcommittee's chairman. Congressman Robert W. Kastenmeier, Chief Justice Keith A. Callow, and Rex E. Lee made up the rest of the committee. Prior to serving on the subcommittee, Judge Posner expressed a healthy skepticism about the need or feasibility for making specialized courts part of the courts of appeals. See, e.g., Richard A. Posner, *The Federal Courts: Crisis and Reform* (Cambridge: Harvard University Press, 1985), 147–66.

39. *Annual Report of the Director of the Administrative Office of the United States Courts,* from 1985 to 1997, Table B-1. It should be noted that in 1992 the Administrative Office changed the way it reports data in Table B-1. The pre-1992 tables used the fiscal year

ending June 30, whereas the 1992 tables (and all subsequent years) employed the fiscal year ending September 30. The Analysis and Reports branch confirms, though, that while the different dates over- or underinflate the data, they still do not substantially affect the percentages reported here. Telephone interview with Marilyn Ducharme, *Statistical Analysis and Reports Division* of Administrative Office of U.S. Courts, on September 29, 1997.

40. See Federal Courts Study Committee, *Working Papers and Subcommittee Reports*, 253–54, especially nn. 51–53. In ibid., at 253 n.52, for example, one treatise on administrative law and one law review article is used to support the subcommittee's position. Moreover, the subcommittee seems to contradict itself when it observed that the volume of direct appeals from agencies may be overstated since it includes consolidated petitions. Ibid., 252 n.50. Ideally, the number of consolidated petitions should be juxtaposed against the number of informal adjudications in the circuit appeals docket to see if one category of appeals offsets the other, which potentially makes the number of direct appeals more representative of the court's workload.

41. Ibid., 257.

42. Using 1988 of the *Administrative Reports* as its exclusive frame of reference, the subcommittee apparently arrived at these figures by dividing the number of cases commenced by the number of authorized judgeships (156) to measure how well the D.C. Circuit compares against the national average in disposing of agency appeals. This is probably an inaccurate measure. And even if it is reliable, the calculations are incorrect in regard to the D.C. Circuit per judge figure (i.e., dividing 1,925 by 12 D.C. Circuit judgeships equals 160.42 cases per judge, not 136). See *Annual Report of the Director of the Administrative Office of the United States Courts 1988*, 2, Table 1, 140, Table B. See also volume 1 of the Federal Courts Study Committee, *Working Papers and Subcommittee Reports*, 255–56.

43. An explanatory note in the *1997 Federal Court Management Statistics* volume states, "Actions per panel provide a more accurate indication of the caseload of an individual judge, since appeals cases are generally handled by panels of three judges than by single judges." *Federal Court Management Statistics (1997)* (Washington, D.C.: Administrative Office of United States Courts, 1997), v. The numerical rankings of the D.C. Circuit for administrative appeals merit terminations are: for 1990, first; for 1991, first; for 1992, first; for 1993, second; for 1994, second; for 1995, second; for 1996, second; and for 1997, second. Furthermore, with the exception of 1991, the number of vacant judgeship months fell within a range of 8.5 months to 29.9 months, thus indicating that the court was functioning with fewer than twelve judges, its authorized number. The numerical rankings of D.C. Circuit merit terminations (prisoner, other civil, criminal) are as follows: for 1990, twelve; for 1991, twelve; for 1992, twelve; for 1993, twelve; for 1994, twelve; for 1995, twelve; for 1996, twelve; and, for 1997, twelve. Ibid., 3 (FY 1990–97).

44. Volume 1 of the Federal Courts Study Committee, *Working Papers and Subcommittee Reports*, 256.

45. Ibid. The subcommittee cited *Vermont Yankee Nuclear Power Corporation v. Natural Resources Defense Council, Inc.*, 435 U.S. 519 (1978); *Motor Vehicle Manufacturers Association of the United States, Inc. v. State Farm Mutual Automobile Insurance Company*, 463 U.S. 29 (1983); and *Chevron U.S.A. Inc. v. Natural Resources Defense Council, Inc.*,

467 U.S. 837 (1984) as "disapproved examples of what the Supreme Court viewed as the D.C. Circuit's interference with agency discretion."

46. Volume 1 of the Federal Courts Study Committee, *Working Papers and Subcommittee Reports,* 256. n.58, citing Wald et al., "The Contribution of the D.C. Circuit," 507. This page correctly attributes the comment in "Contribution" that there is an allegedly "uneasy" relationship between the D.C. Circuit and the U.S. Supreme Court. It does not establish, however, that the Supreme Court has taken and reversed more D.C. Circuit cases than those from other circuits.

47. See Figures 11, 12, and 13 in Chapter 4.

48. Much of the ensuing discussion is drawn from Baker, *Rationing Justice on Appeal,* 221–24, 261–69; Volume 1 of the Federal Courts Study Committee, *Working Papers and Subcommittee Reports,* 153–284; The Federal Courts Study Committee, *Report of the Federal Courts Study Committee,* 72–73, 120–25; Judicial Conference of the United States and the Committee on Long Range Planning, *Long Range Plan for the Federal Courts,* 1–20; and American Bar Association Standing Committee on Federal Judicial Improvements, "The United States Courts of Appeals," 538–39.

49. Baker, "Imagining the Alternate Futures of the U.S. Courts of Appeals," 957.

# Index

effect, 82–85, 157n. 52; 158n. 57; step one of, 78, 80–82; step two of, 78, 82–83. *See also* Judicial deference; Legislative history; Statutory construction

Chrysler Corporation, 59. *See also* Corporate Average Fuel Efficiency

Circuit courts (federal), 1, 92, 140; advocacy practiced in, 128; agenda-setting of, 53, 64, 88; as court of last resort (or final legal policy change), xvi, 1–2, 18, 86, 88, 117, 131; and en banc review, 92–96; and error correction, 126; original purposes of, 126–29; reform of, xiv–xv, 2, 117–19, 127–28, 140, 165n. 23; specialization of, 129–39, 166nn. 32 and 38; traditional (conventional) appellate justice of, 118, 126–31, 162n. 3, 165n. 17. *See also* U.S. Court of Appeals; U.S. Court of Appeals for the District of Columbia Circuit

Circuit Court of the District of Columbia, 8; acting as local and national court, 8–9. *See also* U.S. Court of Appeals; U.S. Court of Appeals for the District of Columbia Circuit

*Citizens to Preserve Overton Park, Inc. v. Volpe*, 46, 152n. 47

*City of Los Angeles v. National Highway Traffic Safety Administration*, 154n. 15

Clean Air Act: Amendments, 32–33; and *Chevron U.S.A. Inc. v. Natural Resources Defense Council, Inc.*, 76–77; and *International Harvester Company v. Ruckelshaus*, 44; and *National Lime Association v. Environmental Protection Agency*, 72–73

Clinton, Bill, 4; and Whitewater scandal, 143n. 11

Coffin, Frank M., 115

Collegiality: impact of caseload crisis on, 128; and interpersonal relationships on D.C. Circuit bench, 5–6, 62, 86, 105; Judge Bazelon's impact on, 11;

and judicial politics of appellate review, 89–90

Commission on Structural Alternatives for the Federal Courts of Appeals, xiv; Final Report of, xv, 142n. 5, 163n. 5, 165n. 21 and 23; political motivation of, xiv

*Committee to Save WEAM v. Federal Communications Commission*, 158n. 56

*Competitive Enterprise Institute v. National Highway Traffic Safety Administration*, 154n. 15

Congress. *See* U.S. Congress.

Consumer Product Safety Act, 32–33

Corporate Average Fuel Efficiency (CAFE): as focus of D.C. Circuit jurisprudence, 57–65, 86, 104; standards of, 57–58. *See also* Access policy-making; U.S. Court of Appeals for the the District of Columbia Circuit

Court of Appeals of the District of Columbia, 9–10, 99

Cranch, William, 8

Danaher, John, 146n. 48

Danger signals. *See Greater Boston Television Corporation v. Federal Communications Commission*; Hard look doctrine

Davis, Kenneth, 33

*Davis v. United States*, 149 n. 19

D.C. Bail Project, 17. *See also* Bazelon, David; U.S. Court of Appeals for the District of Columbia Circuit

D.C. Circuit. *See* U.S. Court of Appeals for the District of Columbia Circuit

DeB. Katzenbach, Nicholas, 23; and private correspondence with David Bazelon, 23–24

Delegation. *See* Nondelegation

Deregulation, xiii, 53–54, 56, 71, 77–78, 85

Department of Agriculture, 150n. 36

Department of Labor, 130

Department of Transportation, 130; and

Department of Transportation *(cont.)*
passive restraints, 74; and *State Farm
Mutual Automobile Insurance Company
v. Department of Transportation*, 73
Dicey, Alfred, 66; and conservative New
Deal ideology, 69–70. *See also* New
Deal; U.S. Supreme Court
District of Columbia, 3; crime problem
of, 25, 27; and inefficiency of criminal
justice system, 27; origin of, 7
District of Columbia Court of Appeals,
29. *See also* Circuit courts; U.S. Court
of Appeals; U.S. Court of Appeals for
the District of Columbia Circuit
District of Columbia Court Reform and
Criminal Procedure Act (of 1970)
(D.C. Circuit Crime bill), xii, 9, 26–
32, 34, 46, 49, 119–20, 148n. 11; as
affecting bail for dangerous offenders
in noncapital cases, 30; as affecting
involuntary commitment and insanity
pleas, 30; as affecting transfer of
juveniles and adult prosecution, 31;
and *Bolton v. Harris*, 30–31; circuit
executive provision of, 29; court
reform provisions of, 28–31; detaining
criminal suspects in lieu of bail
provision of, 27; filing expedited
appeals for government provision of,
32; habeas corpus provisions of, 29;
and House Committee on the
District of Columbia, 30–31;
interlocutory appeals provisions of,
29; legislative history of, 28, 148n. 13;
and *Luck* doctrine, 29; new juvenile
code provisions of, 29; no-knock
search provision of, 27, 31–32;
partisanship motivations of, 27–32;
paternity provisions of, 29; public
defender system provision of, 29;
Senate Committee on the District of
Columbia, 31; sentencing recidivists
provision of, 27, 31; and *United States
v. Alston*, 30; and *United States v.
Leathers*, 30; and wiretapping

provision of, 27. *See also* Circuit
courts; U.S. Court of Appeals; U.S.
Court of Appeals for District of
Columbia Circuit; U.S. Congress
Douglas, William O., 67; and *Textile
Mills Securities Corporation v.
Commissioner*, 93, 106
*Durham v. United States*, 15–16,
146nn. 35, 38; insanity rule's impact
of, 148n. 7

*Easter v. District of Columbia*, 16
Edgerton, Henry W., 15, 146n. 48
Edwards, Harry T., 51–52, 56, 152n. 1;
and *Bartlett v. Bowen*, 161n. 37; and
*Center for Auto Safety v. Thomas*, 60–
61; and *International Ladies' Garment
Workers' Union v. Donovan*, 75–76;
labor relations law expertise of, 124
Ellender, Allen J., 28
En banc review: benefits of, 95–96; and
circuit courts, 100–2; as D.C. Circuit
tradition, 99–100; as element of
circuit court independence, 89; as
final decision, 105–7; and Ginsburg-
Falk study, 107, 162n. 43; history of,
xiii, 91–96; as intensifying internal
conflict on the bench, 90; as limited
procedure, 160n. 22; as part of judicial
policymaking, 115; politics of, xiii–xiv,
52, 61–65, 96–99, 102–6, 115; as
supplemental (exceptional) judicial
review procedure, 87, 94–95, 98, 105,
115, 159n. 2; and Watergate crisis,
161n. 30; weaknesses of, 90, 96–99.
*See also* Access policy-making; Circuit
courts; Collegiality; Justiciability;
Ideology; Panel decision-making; U.S.
Court of Appeals; U.S. Court of
Appeals for District of Columbia
Circuit
Endangered Species Act, 32
Energy Policy Conservation Act, 58
*Environmental Defense Fund, Inc. v.
Ruckelshaus*, 150n. 36